Stuart Library
of Western Americana
University of
the Pacific
Stockton,
California

Also by JACK O'CONNOR

THE RIFLE BOOK (1949, 1964)

THE BIG-GAME RIFLE (1952)

THE SHOTGUN BOOK (1965)

THE ART OF HUNTING BIG GAME IN NORTH AMERICA (1967)

*These are Borzoi Books, published in New York by*

ALFRED A. KNOPF

# HORSE AND BUGGY WEST

# HORSE AND

*A Boyhood on the Last Frontier*

*Illustrations by* IRVING BOKER

# BUGGY WEST

by JACK O'CONNOR

*ALFRED A. KNOPF, New York 1969*

THIS IS A BORZOI BOOK

PUBLISHED BY ALFRED A. KNOPF, INC.

*FIRST EDITION*
 Published in the United States by Alfred A. Knopf, Inc., New York, and simultaneously in Canada by Random House of Canada Limited, Toronto. Distributed by Random House, Inc., New York. Manufactured in the United States of America.

*Library of Congress Catalog Card Number: 68-23938*

For Eleanor, whom I have bored for four decades with these tales of my old home town; for Angus, who encouraged me to write them; and for Bob, who thinks some of them are funny.

# Foreword

I HOPE my readers are not unduly shaken up by the fact that I have put in direct quotes conversations that took place a half century ago. I did so because I think doing so lends pace and interest to this book and also, strange as this may seem, because I can remember (or think I can remember) much of what I said and what others said.

Possibly the passage of many decades has shed a rosy glow over some of the episodes in this book, but if good tales have improved in the telling, so much the better. In many places I have substituted fictional names for real names to avoid causing embarrassment to persons who may still be living.

## Contents

# HORSE AND BUGGY WEST

# 1 · Center of My World

I SUPPOSE everyone recalls some incident of time and place where his connected memory began. I date my own from a time when I was sitting in a dry irrigation ditch in a small Arizona town called Tempe. The ditch ran in front of the two house tents where I lived with my mother and my small sister Helen. The year was 1907 and I was then five years old. I was wearing a curious costume which was in those days inflicted on small children. It was known as "a pair of rompers," and it consisted of a one-piece garment with full, bloomerlike legs. Each leg was held just above the knee with

elastic. The rompers I wore that day had short sleeves, a low neck, and the costume had a flap behind, which unbuttoned. I was barefoot.

At the time when my memory begins I was making a house with damp sand. The ditch was my principal playground. In it I found all manner of interesting things—whiskey bottles, pine cones from the high mountains at the head of the Salt River, baling wire, tin cans.

On this particular day, which has remained forever in my memory, my mother appeared suddenly on the bank above me. With her was my Uncle Jim O'Connor, my father's eldest brother. He was a tall, handsome man with friendly light-blue eyes. At that time he was in his early forties but his hair and his mustache were already snow-white.

"Have you been a good boy?" my mother said.

"Yes, Mama."

"Come on up, Jack," she said. "I have a present for you."

Uncle Jim O'Connor reached a hand down and pulled me up.

My mother's eyes were red and I could tell she had been crying. Some women can be lovely when they weep, but my mother could not. Her eyes quickly became red and so did her rather long nose. She knelt down and put her arms around me. I could feel the wetness of her tears against my cheek.

"Darling," she said, "your father and I were divorced today. Now you have no father, only a mother—only me. Do you understand?"

I only partly understood, but I remember that a feeling of overwhelming sadness and desolation overcame me. Today I have only a few scattered memories of my father before he and my mother parted, but I must have been fond of him or I would not have felt so lonely when I was told he would never come home again.

My mother stood up, unwrapped a bulky package she was carrying. "I bought presents for you and Helen," she said. One was a teddy bear, the other a white cloth rabbit with pink eyes. The

*This book*

*is sent to you with our compliments.*

*We would appreciate receiving two copies of any mention of it which you may publish.*

*But no review should appear before publication date.*

Title: HORSE AND BUGGY WEST
Author: Jack O'Connor
Price: $5.95 Pub Date: 2-26-69

*Alfred A. Knopf, Inc.*

*501 Madison Avenue, New York City 22*

white rabbit within a couple of years became so dirty, bedraggled, and eyeless that it was done away with, but the teddy bear remained around for many years, a charming little figure with shoe-button eyes and a saucy look. I can still remember how my sister Helen and I used to haul it around in a shoe box pulled by a string and how its paws were patched with some of mother's knit underwear. I am certain that the reason the scene the day my mother came home after getting her divorce has remained so vivid in my memory is that it was kept fresh by the presence of the white rabbit and the teddy bear.

My mother, my Uncle Jim O'Connor, and I went into the first of the two house tents which were pitched together and which served as our home. Jim sat down in a chair.

"Could I make you a cup of coffee?" my mother asked.

"No," said Jim. "It's too much trouble. What I could use is a good, stiff shot of whiskey, but I am sure you don't have any. It's been a trying day."

"I know," my mother said. I could see that tears were gathering in her eyes and it made me uneasy.

"Oh, for God's sake, Ida, don't cry any more! I know how you feel, but I think it was the only thing to do. You must remember that Andy is my brother. Well, I must go. Be a brave girl, Ida. It was all for the best."

From the day of my parents' divorce until this present moment, sixty years later, I can remember the main outlines of my life and much detail—the floor plans of the various houses in which I lived, streets of cities I have visited, the faces of friends, books I have read —but before that day my memories are few and scattered.

Perhaps the earliest of all is of an inconsequential incident at the Sutro Baths, an indoor salt-water swimming pool in San Francisco. I was probably about two years old at the time and I was in my father's arms. A girl who had gone down a slide into the pool must have run into difficulties, because my mother, who all her life enjoyed looking at the dark side of things, said, "Oh, the poor girl will drown."

I had no idea what drowning was but I sensed it must be pretty bad business, and this exclamation of my mother's served to fix the whole scene in my mind—the steamy-salty-fishy air of the indoor pool, the screeching and yelling of hundreds of excited swimmers echoing hollowly through the big building, the heads bobbing in the water. The structure that housed Sutro Baths was torn down in the 1960's. In all the years since that girl went down the slide and shipped some water, I have never again been inside the Sutro Baths, although I have passed the place many times. The scene has ever since been indelibly impressed on my memory.

We were living in an apartment in San Francisco at the time. I can remember that it had a bay window and I used to sit in it and look out over the street. This was before the San Francisco earthquake and fire and at the very beginning of the automobile age. Sometimes I used to awake at night. I can remember the clop, clop, clop of the shod hoofs of horses on pavement and I can also remember the whine and clang of streetcars and the brilliant blue sparks made by the trolley on the overhead wires.

My father at that time was a sports writer on one of the San Francisco newspapers, the *Examiner,* I believe. He used to bring home photographs of race horses and prize fighters. I must have had a certain manual dexterity for one so young because I learned to cut them out. I played with them as if they were paper dolls. Because I was very small I remember them as being enormous.

My father had played baseball at St. Mary's Academy at Oakland and at the University of California. After he got out of college he worked on newspapers, had taught in high school, and had played bush-league baseball. He was a catcher and apparently quite a good one, but his baseball career was cut short by a terrible case of empyema, which almost killed him and which kept him in bed for months. I can still remember the big deep scars in his ribs where the drains were inserted. I also remember his scarred and twisted fingers. He told me that when he started playing all he had to protect his left hand was a piece of leather held to his palm by string, and that the pitchers threw the ball as hard in those days as strong high-school pitchers did later. All his fingers had been broken and split at the ends.

Many years later my father told me that Gentleman Jim Corbett held me in his arms when I was very small, and I have heard him speak of Joe Choinski, Willie Meehan, Bob Fitzsimmons, and Stanley Ketchel. My father also knew the famous cartoonist T. A. Dorgan and "Hype" Igoe, the sports writer. Some years after he and my mother were divorced he brought James Montgomery Flagg, the illustrator, with him when he came to see us.

I can remember also a journey along about this time. I must have been in either my mother's or my father's arms when one of them lit the gas lights in a hotel room; I remember the flare of the match, the pop as the gas ignited, and the bright spurt of the flame.

Possibly on the same trip I awoke in the middle of the night and wanted to go to the bathroom. In those days, and much later, every hotel room had a washstand with a heavy china pitcher full of water and a heavy china washbasin. Towels hung on the side of the washstand and a slop jar stood beside or under it. Into the slop jar the water from washing or shaving was emptied. The maid brought fresh water and emptied the slops every day.

Back in the early years of this century the daily bath would have been considered a wasteful, reckless, and even dangerous business that, if indulged in over any length of time, would bring a man down with a bad cold, sap his strength, or even undermine his manhood. The bathroom was always down the hall, just as it is in third-rate British and continental hotels today, and once a week or so the hotel dweller warned the maid that he was about to embark on the serious business of taking a tub bath. The maid laid out towels, and if the bathroom was cold she might start a kerosene heater to "take the chill off." Then, wearing bathrobe and slippers, the bather marched importantly down the hall toward his adventure.

Some cheap hotels, roominghouses, and even homes had no bathrooms at all in those days. In many homes the children were bathed in the kitchen in rotation on Saturday night in a round washtub, and bachelors who roomed at private houses or in roominghouses generally bathed once a week at the barbershop. The price of a bath at the barbershop was twenty-five cents, and many hotels charged extra for baths, just as they do in some European hotels today. Between times, fastidious people took "sponge baths" in their rooms. When a bath cost two bits, the price of a good meal, two shots of bourbon, or five big glasses of beer, you didn't take one lightly.

The toilet was also down the hall in most hotels, and if an emergency arose during the night people were not expected to get out of bed and go traipsing down the cold hall to the toilet. Instead they used the chamber pot, which was under every bed and was the artifact around which many ribald turn-of-the-century jokes were spun.

At any rate, one night when I was very small I awakened with a full bladder. I had been sleeping in a small bed on one side of a large room. I can still remember the shadowy forms of my mother's and father's bodies under the covers on the double bed, their soft and genteel snores, the light from a street lamp that came through the open window.

I remember that I did not want to awaken my mother and father. I fumbled around under their bed for the chamber pot but I did not find it. Instead I found one of my father's shoes. I made do with that. In those days all shoes had high tops. Most were well made, and since their wearers did a lot of tramping around in mud and slush good ones were waterproof. As my father was to find out, his excellent boots not only kept water out but kept it in.

I can still remember his outraged bellow the next morning.

"For Christ's sake, Ida, that kid has pissed in my shoe! Of all the goddam things!"

"How do you know that?"

"I can smell, for God's sake, can't I? If he didn't, you must have. I know damned well I didn't."

"Andy, how you talk!"

"I ought to give him a good paddling!"

I knew what a paddling was and I began to bawl.

"Don't you dare touch him! He's only a baby!"

I can remember my mother cuddling me and drying my tears while my father rinsed out the shoe with water, set it in the window to dry, and got out another pair. His indignant howls forever fixed the incident in my memory.

I owed it to my father that for a time I was desperately afraid of the dark. I believe most small children are nervous about being outside at night alone. During the time when I was four years old and we were living in the mining camp my father discovered that I was afraid of the dark and decided to cure me. He took me outside and made me run around the house while he shouted that a coyote was after me. Naturally I was terrified. When my mother realized what was going on she put a stop to it.

The coyote my father had said was about to get me was very real to me. While I fled around the house I could almost feel his sharp fangs in my tender little bottom. I had never seen a coyote but I knew there was such a thing because every night coyotes howled around the outskirts of the mining camp. They were attracted by the garbage, and sometimes snatched an unwary chicken or someone's cat.

For years after that I hated to be out in the dark alone. After my mother and my father were divorced, I used to have to pick up a lard pail full of fresh milk from a neighbor a few blocks away after the evening milking, and in the winter I often had to go home through the darkness. I was menaced by weird sounds, furtive movements, strange and terrifying shapes. I never refused to run the errands, but I was always frightened.

My Uncle Bill Woolf cured me when I was eight or nine and my mother, my sister, and I were living with Grandfather Woolf in his big new house. One of my mother's younger sisters was teasing me about my fear of the dark and Bill Woolf heard her.

"Jack," he said, "would you like to earn five dollars?"

I was stunned. To me five cents was a very useful sum. I could see a show at the Goodwin Opera House for a dime. For a quarter

I could go to a movie, devour a delicious pineapple ice-cream soda, and still have a nickel left over for a rainy day. I had never possessed a whole dollar in my life. The idea of earning five dollars all at once staggered me. I would have taken on a mountain lion with my bare hands for half that.

"You're not joking?" I asked.

"No," Bill said. He took out a five-dollar bill and laid it on a table. "I'll give you a piece of chalk," he told me. "You go out to the Double Buttes cemetery, go into it, and put an X on a tombstone. Then I'll give you the five dollars."

I thought for a while, wavering between caution and greed.

"Can I have a flashlight?" I asked.

"Sure," said Uncle Bill.

It was a moonlit night in early November, nippy but not really cold. The cemetery was about two miles away. There had been a frost, and big yellow leaves fluttered down off the cottonwood trees that lined the ditch banks. Herds of cattle made dark lumps in the alfalfa fields. Dogs barked at me as I passed lonely farm houses. I had to pelt one dog with stones to drive him away.

Walking through the graveyard in the misty moonlight was an eerie experience, but I nervously made my way to what I judged to be the middle, found a rough spot on a tombstone and marked it with an X. As I walked stealthily toward the gate I got a shock that almost made my heart stop beating. Fifty yards or so away I saw a vague white shape drifting along close to the ground. For a terrified instant I was sure it was a ghost—though I did not believe in ghosts. I turned the flashlight on whatever it was. The beam of light revealed a large skunk foraging among the graves for its dinner. The vague white shape was its tail.

It was as if I were out from under an enormous load. I laughed. I actually loved that skunk. I strolled down the roadway in the cemetery, out through the gate. I enjoyed the two-mile walk home through the moonlight. I even made friends with the dog I had chased away with stones before. Never again was I afraid of the dark. What happened to the five dollars I cannot remember. My mother, who was a very sensible person, probably took it away from me and bought me a stout pair of shoes or a good warm jacket.

In my youth my mother used to put all the blame for their unsuccessful marriage on my father. He was not thrifty, she said. He was self-indulgent, reckless, rattlebrained, irresponsible. Her telling me this used to disturb me greatly, and as a small boy I can remember resolving to be thrifty, sensible, and responsible so my wife, if I was ever lucky enough to have one, would not divorce me. As I in turn look back upon my life I am aware that I have spent much time and energy trying not to be like my father.

In her old age when she was taking stock of her life, my mother blamed the failure of her marriage largely on her mother. My grandmother, she said, had made it impossible for her to establish a home. She was always demanding that my mother return to the ranch and help her out. My mother dutifully did so. My mother was the first of my grandmother's eight children to marry. When Charles, the eldest son, get married when I was not yet three, my grandmother fell as Charles and his bride were driving away in a carriage after the wedding. They were going to catch a train to the "Coast" for their honeymoon.

My grandmother hurt her spine and took to her bed, partially paralyzed. She wired for my mother to come and run the house, and my mother left her husband in San Francisco, took her infant son, and went back to Mama. This was the beginning of the end of my mother's marriage. From that time until her death thirty years later my grandmother always walked with a crutch.

My father threw up his newspaper job, got a position in the office of a mining company in Arizona so he could be near his wife. Later he went back to California as a salesman for a publisher of textbooks.

My grandmother did everything she could to break up my mother's marriage, but I am inclined to believe it was doomed from the start. Nevertheless my father was not the completely irresponsible playboy my mother made him out to me in my youth. Nor was he the fine young man whose life my mother in her old age felt she had ruined. Surely my grandmother's demands caused trouble, but if my father had had as much iron in his soul as I have had in mine, he would have told her to go climb a tree and he would have given my mother a spanking. If he had refused to let my mother leave the first time she was summoned home things might have worked out.

Among other reasons, Grandmother Woolf resented my father because of his Irish name and his free and easy ways. I can remember her saying, "Your father always had a good horse, a shiny buggy, a hundred-dollar watch, a fine shotgun, and a fancy suit on his back, but he never had any money in the bank." Then she'd snort, "Shanty Irish!" The only O'Connor Grandmother Woolf had any use for was my father's brother Jim. "Jim O'Connor's a good man, an industrious man, a clean man," she used to say. "You'd never know he was shanty Irish!" Jim was a university graduate, a successful lawyer, and a man of substance, but to Grandmother Woolf anyone was shanty Irish whose name began with an "O" or with "Fitz" or ended with an "an" as in Brogan, Flannagan, or Hannigan.

I saw my father the last time in the fall of 1937. He was then sixty-four and had three more years to live. He had a bad heart and apparently he knew he was not long for this world. He was then living in Honolulu where he was in the immigration service. He had come back to Arizona for the last time, to see the children of his first marriage, to say goodbye to old friends, and to see what had happened to the Arizona of his youth. He was still lean. His eyes were still light-blue. His wavy hair was still thick but now it was white.

He and my mother had a brief reunion in our house. He said, "Hello, Ida," and she said, "Hello, Andy." He said, "Ida, I would have known you anywhere. You are still lovely!" My mother said, "Tsk-tsk, Andy, that is all in your mind. I am an old woman and you are an old man. But really *you* haven't changed much. I'd have known you anywhere." Then he said, "Ida, I'll probably never see you again. I've got a hell of a bum ticker. May I kiss you?" "Yes, you may," she said. He kissed her lightly and as he turned away I could see one lone tear glistening on the end of his nose. My mother's eyes were wet.

When my father and I drove off he asked me how my wife and I were getting along. I was then thirty-five and she was twenty-nine and expecting our first daughter.

"Very well for the most part, but we pull each other's hair out now and then," I said.

"She's a beautiful girl," he told me. "Take care of her. Work your ass off for her. Try to understand her. I think there is only room in a man's life for one real love and if it escapes him he'll always be filled with remorse."

I spent three or four days driving my father around to see the scenes of his youth and to visit old friends. It was a depressing experience. The hand of death was upon him. Many of his friends were old and ill and wore ill-fitting false teeth. Many had gray faces and hands twisted with arthritis. They laughed and talked of people long since dead, of feats forgotten by all except them. One was an old college friend who had been worth a million dollars at one time but who had lost his cattle ranch and his spirit in the 1921 depression. Another was a cadaverous old man in the last stages of tuberculosis. He and my father had played minor-league baseball together back in the 1890's.

Some of my father's friends were sleek, rich old men with smooth pink faces, shiny shoes, well-fitting suits of rich tweeds and expensive worsteds. They lived in fine houses with Persian carpets on the floor, the smell of good cigars in the air. These men all had plump wives with blue hair and they drove black shiny Cadillacs. But most of my father's old friends were retired people living on tiny pensions in small shabby houses and waiting to die. My father would always bring a fifth of good bourbon to these old men. When they had two or three drinks, they'd get some color in their old gray faces, their eyes would light up, and their tongues would wag.

I watched my father with much interest. Here was a man of many gifts. He was well educated, well read, intelligent. He possessed considerable charm. He talked well. Yet he somehow had lacked stability of character and the ability to plan ahead. He was always looking for an investment that would make him rich at one stroke, for a job with few responsibilities but excellent pay. Like many Americans he felt that the outward symbols of success constituted success. If he drove up to an expensive restaurant in a Packard and entertained with caviar, champagne, *tournedos* Rossini, followed by brandy and cigars, he *was* successful.

He would promise the moon—if only he did not have to deliver right away. I saw little of him, but I was always able to observe him clearly since I was never bound to him by any emotional ties. When we did see each other it used to make him feel more adequate to tell me the great things he was going to do for me in the future. "When you're ready for college," he used to tell me, "I'll send you to Yale, to Princeton, to Harvard. Hell, I'll send you to Oxford! I'll work my fingers to the bone to give you the finest education in the world. Nothing's too good for Andy O'Connor's boy!" Then his eyes would mist with the thought of his generosity and self-sacrifice. He pictured himself toiling away at some dreary job, pinching pennies in order to send his talented son to some fashionable university where he could consort with the rich and well-born. I am sure he pictured it all like a grade-B, tear-jerking movie. He imagined me, his son, who had been successful because of his sacrifices, coming out of a fashionable restaurant probably in evening clothes and wearing a silk hat, with my wife, a rich, highborn, and beautiful young woman, on my arm. I am sure he pictured me helping my rich wife into a glittering chauffeur-driven car (probably a Duesenberg or a Rolls-Royce) while he, old, shabby, broken by the toil that had made all this possible, stood wistfully and humbly by, too proud to reveal his presence.

My father never contributed to my college education. For that matter he did not even inquire about it. From the time I was seventeen until his death when I was thirty-nine I saw him only twice. He was like the cock pheasant that tarries briefly to fertilize the hen and then cackles and flies on.

In Arizona any piece of ground that grows anything, be it animal or vegetable, is known as a "ranch," from the Spanish *rancho.* There are chicken ranches, even fruit ranches. The farm of my mother's father was a "hay ranch," a section of irrigated land on which he grew alfalfa. He ran some cattle on the arid public domain surrounding the irrigated valley, then fattened them on alfalfa hay. He also bought others to fatten. In addition he had a dairy herd from which the milk was sold to a creamery a few miles away.

My memories of the ranch are extremely sketchy, since my

grandfather sold out and moved to town when I was three. I do remember sitting on a pillow in front of my Uncle Bill Woolf's saddle and galloping through the fields. I have no conscious recollection of being butted and trampled by a bull one time in a corral at the ranch. I was told that I was wearing a red coat when I slipped through the fence into the corral and that Bill and a hired man grabbed pitchforks and fought the bull off before it had done more than bruise and terrify me.

Time quickly erased this traumatic experience from my conscious memory, but it must still exist in my subconscious. Bulls have made me nervous ever since. On several African safaris my encounters with bull Cape buffalo have always left me jittery, whereas I have never been in the least afraid of the more dangerous lion. I also remember riding in a six-horse stagecoach, exactly the kind we still see in western movies. This must have been when my father had the job at the copper-mining town. I can also remember crossing the raging Gila River in a rowboat when it was at flood stage.

I have a definite memory of seeing a wild camel on the Arizona desert. Before the Civil War the army brought some camels into Arizona to use as pack stock and even imported an Arab camel driver to take care of them. The experiment was not successful, as the sharp rocks in some areas were too much for the camels' soft feet. They were turned loose to survive as well as they could and for many decades an occasional camel was seen. Descendants of the Arab camel driver still live in Arizona, I understand. It is difficult for a child to sort out what he has seen, what he has been told, and what he has imagined. Probably I didn't actually see that camel.

Grandfather Woolf sold the alfalfa ranch in 1905 or 1906. He had owned it for twenty-one years, had worked hard, and had made a good deal of money. My mother told me that during the last few years, anyway, he netted about $25,000 a year. In the early years of the century when many working men toiled twelve hours a day for a dollar, that was a lot of money.

At the time my grandfather quit ranching and moved to the town of Tempe, his three oldest children were married. Charles, the eldest, had law offices in Tempe and in Phoenix nine miles away. My mother was in the midst of an off-and-on marriage, and my Uncle John, the second-oldest boy, had recently married. He was the wild one of the family, a rootin', tootin' vaquero all his life. For years he was the manager of the enormous Green Cananea cattle ranch in northern Sonora.

Bill Woolf was a great friend of Carl Hayden, who as I write this is a very ancient man and who has been in the United States Congress ever since 1912 when Arizona became a state. Hayden was elected Arizona's first congressman in 1912, but he became a senator in 1924. Hayden was the first white (meaning Anglo-Saxon) child born in Tempe, and his father founded the town. At the time my grandfather sold his ranch Hayden was just beginning his career as a politician. He had been elected Maricopa County treasurer. My Uncle Bill Woolf was his right-hand man. Later he ran for sheriff and was elected. Bill became undersheriff. Bill was captain of the local company of the Arizona National Guard. He was a fine rifle shot and competed at Camp Perry. Carl Hayden, who had the happy faculty of always being No. 1 boy, was either the colonel or a major in the First Arizona.

My Uncle Jim Woolf, who was the family eccentric and of whom more will be told later, had long since shaken the dust of Tempe from his shoes, but Arthur, the youngest of my father's brothers, was in and out of my grandfather's house. My mother's two sisters, Irene and Mabel, were in their late teens and were attending the normal. Mabel had brown hair. Irene was a golden blonde like my mother. They lived together in a big room filled with mysterious garments, interesting smells, whispers and giggles. I loved them both!

# 2 · Ancestry

AFTER dinner one night in the spring of 1923, when I was winding up my two-year course at the Tempe Normal, the telephone rang and the operator said nervously that there was a long-distance call for me.

My mother's face blanched. "Oh, dear," she said. "I hope it's nothing serious!" In the early 1920's people did not make long-distance telephone calls lightly. Generally long distance was used only in cases of utmost urgency when the cheaper telegram would be too slow—in case of a very serious illness or accident, the death of a child or a parent, or perhaps the bringing in of a gusher in Texas or Oklahoma. Now and then some love-struck young man would call a distant sweetheart, but such goings-on were frightfully expensive and also unsatisfactory, as generally neither could hear half what the other said.

In those days long-distance telephoning was a long, long way from being the smooth and routine operation it has since become. It usually took from fifteen minutes to an hour and a half to make the various connections. Since the voice was not amplified it was necessary to yell, and the voice of the person you were talking to sounded like that of someone with laryngitis shouting through a one hundred-foot drain pipe during a storm. It was difficult to make out what anyone said over the hum of the telephone wires and the crackle and pop of electricity.

This time the voice of whoever had made the call came all the way from Globe, a copper-mining town about a hundred miles from Tempe.

"You Jack?" the voice shouted.

"Yes."

"This is Jim Follingsbee," the distant voice went on.

"Oh, yes," I said politely. I didn't have the faintest notion who Jim Follingsbee was.

"What in the hell are you going to do with that damned motorcycle?"

"What motorcycle?" I asked, astonished.

"You're Andy O'Connor's boy, ain't you?"

"Yes."

"Well, goddammit, I want you to do something with that motorcycle or I'm going to throw it away! Andy left it here a hell of a long time ago. Said he'd be back next week. I ain't seen hide nor hair of him since. Whatever happened to the crazy bastard anyway?"

I told Mr. Follingsbee that I didn't know where my father was at the moment but I'd come up and see about the motorcycle. One of my pals at the normal lived in Globe and owned a Model T Ford that he drove to Globe and back about once a month to see a girl, and he was always glad to have someone along to help him change tires and to pour water in the radiator when it boiled going up Fish Creek hill. I got a ride with him, looked up Mr. Follingsbee, and inspected the motorcycle. Mr. Follingsbee was a bachelor about seventy-five years old, an ex-prospector, an ex-rancher, an ex-sheriff, and ex-Indian fighter. He lived about two miles from town in a little adobe house with about a dozen hounds. The motorcycle was in his barn. It was a 1912 two-cylinder Thor with less than a thousand miles on the speedometer. Mr. Follingsbee told me that my father had asked him back about 1912 to keep it for him for a week or two and he'd come back and get it. He had not heard from my father since that time.

The motorcycle was covered with dust and the tires were hard and brittle with age, but otherwise it looked new when I wiped the dust off. I pushed it into downtown Globe and sold it for twenty-five dollars at the first garage I came to.

My father was always buying gadgets, then tiring of them and discarding them. He did not remarry until he and my mother had been divorced for about ten years, and in the decade that he was single he left behind him a trail of Swiss watches, shotguns, mounted deer heads, unabridged dictionaries, and complete sets of O. Henry. He would buy a gadget, play with it for a time, then lose interest in it and forget it. He had probably ridden the motorcycle to Globe and had then suddenly decided that riding a motorcycle was no way for a gentleman to travel and that he would go back to wherever he came by some other means. Then he had probably forgotten about the motorcycle.

One of the gadgets my father had left behind when he and mother parted was an Edison phonograph. It had a tin horn that hung by a chain from a little L-shaped metal crane. I thought the horn beautiful; the inside was painted to resemble a morning glory. The phonograph wound up by a crank and played cylindrical records. When we were living in the tents and my mother was away teaching I used to amuse myself and my small sister for hours, playing the records. All began with a stuffy, self-important voice saying, "This is an Edison record," just as radio and television stations identify themselves today. My father's taste in music must not have been very elevated, since most of the records were "coon songs" and "ragtime."

In the early years of this century being a Negro was considered exceedingly funny. Traveling minstrel shows still played the small towns with the all-white members of the troupe made up to resemble Negroes with wide red lips and greasy coal-black skin. The makeups of Al Jolson and Eddie Cantor were in the black-face minstrel-show tradition. Stories about Negroes were all the rage and so were coon songs. The Negroes in the stories and the songs were almost always named Rastus and Sambo, just as the stories about

Irishmen, who were considered almost as funny as the Negroes, were always about Pat and Mike. Jews were likewise considered a riot and those in the stories were always named Abie and Ikey.

I can remember only one of the coon songs I used to play on that old Edison phonograph—and I remember it only vaguely. It was about a preacher and a bear and how the bear put the preacher up a tree. Another (not a coon song) concerned a young lady who was to have been a bride at a church wedding, but the groom did not show up. It was called "Waiting at the Church." Since it contained a story I played it again and again. The punch line was contained in a note from the boy friend:

> I can't get away
> To marry you today.
> My wife won't let me!

The small end of the horn of the old Edison was connected with the part of the phonograph that moved across the record and made the sound by a cylindrical piece of rubber. One day while my mother was teaching and I was entertaining my sister Helen, then about two, the brittle rubber broke. I went next door and reported the catastrophe to my Grandfather Woolf. He substituted a fired 12-gauge paper shotgun shell with the brass head cut off and it served just as well. The Edison phonograph did not survive our move to Grandfather Woolf's big new cement-block house on Myrtle Avenue. My mother probably gave it away. It was about time, because the needles and records were pretty well worn out.

When, after an absence of some years, I returned to Arizona with a wife and a baby in 1931 my father had been living in Honolulu for some time. Nevertheless I continued to fall heir to various of his discarded possessions until I moved away from Arizona in 1948. Elderly people I had no recollection of used to drive up to our house in Tucson and leave various oddments. One thing I appreciated was a Remington double-barreled trap gun of good grade, complete with leather leg-of-mutton case. My father had probably bought it thinking that it would cure his tendency to flinch or stop his swing, and that once he had it he would never drop a target. When he discovered that he could miss just as often as he had before he probably handed it to someone and said, "Do you want to use this damned gun for a while? I'll pick it up sometime."

Among other of his possessions that turned up were a Stevens target pistol, another shotgun—an Uncle Dan Lefever with Damascus barrels—a cheap pair of opera glasses, an autographed book by Jack London, the complete works of Francis Parkman, the Yukon edition of the novels of Rex Beach. Just as my father was always buying trap guns and then discarding them when he discovered he could miss with them, he was constantly buying watches and giving them away when he discovered that they did not keep perfect time. My sole legacy from my father was a Hamilton railroad pocket watch which he sent me a year or so before his death.

IT IS LITTLE WONDER that my mother and my father did not hit it off, as they were entirely different in personality and in background. My father and a dollar were soon parted, but my mother believed in the adage that a dollar saved is a dollar earned. She was born in Kentucky in 1873 but her young parents took her west with them when she was less than two years old. She grew up on a cattle ranch in a mountain valley on the New Mexico–Colorado border and on a large irrigated farm in the Salt River valley of Arizona. It was only a few miles from where she taught for many years in the school that evolved through the years from Tempe Normal School to Arizona State Teachers College to Arizona State College and finally to Arizona State University. She died in 1962, a few miles from the farm where she had spent the last years of her girlhood.

On the Colorado ranch, my grandfather thriftily shot deer for the table when the animals were fat, and saved his cattle to sell. He had a kitchen garden, a patch for beans and one for potatoes. My grandmother put butter up in tubs, made cheese, smoked ham and bacon, even cast her own candles in a mold. My grandfather tanned his own cowhides for shoes. My grandmother made clothes, knitted socks and sweaters.

My mother's thrift was that of the American pioneer farmer, who never bought anything he could make, never discarded anything he could repair. In such families the father's worn-out suits were cut down for one of the boys. Younger boys inherited the outgrown clothes of older ones. The mother's wedding dress was made over for a daughter's graduation from eighth grade. Nothing was wasted. Flour sacks were ripped open and used for dish towels —or even for underwear. The old story about the girl who took a tumble and who displayed PILLSBURY'S BEST on the seat of her panties was based on truth.

My father grew up in the easier climate of California. My mother was the oldest girl in a large family, and from the beginning she had considerable responsibility thrust upon her. She helped her mother with the cooking, the washing, the ironing. She helped take care of the younger brothers that came along. My father, on the other hand, was the youngest boy and the youngest child in his family, the pampered pet of his two brothers and two sisters as well as of his mother. My mother took care of others. Others took care of my father when he was young.

My mother's family were Baptists—and Southern Baptists at that. Both Grandfather and Grandmother Woolf were mostly of British descent—English, Scotch, and "Scotch-Irish," with the tradition of a Dutch ancestor somewhere. My father's father was an Irishman of good family. He died when I was very small. I am not sure that he ever laid eyes on me, his first grandson. He was then a very old man. Before he came to San Francisco by ship in January 1850 to look for gold he had been to a military school in England, had served as an officer in the army of the East India Company. An ancestor of his had become a Protestant in order to hang onto some land, but from what I could learn from my father and my uncles he was an agnostic. Grandmother O'Connor was also Irish but a Catholic. As far as I know all of the children were nominally Protestants or were agnostics.

My mother's people, the Woolfs, were thrifty. The O'Connors lived it up. The Woolfs were prohibitionists, believed that whiskey should be used for medicinal purposes only. The O'Connors drank wine with every meal. When the soles of the Woolf shoes had holes they were half-soled again and again. When O'Connor shoes got holes in them, the O'Connors threw them away and bought new ones of the best quality. Grandfather Woolf left a small fortune when he died, but if Grandfather O'Connor left much behind I never heard of it.

My mother clung to possessions. Her living out most of her life in a small area made this easy to do. My father moved often, left things strewn around Arizona, California, Mexico, and the Hawaiian Islands. My thrifty mother saved out of her small salary and from the inheritance she received after Grandmother Woolf died (not a great deal when the estate was divided among eight children) and invested wisely. When she died, her estate was by no means inconsiderable. When my father died in far-off Honolulu I doubt if he left anything besides a house, an automobile, and a life-insurance policy.

This ill-assorted pair would never have met if my father's brother Bill had not got into an embarrassing situation with a young lady while he was in his senior year in law school. He solved the dilemma in the classic manner by running away from it. He landed in Nogales, Arizona, on the Mexican border, got a job teaching school. He studied for the Arizona bar, passed it, and quickly established a remunerative law practice. He wrote my father's eldest brother Jim that the rubes in Arizona were a soft touch for sharp young California-educated attorneys, so Jim, who was not getting rich in California, came to Arizona and began practicing law in the desert town of Florence, about sixty miles from where I grew up in Tempe. My father met my mother when he was on a visit to his brothers. My Uncle Bill's ill-advised romance set a great many wheels in motion!

ONCE AT A DINNER PARTY in Connecticut, a New

England woman of the D.A.R.—Colonial Dames variety—very snootily asked me if I were all Irish. It was plain to see that she entertained considerable doubt as to whether the Irish were Caucasian. I told her politely that my mother was from very old American stock that had settled in Virginia and North Carolina so long ago that as far as I knew there was no tradition about when any of them had landed on these shores or what part of Great Britain they had come from. I added that all my Southern forebears had moved to Kentucky right after the Revolutionary War. The old girl looked down her nose at me and observed, "All were descended from indentured servants, no doubt!" She had me on both counts.

She may have been right—at least partly so. It is usually not the rich and well-born that emigrate. Most Americans are the descendants of European peasants—just as most Europeans are also descended from European peasants—simply because there were more peasants, small tradesmen, and shopkeepers than there were nobles and gentry. My father's family never forgot that my grandfather had been an officer and a gentleman, but they found it difficult to remember that his wife was a peasant girl.

My grandfather's people, the Woolfs, must have arrived in North Carolina very early. In a *Who's Who in Arizona* published about 1905 I see that my grandfather's people came from England in the late seventeenth or early eighteenth century and that my grandfather's great-grandfather served with "honor and distinction" in the Revolutionary War. I once knew a fusty old maid who in her declining years became a genealogy nut. She had a copy of the first census of North Carolina made right after the Revolutionary War. In it were dozens if not hundreds of Woolfs. Some of the names were spelled Wolfe, some Wolf, but I would assume that they all came from a common ancestor. My Grandfather Woolf's family had some vague connection with the Custis family of Virginia. What it was I have no idea. Perhaps a Woolf boy once married a Custis girl, or maybe a Woolf was an overseer for a Custis and horsewhipped the slaves for him. At any rate, it was traditional with the Woolfs to use the name Custis as a first or middle name. My mother's oldest brother, a very successful Arizona attorney and banker, was named Charles Custis Woolf.

My Grandmother Woolf's maiden name was Mary Ann McConnell. Like my grandfather she came from North Carolina and Virginia forebears. She was of Scotch-Irish and English descent but her coal-black hair and high cheekbones used to make me wonder if there were not an Indian somewhere on the family tree. I remember that my grandmother's mother's maiden name was Brown and Grandfather's mother's was Baker. I am told that the McConnells are a branch of the clan McDonald and that most of them were moved from Scotland to northern Ireland after Cromwell had butchered most of the native Catholic Irish there.

My maternal grandfather, James W. Woolf, was a compact, powerfully built man about five feet eight inches tall. He had yellow hair (which my mother inherited and which in turn I got from her) and bright, steely-blue eyes. My grandmother was a slender little woman with an oval face, rather large gray eyes, dainty, prettily arched eyebrows, a straight, delicately shaped but rather long nose. Her hair was black and remained black until the day she was buried in her eighty-eighth year. Pictures of her as a girl show her as rather aristocratic-looking and very pretty.

For many years I boasted that I was the only American of Southern descent whose ancestors had not owned slaves. I said that once before my mother and she told me that I was in error—that my Great-grandfather Woolf owned about a dozen slaves, but that he was not above working beside them in the fields. He was not a "planter" but a farmer and a very successful one. When my grandfather wanted to marry his black-haired, gray-eyed cutie my great-grandfather told him he would lease two farms to him and when he had learned enough about farming to make them pay they were his. He gave another son $25,000 in gold to buy a cattle ranch in Texas. This son was murdered for his bag of gold on the Staked Plains of Texas in the neighborhood of Amarillo in the 1870's.

The McConnells were not as well off as the Woolfs and as far as I know owned no slaves, but oddly enough the members of the McConnell clan were staunch Confederates and the Woolfs just as loyal Unionists. At least two of my grandmother's brothers served in the Confederate army and at least one was killed. My grandmother remained a Confederate as long as she lived. My Grandfather Woolf put in a few months in a Kentucky regiment, but I somehow got the idea that it was a home guard outfit.

My maternal grandparents came West in 1875. At that time they had two children—my Uncle Charles, then about three and a half, and my mother, then about two. They came most of the way by railroad and then went on by wagon. My mother told me that her earliest memory was standing up in the wagon bed where she had been put to go to sleep and looking out to see her parents seated around a campfire and talking.

My Grandfather Woolf established his ranch not far from Trinidad, Colorado, in New Mexico just south of the Colorado line. He and his family spent the first winter in a one-room log cabin built by my grandfather. It had a puncheon floor—logs split in two with the flat sides up to form the floor. Cooking was done on a fireplace and this was the only source of heat.

My grandfather was a man of great energy. As time passed he enlarged the house, built up a good herd of cattle. He was a passionate hunter and every time he drove to Trinidad for supplies he filled the wagon with the carcasses of mule deer to trade for flour, beans, coffee, and other staples. Once a year an itinerant shoemaker showed up and used the leather of the hides Grandfather had tanned to make shoes for the family. My grandmother produced a baby about every fourteen months. My grandfather, who had a do-it-yourself medical book, delivered them. Once when my grandmother was expecting she asked him not to go hunting as she felt as though she might be going into labor. He told her not to be foolish, that the child was not due for over a month, and went hunting anyway. He got home a few minutes before my Uncle Jim Woolf was born prematurely. Jim turned out to be the family runt and eccentric and my grandmother always blamed my grandfather because Jim didn't have quite all his marbles.

My mother always looked back on her life in New Mexico with great nostalgia. It must have been a delightful life for a child. She and her brother Charles explored up and down the valley with a brave and intelligent old dog named Crook, who growled at bears they saw but who was smart enough not to chase them. Once when they were a couple of miles from the ranch they came face to face with a mountain lion. Charles took hold of one of Crook's ears, my mother of the other, and they all fled to the ranch house. Luckily Crook was a hound of some sort and had large ears.

At that time most of the hostile Indians had been herded onto reservations, but occasional war parties broke out to murder settlers, burn ranch houses, and steal cattle. One of Mother's tales was about a twelve-year-old girl who lived on a ranch in the area and who was carried off by the Indians. She was on a horse behind one of the Indian warriors and she had presence of mind enough to unravel her red sweater and leave bits of yarn on the bushes. My grandfather was one of the posse of ranchers that tracked the

Indian war party with the help of the pieces of yarn, found the Indians in camp, and killed them all. The girl was rescued unharmed.

On another occasion a war party came to the ranch when Grandfather was away. The leader demanded that my grandmother feed them. She told them that they were filthy and that they could not come into the house until they had washed up at the horse trough. She gave them soap and towels. They all washed thoroughly and then sat around in the sun picking lice out of each other's heads until Grandmother had fried a great quantity of venison in three Dutch ovens and had cooked an enormous pot of potatoes and one of cabbage.

While the Indians gobbled the food, the little children stood around and watched wide-eyed. John, who was in age next to my mother, and then about five years old, asked: "Are they going to kill us, Mother?" My grandmother said, "Of course not!" But the leader glowered at John and said: "Maybe kill you. Maybe eat you, too!"

When the Indians had eaten everything in sight, including all the loaves of bread in Grandmother's weekly baking, they all shook hands with Grandmother, patted the children on the heads, and rode over to the next ranch, about ten miles away, burned the ranch house down and killed and scalped the entire family.

Life on Grandfather's wilderness ranch must have been a bit like life with the Swiss family Robinson. My grandfather and grandmother added milk cows to their herd, made their own butter and cheese, struggled to save enough chickens from the skunks, weasels, coyotes, and coons so they could have fresh eggs and an occasional chicken dinner. Grandfather built a spring house that kept milk cold on the warmest day of summer. He dammed the creek to irrigate a garden plot. He built a little sawmill run by water power from the creek. He was a carpenter, stone mason, blacksmith, veterinary surgeon. He added new rooms to the house and put in floors made from the yellow pine logs he sawed in his little homemade mill.

He would take a blanket, some "jerked" (dried) venison, his Model 1876 Winchester, and his dogs and would follow a big, mean cattle-killing grizzly to the death. In late summer he used to take a pack horse, a saddle horse, and a light pack outfit and camp up around timberline to hunt bighorn sheep.

As the children came of school age, he built yet another bedroom onto the ranch house and put up a little one-room school complete with fireplace, homemade desks, and benches. Then he imported a pretty blonde from the East as the children's first teacher. But in the woman-hungry West the teachers always got married at the end of the term.

My mother retired from teaching when she was sixty-four from what is now called Arizona State University, but which was humble Tempe Normal when she had joined the faculty. She had always said that when she quit teaching she was going to write a book about her pioneer girlhood in New Mexico and Arizona. She never did. She was an excellent storyteller as long as she did not try to write down what she wanted to tell. But like many amateur writers, she became self-conscious when she was confronted with paper and pen. Her stuff was then stiff, stilted, and literary. She wrote one chapter, showed it to me. I told her that it wasn't very good because it was too stiff. As far as I know she never wrote any more. It is my feeling that anyone who waits until the age of sixty-four to start writing probably is not a natural-born writer.

My grandfather had thought he was settling on the public domain when he came West but he discovered his land was on an ancient Spanish grant, the title of which had been owned by a pioneer named Pete Maxwell but which had been sold to speculators. Since trouble was brewing because the squatters were shooting the hirelings of the owners and the hirelings were shooting the squatters, my grandfather, who had a family of young children, sold his cattle and improvements and moved to the Salt River valley of Arizona a few miles from Tempe. The town of Maxwell, New Mexico, is located at the site of my grandfather's old headquarters ranch. As far as I know no member of the Woolf family has ever been back. In Arizona he bought a section of irrigated land, raised alfalfa hay, fattened cattle which he raised on nearby desert land.

# 3 · Meskin Town

WHEN my mother decided to leave my father and to get a divorce the only assets she obtained were a shiny, rubber-tired buggy with a round fringed top and a high-stepping standard-bred mare. These she sold for several hundred dollars. My grandparents had moved to Tempe and had rented a big, sprawling, stuccoed adobe house across from the normal-school campus. My grandfather had bought an entire city block near the high school. He planned to sell half of his block as building lots but keep the other half for his own house and for an orchard, a barn, chicken runs, and a pasture for a cow and a horse. In those days in Arizona it was only the feckless who did not produce their own eggs, milk, and fruit.

Like many women, my grandmother liked to pretend that her husband was an impractical dreamer who would be unable to exist without her sage advice. Grandfather drew up the plans for his house, and with the aid of two hired men made all the cement blocks used in it. He hired carpenters and worked with them, contracted for the plumbing and wiring. My grandmother disapproved of the whole project from the start, refused to visit the building when it was under construction, even refused to believe in its existence until she actually moved in. She always referred to it as "another one of Jeems's pipe dreams."

She always called my grandfather "Jeems," the old-fashioned pronunciation of James. Both she and my grandfather had lived in the West so long that they had lost their Kentucky accent and used the Far Western variety of the standard American pronunciation. She had had very little formal education, but her grammar was perfect. She did, however, use some expressions that were both old-fashioned and Southern. If someone consumed a large quantity of food, she said he "certainly ate a bait." If anyone displayed a remarkable appetite, she said he "relished his vittles." A comfortable bed was one that "slept well." She spoke of a "mess of peas," a "mess of beets," a "mess of quail."

My mother was too "proud" and too "independent" to ask her well-to-do father for financial help when she and my father parted company. In turn my grandfather was too unobservant to see that she needed it. Her mother, who had done everything possible to break up my mother's marriage, knew very well that my mother was having a hard time, but as she expressed it, "Ida's made her bed, so let her lie in it." I remember her saying that to one of her other daughters. I thought it a very odd statement because my mother was not one to lie abed.

Too proud to move in with her parents and yet too dependent on them emotionally to be far away from them, my mother used part of her money to buy two wall tents. She had floors and wooden frames for them built. The tents were stretched over the frames to make a two-room dwelling. My mother used one as the kitchen, dining room, and her own bedroom. When we moved into the tent house my sister Helen was but a few months old.

I did not realize it then, of course, but we were very poor. My mother had been a teacher before her marriage, but the local school board had a rule against employing married women. She could not get a teaching job until her divorce came through. In the meantime we had slim pickings. To stretch what little money she had, she raised a kitchen garden on the vacant lot where the tent was pitched. As a girl she had learned to cook Mexican dishes from her mother's servants. She made marvelous tamales, and to pick up extra money she took orders from churches and lodges to furnish tamales for "Mexican suppers." Since she did not have room in the tents she made them next door in her mother's big kitchen.

I followed all the steps in tamale making, and even today if I had to I am sure I could start from scratch and turn out a creditable tamale. Let me assure anyone who has unthinkingly wolfed down tamales that their manufacture is a long, detailed, painstaking, and tiresome process and one not to be undertaken lightly. In Mexico, because of all the toil and trouble involved, tamales are holiday food, festival food eaten only at Christmastime and on important saints' days. A Mexican would no more think of living on tamales than an American would think of living on roast turkey with sage dressing. Even the delicious and much easier to make enchiladas (corn cakes fried in deep fat, dipped in chili sauce, and sprinkled with chopped onions and olives, grated cheese, and chopped lettuce) are pretty fancy food for the poor Mexican. He lives on tortillas (balls of dough patted thin and cooked on a piece of iron over a fire), frijoles (red Mexican or pinto beans, the most delicious of all beans), strong coffee flavored with crude cakes of sugar called pinoche. If the poor Mexican gets some beef, mutton, goat meat, or venison he makes it into a stew with chili. If he has eggs he probably concocts a delicious omelet with onion, green pepper, and perhaps a little chili—the basis of the Denver sandwich.

To make tamales my mother would buy great quantities of corn shucks. These she would wash, soak, and trim. She would buy and boil cheap cuts of beef, then she would cut the beef into cubes about half an inch square. She would soak vast quantities of corn kernels in a lye solution so the outside coat of the kernels would fall off. Then she would wash the kernels and run them through a hand grinder. They came out in the form of a damp white flour called masa, which is the basis for all of the delicious Mexican-Indian cookery that employs corn. While all this was going on she bought strings of red chili peppers, soaked them, opened them to remove the seeds, then ran them through the same hand mill she had used to grind the corn. The resulting chili sauce was then mixed with the cubed beef. The final step in the preparation of masa was to mix it with lard, salt, and broth from the boiled beef. Then one large shuck or two smaller overlapping shucks put together were held in the left hand and spread with the masa. Then about two tablespoonfuls of the chili-meat mixture were dabbed on the masa and the cornshuck folded around it. Several dozen tamales were then stacked tightly together and steamed until the masa was done.

When Mother was in the tamale business she didn't have much time for other cooking. Fortunately I liked tamales then—and I still like them. I used to turn the mill for my mother, and when she had a batch of tamales ready for a supper for the Methodist Church or the Odd Fellows' lodge, I delivered them in my little red wagon, lard bucket after lard bucket filled with closely packed tamales kept warm and protected from dust and germs with clean flour sacking. My mother also had standing orders for a few dozen tamales from various housewives every time she made a batch. I delivered those and collected the money. I still remember the price —fifty-five cents a dozen.

If some tamales remained I sometimes took a couple of lard buckets full and peddled them at the boys' and girls' dormitories at the normal school. Because I was small and very young (less than seven) I was allowed to hawk the tamales through the sacred halls of the girls' dormitory, and go into the rooms with scantily dressed young ladies and sit big-eyed on a chair and watch while they chattered, giggled, and devoured tamales at five cents each.

In 1908 there were surely no more than a dozen four-year high schools in all of Arizona and possibly not more than half that many. The Tempe Normal School maintained an "academic department" that taught four years of high school so youngsters from lonely mines and ranches and forlorn little desert towns could get a high-school education. The young girls who attended were fed three good wholesome meals a day at the dining hall. They were warmly housed, closely watched. For a decent young girl to go out with a date unchaperoned and after dark was in the Arizona of those days considered as wild and reckless as mixed bathing in the nude.

Whenever I had a few dozen tamales to peddle I generally hit for the girls' dormitory. I could sell them quicker to the boys, as often one hungry young man would buy a half-dozen and eat them one after another. But I liked going to the girls' dormitory best. The girls were pretty, sweet-smelling, warm, mysterious. Once a young lady returned from the bathroom, shucked off her kimono, saw me. She gave a little squeak and said, "You oughtn't to have that kid in here." One of the other girls told her I was only six. "I don't give a damn how old he is," she said. "I don't like the look in the little bastard's eyes!"

We must have lived in the tents at least two years, perhaps three. I was not five when we moved there and I was eight when I started to school. But then we were living in my grandfather's big new house. Like many other members of my generation I learned to read from *Peter Rabbit* about the time of my fourth birthday. My mother used to read this fascinating story to me before she put me to bed, and presently I discovered that I recognized the same words elsewhere. I asked my mother about strange words. Presently I found that I could recognize enough words to get some meaning out of other simple books. I learned the numerals by copying them from calendars before I was five. At Christmas, about a month before my fifth birthday, someone gave me a child's edition of Grimm's *Fairy Tales.* I sat down by the Christmas tree in my grandmother's house and began to read the book. I must admit, however, that there was a great deal of ham in the performance, as I gloried in hearing the adults comment on my precocity. Within a year I read very well, but I mispronounced many words. Even today the word "misled" doesn't have nearly as much meaning for me as "mizzeled," which is the way I pronounced the word when I was young. The older my mother got, the younger she had me reading. A year or two before her death in 1962 she said I was reading when I was eighteen months old.

Learning to read at an early age has advantages but it also has its drawbacks. When we were still living in the two tents and long before I started to school, I used to go over to the house of my grandparents next door and read the *Arizona Republic* that was delivered in the morning and the *Gazette* (Democratic) that came in late afternoon. I read the comic strips first and then turned to the front page. I understood most of what I read quite well, but I was confused by some of the euphemisms in use at that time.

In those years when I was learning to read well one of the principal domestic stories of the day was that of prostitution and the red-light districts that existed in most cities. I read all the stories but I didn't get much out of them. It was some time before I knew that a disorderly house was not a place where people left their toys and bits of paper lying around. I was always being accused of being disorderly for those reasons. I read of young women being "assaulted" and I presumed that powerful and wicked men had beaten them up. Girls who were discovered to be in a "delicate condition" I thought were so ill they were almost at the point of death. For some reason I always pictured "white slaves" as young women, blond and pretty, who wore golden chains while they picked cotton and sang. Every now and then some cruel man assaulted one of the poor girls.

I was four and a half in June 1906 when Harry Thaw bumped off Stanford White for reasons that were a bit obscure to me at the time, but the next year when I followed the trial in the Phoenix papers I realized the hanky-panky that had been going on and began to have some intimations as to the doings of the birds and the bees.

I also drew endless pictures of horses and cowboys. I played in the irrigation ditch in front of our tents. The bottom of the ditch was covered with clean white sand. I used to build dams across the ditch to hold back the water when it was turned on from the main canal once a week or so. It was always dramatic to see the water sweeping down the ditch bearing on its foaming crest twigs and pine cones from the cool mysterious mountains that fed the Salt

River. When the head of water struck my dam it stopped and began to rise. As I piled on sand the water rose higher and higher. Then a trickle would lap across the top. Quickly it would cut into the dam. Then a stream became a torrent—and my dam was gone.

I played alone because there was no one to play with. We were a lonely enclave thrust into what was called "Meskin Town"—Mexican Town—and separated from it by a high board fence. Across the street was the grassy, shaded normal-school campus where young Mexican couples crawled under the bushes to make love and where Indian and Mexican drunks slept off their benders.

Now and then a Mexican child peeped through the fence at me or a group of little Mexicans yelled taunts at me from the sidewalk in front of the normal-school campus across the street. Until my mother heard me I always shouted, "Go to hell, you little greasers!" —a reply taught me by my Uncle Arthur. Exactly what the word "greaser" meant I do not know; nor do I know what its origin is. But it was a term of contempt applied to Mexicans by Americans in Texas and in the Southwest fifty and sixty years ago. Its use goes back many years—perhaps as far back as the Mexican War and the word "gringo," a term of contempt applied to Americans by Mexicans. I have not heard a Mexican called a greaser for many years.

The Mexicans in the Salt River valley of Arizona during my childhood were almost altogether poor peasants from Sonora who had come north to find work after the valley was developed by American farmers like my Grandfather Woolf. The Spanish had made no permanent settlements in Arizona north of Tucson. The Apache Indians were just too tough. In the valley it was the gringos, not the Mexicans, who were the pioneers.

These Salt River valley Mexicans who lived in Mexican Town on the other side of the high red fence were almost entirely Indian in blood. They had Spanish names. They spoke Spanish, but their features were Indian, their cooking was Indian, and they lived the bare and simple life of Indians. They dug ditches, irrigated, collected garbage, toiled in the mines and on the cattle ranches. They were neat, placid, uncomplaining workers who labored long hours for poor pay.

In the settlement at Tempe the Mexicans had attempted to re-create a Sonora village. It consisted of one street five or six blocks long lined with flat-roofed adobe houses set flush with the street. There was a saloon in those early days, a pool hall, and, I have been told, a bordello with three inmates. The Mexicans bought some of their dry goods and hardware at Markovich's store. Markovich was a Jew who was married to a Mexican woman. Most of their groceries they bought at Moe Levitsky's—and of the tribe of Levitsky more in a later chapter. Some of the Mexican women took in washing, and some, generally girls who were born in the United States, had gone to school, and spoke English, worked as maids in various homes in the town.

In one corner of the back yard of my grandfather's place was a one-room house of raw adobe and in it lived Lupe, a Mexican woman who helped with the housework, did some of the cooking, and all of the washing and ironing, a process which I found fascinating. First she soaked all the clothes overnight in cold water. Then she shaved up cakes of laundry soap to put in the water with the clothes. Then she put the tubs on stones and built fires of mesquite wood under them. As the water heated she poked at the clothes with an old broom handle. I often assisted with this chore.

When Lupe decided the clothes had boiled sufficiently, she put them in the tub, rubbed more soap from a cake on them, scrubbed them thoroughly on the corrugated washboard, wrung them out, and then tossed them into a tub of clear water. When this tub was full, she wrung them out once more, put them into another tub of clear water. Then they were wrung out again and put in a tub of water to which blueing had been added. Next the clothes were hung on a line to dry under the hot Arizona sun. Lupe no sooner finished one washing and ironing than she had to start another.

I was very fond of Lupe. She did her own cooking on a fire in the back yard. She always had a pot of coffee on the fire and a pot of frijoles gently simmering. Her stove was a sheet of iron perched on four piles of stones. On it she baked delicious tortillas which were about the size of bicycle wheels and of the consistency of wet buckskin. The pat-pat-pat of Mexican women shaping tortilla dough is one of my earliest memories. Lupe would start with a piece of dough about twice the size of a golf ball. At each pat she spread her fingers and turned the growing tortilla first on one side and then on the other. At each pat the tortilla grew bigger. When it was two feet or so in diameter she'd slap it on the hot sheet of iron.

A tortilla half cooked on sheet iron had body. Since it was hard to digest it stuck to a poor working man's ribs. Put a few tablespoonfuls of fried beans in a tortilla and roll them up in it and you have a "burro," a delicious lunch. The poor Sonora Mexicans all carried two or three burros to work with them for lunch.

Lupe was homely, skinny, cross-eyed, very dark of complexion. A couple of years before, she and a younger, prettier sister used to sleep in the summertime on cots in the back yard. Conception, the younger sister, had a boy friend who used to sneak in at night and crawl in with her. One night he made a mistake and crawled in with Lupe. Perhaps the night was dark. Perhaps the boy friend had been drinking. At any rate he made a mistake. Poor homely Lupe, possibly thinking it was an interesting experience and it might be her only chance, said nothing.

When Lupe's figure made her condition unmistakable, my grandmother asked her about it. She answered frankly that Chico, the boy friend, had made a mistake. If it had been a white girl my grandmother would have been shocked. As it was, she was amused. When the baby boy was born, Grandmother furnished a layette and Grandfather gave Lupe a twenty-dollar gold piece.

"Just like a goddam greaser!" my Uncle John Woolf commented. "They all screw like jackrabbits!"

In the early years of this century the area under irrigation in the Salt River valley was much smaller than it is now and as a consequence it was less humid and the air cooled off more at night. When the hot weather began in earnest in June all of the Woolfs and Mother and her two children moved heavy Mexican cots into the back yard. Days might be fearfully hot with the thermometer going up to 120 degrees in the shade and with sidewalks so hot they would quickly fry eggs, but once the sun went down the air cooled rapidly and by the time darkness had fallen and I was told to go to bed the sheets were delightfully cool. I would lie there watching the myriads of close and brilliant stars, listen to the wind whispering through the cottonwood and chinaberry trees. Lupe also slept in the back yard, discreet and modest behind a screen of cottonwood branches beside her little adobe house.

The last summer we spent in the two tents was that of 1910 and I can remember the great glowing sweep of Halley's comet in the sky. I used to lie on my cot in the cool sheets watching the comet and thinking sadly that the next time it visited the earth I would be in my grave.

My sister Helen, who had been born in December 1905, and I had all the children's diseases known to man while we lived there in the tents. For a woman with practically no income and with dwindling capital, the drug and doctor bills must have been staggering. We went through measles, whooping cough, scarlet fever, chicken pox, all varieties of colds, and whatnot. We were inoculated against diphtheria and suffered horribly from hives, only to come down with the disease exactly three months after we were inoculated. Somehow we escaped the mumps, and I didn't fall prey to this miserable disease until many years later when I was trying to make hay with a beautiful University of California co-ed by throwing away my money to take her to dinner and dancing at Tait's Downtown, a very sleek night spot of the early 1920's in San Francisco. I felt like hell. Even a few fingers of bootleg Canadian rye in ginger ale failed to arouse me. My date told an Arizona friend with whom I was double-dating the two glamorous Kappas that I was moody. I was worse than that. I awakened the next morning with a real case of mumps.

When my sister and I were sick we were purged, given enemas, and the moment I had as much as a sniffle my mother started giving me "a good cleaning out." Luckily my sister and I had strong constitutions or the cascara, Epsom salts, calomel, and castor oil we downed would have killed us.

My mother got a job teaching after her divorce went through, and although grade-school teachers were not very generously paid her salary was enough to support her and her two children, and to help her to start paying off the bills she had run up while my sister and I were sick.

I started in first grade when I was seven in the fall of 1909. The year before, when I would ordinarily have started, I had been sick with scarlet fever. My mother was teaching at another school so I had to report to the first-grade room alone.

Almost all the children were being towed to school by their mothers. Half of them were bawling. The other half were pummeling each other or pulling each other's hair. I took one good look and decided that this was not for me. I didn't bawl. I didn't run. I didn't go over to the other school where my mother was teaching. I simply went back to our tents and drew pictures of cowboys.

When my mother got home my sister, then almost three, and I were happily building a sand castle in the ditch. She asked me how I liked school. I told her I didn't like it and wasn't going to go. For whatever the reason, she let me stay out of school another year. I was reading just about everything about that time. My Uncle Arthur made me a slingshot and I grew very skillful at knocking doves and blackbirds out of the cottonwoods. Once I even killed a cottontail rabbit.

I was invited to the birthday party of a boy named Gordon Goodwin, who lived four or five blocks down the street. He was six months older than I and he and I were friends through most of my youth. At first the presence of all the other children made me very shy, but presently I warmed up and was racing around, screaming, pushing other children in a frenzy of sociability. Suddenly one of my sandals flew off. The other children laughed. I began to weep, fled home with but one shoe, and refused to go back.

# 4 · Grandfather Woolf

WE moved into Grandfather Woolf's new house in the late summer of 1910. Although he never said as much it was apparently Grandfather's secret wish to gather his clan about him in his fine new house and reign as a patriarch forever. At that time his two youngest children, my Aunt Mabel and Aunt Irene, were still living at home. They were teaching school, just about the only respectable thing for a middle-class girl to do in those days in the interval between school and marriage. However, both girls were nubile. Eligible males were constantly sniffing around and to my vast disgust "spooning" with the girls in the living room or on a sofa in the front hallway. I used to lurk at the head of the stairs and listen to the low murmurs and the loud smacks as they kissed.

My Uncle Charles Woolf was a successful attorney with offices in both Phoenix and Tempe, the father of two red-headed children. Uncle Bill Woolf was living in Phoenix, where he was undersheriff, Carl Hayden's right-hand man. By this time my Uncle John Woolf with his wife and infant daughter was in northern Sonora managing the great Green Cananea cattle ranch, shooting bandits and worrying about the new Mexican revolution. Arthur Woolf made the house his headquarters, but he was just getting into the business of buying cattle and was away a great deal.

Jim Woolf, the family runt and eccentric, had always refused to have anything to do with responsibility, respectability, or property. He lived most of the time in southern California in cheap hotels and he worked intermittently as a fruit packer. Whenever he was broke he wrote home for money and Grandfather always sent it. Jim was a little man not over five feet three or four, with light hair and small, hostile green eyes. For his size he was one of the best rough-and-tumble barroom and whorehouse fighters in the West. He would have done well if he had stayed in his own weight class, but when he was in his cups he would tackle anyone. He often got beaten up by bigger and stronger men, but he never seemed to learn as he was always ready for an eye-gouging, ear-biting, nut-squeezing brawl.

Many years later when I was in college I worked one summer in a mine. I once mentioned to a grizzled miner that I was from Tempe.

"I used to know a guy from Tempe," he said. "Knew him in California. Meanest little son of a bitch I ever run into. Let that little bastard get a few snorts in his hide and he'd fight a buzz saw. Everybody who knowed him was a-scared of him. They thought he was crazy!

"Christ, I remember one night in Fat Minnie Schultz's whorehouse in Colton. This little fart came in there all liquored up. They had a bar and one of these-here player pianners on the lower floor, but the girls, they done their tricks upstairs. Anyway, this guy Jim he come upstairs and got into some kind of an argument with a pimp. Jim knocked him on his ass, then picked him up and throwed him downstairs. His legs was short but his arms was big and long and real powerful.

"Fat Minnie come up to see what the hell was going on and this guy Jim throwed *her* downstairs. Somebody called the cops. They was three of them harness bulls. They started upstairs after this crazy little bastard and he throwed a red-headed whore at them. These cops they never laid a hand on him until he run out of whores to throw. They grabbed this guy and beat hell out of him and throwed him in the hoosegow for thirty days. They slapped a big fine on him too but he had a rich father who sent the dough to pay that off. That was a long time ago—1913 or 1914."

"Was his name Jim Woolf?" I asked.

"Christ, yes! Do you know him?"

"He's my uncle," I said.

The miner looked at me with sudden respect.

"Well, I'll be goddamned," he said. "I'd better be careful around you. If a guy was as big as you are and was as strong and as mean for his size as Jim Woolf there'd be no holding him. Yeah, I see you're his kin. You got them same kind of mean little green eyes that little son of a bitch had. You ain't got that same crazy look in them, though."

I can only remember seeing Jim one time during the years we lived in the big house. Later he did not even come to his father's funeral. I knew there was such a person as Jim, but I had not seen him since I was very small and was a bit vague about him.

I was in the front yard one day when a little red-faced man with thinning light hair, a broken nose, and a scowl on his face strode up to the front gate carrying a tight, neatly rolled "bindle," or bedroll. He opened the gate and walked in as if he owned the place. I thought he was a tramp and was about to tell him to go away, but he fixed me with his penetrating little green eyes and snarled: "Who in the hell are you?" "Jack," I answered. By that time I was nine and almost as tall as he was. "I might have known it, you fat slob," he snarled. "You're built just like your mother. You haven't got any more ass than a snake. Quite a dump the old man's built here. Where in the hell is he?"

Just then my grandfather appeared on the porch.

"Oh, hello, Jim," he said, as if his son had just come back from the post office. "You look tired. Come in and we'll fix you something to eat."

"I am kind of tired, Dad," he said. "I rode a freight in. I haven't had a bite for twenty-four hours."

He and my grandfather disappeared into the house and a few

minutes later I could smell bacon frying and coffee boiling. Jim stayed around for two or three weeks, quarreling with everyone, rolling Bull Durham cigarettes, spilling tobacco and ashes on the carpets. He had got some money from his father and was apparently drinking in his room; I could smell liquor on his breath.

The blowup came when one of Mabel's suitors showed up to spend a weekend. He was a doctor in the United States Navy, a tall, handsome, well-educated, well-dressed young man from a distinguished Eastern family. The very sight of him enraged Jim. He found out that the young man was of colonial Dutch descent, a Republican, an Episcopalian, and a graduate of Harvard Medical School.

Jim hung on the young officer like a leech, much to Mabel's distress. He called the Dutch squareheads. He said that he had never known a Republican who wasn't a bastard or a Harvard graduate who wasn't a fairy. The officer refused to argue with him, regarded him with detached amusement as one might regard an extraordinarily large, fuzzy, and rather repulsive caterpillar. This infuriated Jim. Finally he called the officer a big tub of guts.

Mabel had left the room and except for me the two were alone. The young officer's eyes glinted coldly. "Listen, you little horror," he said. "If you weren't Mabel's brother and were anywhere except here I'd slap your nasty little face—"

Jim jumped to his feet and threw a punch, but the tall young officer's left hand was in his face. Just then my grandfather shot out of his study, blue eyes blazing behind steel-rimmed spectacles. He grabbed Jim's left ear between thumb and forefinger and led him out of the room.

Jim did not show up for supper that night, nor for breakfast the next morning. By peeking into his room I ascertained that both he and his bindle had disappeared. A week later someone entered the house by the unlocked door on the back screen porch, stole all my mother's wedding silver, a freshly baked and frosted cake, a large and expensive Navajo rug, and my grandmother's little hoard of change from which she paid Chinese vegetable peddlers, Indians who brought mesquite wood, the ice man, and various tinkers and peddlers. The local constable came up, looked around, and said it looked like an inside job to him. He said if it wasn't, how in the hell would anybody know where Mrs. Woolf kept that money and how would anyone have known that the silver he got away with was sterling or the rug was worth two hundred bucks. Grandfather said to let it go. Bill Woolf, who thought he was funny, said that a posse from the Maricopa County sheriff's office had found an unidentified tramp stone dead, wrapped in a Navajo blanket, and surrounded by cake crumbs. They had simply dug a hole and dumped the tramp into it, still wrapped in the rug. He said he wasn't the least surprised at what had happened to the guy because Ida had always baked lousy cakes anyway. Everyone suspected that Jim had been the thief.

Grandfather's big house was made of concrete blocks cast to suggest cut stone, one of the ugliest and phoniest building materials ever invented. It had two bay windows in the living room, an open porch that ran around two sides of the house, and a screen porch in the rear. It was the first house in Tempe with central heating. There was a big coal-gobbling furnace in the basement and hot-air registers in every room. In the kitchen was an enormous walk-in refrigerator that took 1,200 pounds of ice and seared my grandmother's thrifty soul.

On the ground floor were the living room, the dining room between it and the kitchen, the entrance hallway, my grandfather's large study where he sometimes slept and later died, a bathroom, and my grandfather's and grandmother's bedroom. Upstairs my mother, Helen, and I had two rooms. One of them, which served as our sitting room and my bedroom, had a fireplace connected to the same chimney as the fireplace in the living room. There were three other bedrooms on the second floor, one of which Irene and Mabel shared. Another was a guest room, where the girls' suitors were put up, and in another Arthur Woolf kept his clothes and slept when he was home. At the end of the hall was a large bathroom, but since it was the only one on the floor traffic was often heavy.

Behind the house was an orchard with peach and apricot trees and grapevines, and in the front and side yards were several orange and grapefruit trees. Grandfather had foresightedly planted these long before he built the house. Behind the orchard was a barn where Pet, grandfather's fine trotting mare, Pet's hay and grain, and the buggy were kept. A Jersey cow with the not very original name of Bossy had a feed trough and a shed; and a substantial flock of white leghorn chickens had a house and a run, but most of the time they foraged for seeds, bugs, and grasshoppers in the orchard and in the pasture. At the time we moved into the big house the whole block was enclosed by a barbed-wire fence. All was good Bermuda-grass pasture, where Pet and Bossy grazed, but within a couple of years my grandfather sold the lots on the east side.

In those days early in this century, almost everyone in small Arizona towns kept chickens, and anyone who has lived at that time well knows what "cock crow" means. It was as definite a designation of time as sunup and sundown, as moonrise and moonset. About a half hour before sunup, when the first pale luminescence began to show on the horizon, a particularly alert and perceptive cock would crow. Then another and another. Then cocks would be crowing all over town. It was the first sign of approaching day. I thought of this many years later when I was a middle-aged man and was hunting tigers in India. I had sat all night in a machan above a tiger kill. The tiger had come and had tramped around in the dry leaves, but he had got suspicious and had left. I was dozing in the machan when I dreamed I was a child back in Arizona, that it was morning and all the cocks were crowing. As I awakened I realized I had heard the crowing of the jungle cocks, the ancestors of all domestic chickens. They had made the long journey from the Indian teak and sal forests to the oasis on the Arizona desert where I grew up.

Genuinely thrifty Arizona people had cows. There was no dairy in town and if a cowless family wanted milk it was necessary to make arrangements with someone who had a cow. There was always a small boy mixed up in the business somewhere. If the cow owner had a boy he delivered the milk in a lard pail. If the family that had no cow had a boy, he went after the milk. When we lived in the tents across from the normal, Grandfather had no cow, as he had no place to graze one. Where his family got milk I cannot say, but I know that every night I took my little lard bucket, crossed the street, and walked along the sidewalk on the edge of the campus to a house about four blocks away where a cow was kept in the back yard. The people milked late, and in the winter it was dark when I came back along the dark and spooky walk between the normal-school campus and the ditch. It was shaded by ash and cottonwood trees. Often the ditch bank grew up with weeds and Johnson grass, and there were bushes and shrubs on the campus side of the sidewalk.

For me those dark and lonely blocks were fraught with mystery and terror. The wind made strange sounds in the trees. Now and then a Mexican dog crossed the street to bark and snarl at me. Mexican couples necking in the bushes made strange and spooky noises. "Of course you are not frightened," my mother said when I told her this walk scared the hell out of me. "You are Mother's brave, big boy!" I wanted to tell her I was Mother's little cowardly boy, but I swallowed and went out anyway. I was then about six.

One night the people who owned the cow were especially late in milking and when I set out with my little pail of milk it was both cold and dark. A wind was blowing. Not a star showed, and, as my grandfather used to say, it was coming on to rain.

I had skittishly entered the worst part of the walk, when suddenly there was a strange and horrible sound and a human figure rolled out of the dead Johnson grass by the ditch into my path. I shot around whatever it was and, holding the pail in front of me, ran like an antelope. My feet have never felt so light. I was so frightened and so vague about what I had seen that my mother went next door and told my grandfather. He investigated. I had seen a dead-drunk Indian and the sound I had heard was his vomiting. I continued to get the milk but I hated the job and for a long time darkness made me nervous.

TODAY THE WORDS "rich" and "poor" are seldom used. It is well known today that many people have a great deal of money or property, but ever since the depression of the 1930's the word "rich" has been considered both unfashionable and unlucky. Likewise the word "poor" is seldom used. Instead of being poor people have substandard incomes, are underprivileged or deprived. It is considered that their plight is not their fault but the fault of society.

Back in 1910 it was thought that rich people were smart, thrifty, and had worked for what they had and if people were poor it was their own damned fault. There were various grades of economic being. The rich were a race apart. They lived in large houses built on large, well-landscaped grounds. They had servants, coachmen, or chauffeurs who touched their caps and wore uniforms, maids who wore white aprons and white lace dinguses on their heads. The rich had tennis courts in their back yards, owned automobiles, and when they went someplace they traveled by private railway car. They also had been to Europe and owned steamer trunks plastered with stickers from foreign hotels and steamship lines. To be *rich* you should be a millionaire or even a multimillionaire.

The next grade below the rich were the well-to-do. These people lived in smaller houses on smaller grounds, but by modern standards they were still large. Instead of chauffeurs, butlers, and gardeners they had a hired man who mowed the lawn, cleaned the stable, cut the wood for the fireplace, trimmed the hedges, washed the carriage or the car. Instead of cooks, upstairs and downstairs maids, and even butlers, the well-to-do had a hired girl. The well-to-do almost never went to Europe, and few of them went as far as New York. When they wanted a touch of city life those who were well-to-do and lived in Arizona went to the "Coast"—Los Angeles or San Francisco. Most of the well-to-do who had made their money in cattle had been to Chicago. It was considered something of a status symbol of the well-to-do to spend part of each torrid Arizona summer either on the beach in southern California or in the mountains in northern Arizona. My grandfather owned a cabin at a summer resort north of Phoenix at an altitude

the ranch to the rented place across from the normal-school campus and from there to the big new house on Forest Avenue. There, as long as he lived, it gathered dust in a corner in the furnace room. As soon as he died my grandmother had it carted away with the garbage.

Arizona had once teemed with mountain sheep, desert and Rocky Mountain mule deer, pronghorn antelope, Arizona whitetail deer, black bears and grizzly bears, and elk; but by 1900 the elk were extinct, and other animals had been thinned out by market hunters. Hunting of sheep and antelope was forbidden by law by 1910, but because grizzly bears killed an occasional cow they were bedeviled until they became extinct along about 1920. Even deer were rare, and anyone in Tempe who actually shot a deer was something of a local hero.

Bird hunting was grandfather's dish, and a well-to-do Arizonan who hunted was supposed to have at least one good shotgun. My grandfather was something of a gun nut. He had not one good shotgun but three. All were double-barreled. One was an Ithaca. One was a Parker of good grade. The other, the pride of grandfather's old age and his secret sin, was an English Purdey with two sets of barrels. He kept the other two shotguns in an open gun rack in his study along with his Winchester Model 94, .30/30 carbine, his Model 86 Winchester .45/70, an old Winchester Model 1876 he had used on his Colorado ranch. Every now and then when I was mooning around his guns he would pick up the old '76, sigh, and say, "Boy, I've shot right smart head of game with this old rifle—grizzlies, mountain lions, bighorns, tons of deer. I wish I had this old rifle and was back in New Mexico right now!"

But the Purdey he kept in its oak-and-leather case. He used to let me admire it. I loved the way it was nested in red billiard cloth in cunningly contrived compartments. I admired the chaste scroll engraving on the side plates, the rich and elegant sheen of the brown walnut stock streaked with dark lines, the monogram JWW on the gold oval crest plate near the toe of the stock.

Sometimes when we were ready to go hunting my grandfather

would say, "Boy, do you think we ought to take the Purdey today?" And when we were out in the country and had tied Pet up and were preparing to hunt he would open the case, take out the butt portion of the Purdey. "Boy, what do you think? Shall we use the choke or the open barrels? The birds are flying kind of high."

His principal shooting pal was a banker named Frank Peck. Peck was the cashier at the Tempe National, where Grandfather was chairman of the board. The two had hunted together for years, but Peck never called my grandfather anything but Mr. Woolf. Grandfather called the cashier Peck. When the two hunted together, opening the oak-and-sole leather case with brass corners was a ritual. Peck always said, "Lovely gun, Mr. Woolf. I wish I could afford a really fine gun like that!" Grandfather always replied, "Nothing wrong with that sixteen-gauge Fox of yours, Peck, and you can certainly handle it!" And the cashier would say, "Thank you, Mr. Woolf."

My grandfather's guns fascinated me. So did his case of fine British razors, one for every day of the week. He subscribed to *Field & Stream, Outdoor Life,* and *Outdoor Recreation.* I used to slip into his study when he was working on his accounts, sit by the window, and read about hunts for mountain sheep, grizzly, and caribou in the Cassiar, quail shoots in Georgia. I read all the ads as carefully as I did the text. I filled out coupons and obtained gun catalogues, samples of dried food, brochures of resort hotels. By the time I was ten I could quote ballistics by the yard, knew the range of all American game animals, and was planning my battery for a safari in East Africa.

My grandfather was an important man. He was known not only in Tempe and the Salt River valley but all over Arizona. He had been a member of the Arizona delegation that went to Washington to lobby for the Roosevelt Dam. He was on the board of directors of the Tempe Canal Company, the Tempe National Bank, and the Hayden Flour Mill. At the time he sold his ranch he was worth about a quarter of a million.

Like many men who make money in one business he lost it in

others. A friend of mine made a million manufacturing lace, about which he knew a great deal, and lost it trying to mine gold in Mexico, something about which he knew nothing. My grandmother wanted Grandfather to take the cash he got from the sale of the hay ranch and put it in bonds and good safe 8 per cent mortgages. But he was too restless for that. He lost a good deal of money in a gold mine, more in a Los Angeles company that was trying to perfect a tubeless, puncture-proof automobile tire—a problem that was not solved for fifty years. He started a company to make concrete blocks, concrete pipe, and headgates for irrigation. My grandfather was an expert rancher and farmer, a catch-as-catch-can veterinarian, a pretty good carpenter, bricklayer, bronco-buster, Indian fighter, and dove shot, but he knew absolutely nothing about gold mining or making tubeless tires, and what he learned about the manufacture of concrete pipe and headgates he learned painfully and expensively.

My grandmother considered him a financial incompetent. She called his business ventures after he had sold the ranch those darned-fool, harebrained schemes of Jeems's. She said the only reason he had ever made any money was because bulls lusted for cows. "When you have a ranch," she said, "you can go sheep hunting and bear hunting and trout fishing and the bulls will cover the cows and the cows will have calves and you can sell the calves for money. Anything else, somebody takes your money if you go fishing and don't watch them."

She was particularly bitter about the Purdey shotgun. Grandfather had been quite vague about what it cost. He intimated that through some bit of chicanery he had got it at a rare bargain, had practically stolen it, in fact.

But she was suspicious and snooped around until she found the canceled check made out to the New York gun store that had handled the importation.

"You haven't got a lick of common sense!" she told him. "Six hundred dollars for a shotgun! Jeems, I think you're teched!"

My grandfather died in 1915. Not long before his death he

called Grandmother in and asked her in my presence to be sure that I got the Purdey. None of his sons appreciated a fine gun, he said, and they wouldn't take care of it.

Grandfather was hardly in his grave when Grandmother gave my Uncle Charles the Purdey. She did this deliberately to get even with her dead husband, I am sure, because of all the sons Charles was the one who never hunted, didn't know one gun from another, and was bored stiff by the very thought of hunting. Charles lent the Purdey to friends who thought they might like to shoot a few quail or doves and didn't own a gun. Now and then I'd see it at his house in a broom closet next to the O'Cedar mop.

After I was grown and married I asked my uncle what had happened to it. "You mean that old English gun in the leather box?" he asked. "Darned if I know. I used to lend it out and somebody forgot to bring it back."

So Grandmother used the Purdey to get her revenge. She always held that it was Grandfather's fault that Jim Woolf was so runty and so mean. In spite of her protests Grandfather had gone hunting and when he got back Jim was in the process of being born.

"The fright I got at starting to have that baby all alone out in those hills with the coyotes howling and the catamounts screaming stunted Jim's growth and made him teched," she said. "If Jeems had stayed with me like I asked him to instead of going hunting, poor Jim would be a fine man like my other boys!"

# 5 · Climate and People

IN 1907, the time when I first remember Tempe, the town was not a great deal over thirty years old. It had been named by an English remittance man named Darrel Duppa. Widely traveled, he said that the valley around Tempe reminded him of the vale of Tempe in Greece. For some reason the name of my home town has always been accented on the last syllable whereas that of the Greek valley is accented on the first. Duppa also gave Phoenix its name. In its early days as a settlement the place burned down and was immediately rebuilt. It rose from its own ashes. Hence the name.

It was generally believed that Duppa was a graduate of Oxford and came from a noble English family, but in those days the unsophisticated frontiersmen thought every Englishman who didn't drop his aitches and was so refined that he blew his nose in a handkerchief instead of on the ground was a member of the titled gentry; and since Oxford was the only British institution of higher learning anyone in Arizona had heard of, those refined limey dudes automatically became Oxford graduates. Duppa was often called "Lord" Duppa. Like many early Arizonans he had tuberculosis and trouble with the bottle.

Before Duppa tacked the name of Tempe on my home town, Charles Trumbull Hayden, father of Carl Hayden, had built a house and flour mill there. Water was brought to the fertile desert land by digging canals and ditches and diverting water from the Salt River by building dams of brush and mud across it. This was not too satisfactory, as there was too much water in the spring when the snows melted in the high mountains that fed the Salt and its tributaries and not enough at other times of year. My Grandfather Woolf was one of the Salt River valley farmers who went back to Washington to lobby for the Roosevelt Dam. When this great dam was built it impounded an enormous quantity of water which otherwise would have gone down the Salt unused into the Gila and then into the Colorado and into the Gulf of California.

At one time the ancestors of the Pima and Maricopa Indians had irrigated and farmed much of the valley. Remains of the canals, their villages, their burials were found all over the area, but when the Anglo-Saxon pioneers arrived most of this old farm land had long since grown up in brush, mesquite trees, and cactus, and the Indians themselves lived in small villages close to the river where irrigation was simple. Possibly the Pimas and Maricopas abandoned much of their land because of harassment by the warlike Apaches. Possibly a rising water level from long-continued irrigation had brought alkali to the surface.

When the brush was being cleared from the low desert lands and canals and ditches were being built tons of Indian artifacts were dug up. At my grandfather's house all the door stops were beautifully shaped and polished stone axheads. Grandfather's chickens were fed out of metates hundreds of years old. They were hollowed out of a hard volcanic stone called basalt and were used for grinding corn. My grandparents also had many handsome pots that had been dug out of ancient graves. What happened to any of these I have no idea.

The men who settled the valley were real pioneers. When my grandfather brought his brood there in 1885 the valley must have been a pretty raw-looking place, but by the time of my first memories there were big cottonwoods along the ditch banks, trees around most of the ranch houses, and trees throughout the town of Tempe.

The house my grandfather built shortly after he arrived in the valley in 1885 was by no means palatial, but it was one of the larger ranch homes in the valley. Most of the farmers lived in small, ugly lumber houses set in barren yards cluttered with farm implements, broken-down wagons, tin cans, and generally swarming with chickens. Winters in southern Arizona have always been very pleasant. When the sun shines it is warm at midday but in December and January there is often frost on the grass in the mornings and sometimes water freezes. The distant mountains are generally capped with snow.

But snow almost never falls in the valley, although Tucson, which is 1,000 feet higher than Tempe and Phoenix, gets a snow every two or three years. I was well along in adolescence before I ever saw snow except as something white and far away on the tops of mountains. But summers were and are both hot and long in southern Arizona. Generally the thermometer would start going above 100 degrees by the middle of May. Junes were very hot but dry. Along in the first two weeks of July the clouds would start rolling north from the Gulf of California. Then it would be not only hot but sultry. Sometimes it would be weeks before the rain would fall. The rain would often be heavy and violent with thunder and lightning and walls of muddy water rushing down arroyos that had been dry for months. As a child I used to revel in these summer thunder showers. After rain had fallen for a few minutes it would be delightfully cool and thousands of frogs that had been hidden in the dry earth for months would emerge and begin a tremendous croaking. Lightning would bring the distant mountains into sharp relief. Then the stabbing lightning would get less frequent and farther away. The cannonading thunder would roll off into the distance and the rain would slacken.

An occasional rain brought some relief from the heat in July and August, but the dweller in southern Arizona could count on being uncomfortably hot most of the time from the middle of May until the first of October. When I was a child and for many years later there was no air conditioning of private homes, but along in the 1920's some theaters and department stores in Phoenix established air-conditioning systems. There was, of course, no electric refrigeration, but those who were not too far from an ice plant bought ice to keep perishable food fresh in iceboxes. Those who could not get ice had coolers with burlap sides that hung in the wind. If the burlap was kept damp, the evaporation in the dry air lowered the temperature just as the earthenware vessel, the olla, did.

The adobe houses of the Mexicans were ideal for the hot Arizona climate. Their walls were thick. The roofs were made of brush piled on timbers and covered with earth. Mud and straw for adobe bricks were cheap and there were many Mexicans who for small wages would make the adobes and build houses. But the American pioneers with few exceptions imported expensive pine lumber to build their wretchedly hot houses.

In spite of the fact that I grew up in a desert valley and have spent more time in southern Arizona than anywhere else, I have always hated heat and have fled from it at every opportunity. All of my ancestors came from northwestern Europe, most of them from the cool, foggy British Isles, and I am simply not a creature adapted to heat. I have hunted desert antelope and Barbary sheep in the southern Sahara, gemsbok in the Kalahari of South Africa, black buck and nilgai in the burning plains of India north and east of Delhi just before the monsoon. I have been very uncomfortable in all those places and the heat of southern Arizona is just as bad as it is anywhere.

The dwellers in hot climates in most places—in Mexico, in Spain and Italy, in North Africa—knock off in the middle of the day when the heat is fiercest. They eat big meals, lie down in a darkened room behind cool thick walls, take a siesta. But not the Anglo-Saxon pioneers in the Southwest! Just as they spurned adobe as building material, so they spurned such "degenerate" Mexican habits as the siesta. They worked just as hard at midday as they did in the cool of the morning. The Mexicans thought they were crazy.

A Mexican institution adopted by a good many Americans was the ramada, a brush shelter open on four sides. This gave shade and allowed the breeze, if any, to circulate. The heat was much less oppressive under a ramada than it was inside those awful little lumber houses, where no breeze stirred and it was as hot as a bake oven. A fixture of the ramada was an olla, a large vessel of porous pottery made by Mexicans and Indians, that hung in the breeze and was cooled by the water that evaporated as it seeped slowly through to the outside. A tin cup was always attached to the olla by a string. People were less conscious of germs in those days than they are now.

Small boys who were not sissies always went barefoot as soon as the weather warmed up. Actually I doubt if any of us enjoyed it, but anyone who fancied himself a real he-boy and who didn't want other he-boys to poke fun at him took off his shoes. I was always getting thorns in my feet, cutting them horribly with broken glass, bruising them on stones, having them stung by bees. Making a trip across town with bare feet was for me almost as much of a test of fortitude and faith as it is for the Polynesians who walk barefoot across beds of glowing coals. As I went across town I would skip from one less fiery bit of footing to another. I soon found that cement sidewalks were very hot, that black stones were hotter than white ones, that soft dust and sand were not bad to walk on because the feet sank quickly through the burning surface layer. Some white children from very poor families and many Mexican children went barefoot the year around. Their feet developed heavy cracked epidermis that looked not unlike the bottoms of elephants' feet. They did not seem to be bothered by the burning ground. I was never wild about this barefoot business and I was relieved when I reached the shoe-wearing-in-summer age.

Summers, when I was small, my uniform consisted of a blue chambray shirt and a pair of blue bib overalls. Period. In one of the back pockets of the overalls I always carried a "sling shot" or "nigger shooter." This weapon I always made myself after I had seen an uncle construct my first one. The V-shaped handle was cut from a forked cottonwood branch and all the bark was removed. Only the V was left, and the completed weapon was grasped on the lower part with one hand. If a boy left a handle below the V he was a sissy. The propellent force was supplied by two rubber bands about half an inch wide and about eight inches long attached (preferably with thin rubber bands) to the top portions of the wooden V. The pouch for the missile was made of the upper or the tongue of an old shoe—or a shoe not so old if a discarded shoe was not available. I became very skillful with my sling shot. I could generally knock a dove out of a tree at from twenty to forty feet, hit a dog at forty and fifty yards. Along my route from one friend's house to another officious dogs would still bark at me, but after I had pasted them a couple of times with nice round high-velocity stones from my sling shot they would flee the instant I reached for my hind pocket. One of my chores used to be to accompany my mother to carry bundles for her on her Saturday shopping, banking, and bill-paying expeditions. She used to marvel that I had but to look at a barking dog to send it skulking. She would have been shocked to know they fled because they saw me reaching for my back pocket and were afraid they were about to get a stone in the ribs.

During my youth I never wore a hat, and in the summer when I was out in the sun a great deal my hide gradually grew deeply tanned until I was almost as dark as an Indian. For a blond I certainly had plenty of pigment. As my skin darkened, my hair, which was naturally yellow, gradually faded until it was yellow-white. I must have made a strange appearance with my green eyes and fair hair in contrast to my brown cheeks. Pigment is something one loses with age, alas, but I have a picture of myself taken when I was thirty-three or thirty-four one summer in Sonora with a couple of bighorn rams I had shot. I was as dark as any Mexican.

It is impossible for the people of two cultures to live side by side without some of the vocabulary and customs of each rubbing off on the other. The Mexicans in the valley picked up many English words, "mechee" instead of *fosforo* for match, for example; "trocke" instead of *camion* for truck, "el tren" for a railway train instead of *ferrocarril.* Americans took a *welta* instead of a turn and a *pasear* instead of a walk. They were just as apt to get on a *caballo* as a horse and to pick up a *riata* as a rope. Little Mexicans cursed little Americans boys in fractured English: "You sonomobeechy, you goddam," and the little Americans said, *"Bese mi culo, huidido."* Most Americans who grew up in Arizona in those days picked up the Mexican habit of ending a sentence with no to ask a question: "That is a pretty girl, no?" When they bade each other farewell they were more apt to use, *"Adios, amigo"* than goodbye, and when they wanted to say that someone didn't quite have all his marbles they were apt to say he was *poco loco.*

When I was in grade school little children of Mexican descent started out with the little English-speaking children, but many of the little Mexican children spoke no English and they had a pretty tough time. By the time the members of a class had moved up to fifth or sixth grade most of the children of Mexican descent had dropped out. Not many finished the eighth grade and very few went to high school.

Until the Anglo-Saxon Americans moved into Arizona, herded the warlike Apaches into reservations, began farming in the Salt River valley and developing mines, there was no permanent Mexican settlement north of Tucson. But as the territory developed, labor was needed. Poor Mexicans from Tucson and the settlements in Sonora south of Nogales moved into the Gila and Salt River valleys to get work. Mexicans also came up from Sonora. Most were poor, simple, illiterate, honest, hospitable, and hard-working people. They were very useful citizens of Arizona. Every *paisano* in Sonora knows something about mining, running cattle, and farming by irrigation, and these were the skills needed in early Arizona.

Since the Anglo-Saxon American was top dog he looked down on the ordinary Mexican. He called him a "greaser" and a "cholo." Little Mexican children that started to school were poorly clothed and often dirty. Most of them had head lice and the schoolteachers used to come armed with kerosene to delouse them. In my day there was little association between the Americans and Mexicans. It was not entirely the fault of the American children, as the little

Mexicans played together at recess and went back to Mexican Town when school was out. A good friend of mine for many years was a boy of Mexican descent called Huero, which is Spanish for blond. He had green eyes, fair hair, but Indian features. The last I heard of him he had studied law and had a good government job.

In the early days when there were few women in Arizona of Anglo-Saxon descent many American pioneers married Mexican women. The offspring of these marriages were known as "half Mex." Some were said to have a "Mexicanny look." A very good friend of mine who is from a distinguished Tucson family and is now the head of a large and prosperous law firm in Mexico City is half Mexican on both sides—German and Mexican on his father's side, English and Mexican on his mother's. A friend and hunting companion of my Uncle Jim O'Connor in Florence was a big, tough, blond American of Irish descent. He married a Mexican girl. They had two children—a very pretty daughter who was a blue-eyed blonde and who could have been Irish, English, Swedish, or Dutch, and a son who looked pure Indian. Another American-Mexican cross, the sons of which were friends of mine, produced a very successful lawyer and also a very successful physician.

Because the Mexicans were looked down on by many, the better educated and more ambitious among those in Arizona claimed to be of Spanish descent, but even the most Spanish of them were quite plainly largely Indian. Sonora was Mexico's frontier, its wild West. Far more pioneer males of Spanish descent went to Sonora than females. It was a long way back to Mexico City, so many men of the purest Spanish blood took Indian wives. The part-Spanish mestizos who came along also took Indian wives. An Indian who got a job on a Mexican rancho, became a Catholic, learned to speak Spanish, and took a Spanish name became Mexican and was just as good as any other Mexican of his class.

Most Sonora Mexicans of whatever class are dark, but some families with considerable Indian blood produce individuals who are fair. One family I know is of Basque descent, owns property in both Arizona and Sonora. Some members of the family are citizens of Mexico, some of the United States. This remarkable family surely must have a large infusion of Indian blood and some of the members appear to be pure Indian but it regularly produces blonds and tall, freckled redheads that look like everyone's idea of tough Irish cops.

Apparently a rather high percentage of the early Spanish settlers in central Mexico were from Galicia, León, and Aragon, where many of the people have fair hair and light eyes. When I was visiting in Mexico City in 1963 I was astonished to discover that somewhere around half the members of Mexico City's upper crust that I met had light eyes and about a fourth were blond. But today among sophisticated and well-born Mexicans it is fashionable to boast of having Indian blood, as in Mexico it is the Indian who is considered the real Mexican, the founder of the Mexican culture. A friend of mine in Mexico is a handsome lawyer in his early thirties. He comes from an ancient and wealthy Mexican family that came over from Spain not long after Cortez. My pal proudly claims to be part Comanche. He may well be, but with his fair hair, his blue eyes, and his well-tailored conservative suits he looks like a young New York lawyer not long out of Yale.

All Mexicans resent the tendency of southwestern Americans to look down on them and to refer to them as greasers and themselves as "white," as if the only Caucasians were those from northwestern Europe.

Among the pioneers in the Salt River valley were settlers from all over the United States and some from foreign countries besides Mexico. There were some English and Irish remittance men, one authentic Danish count, some good, sturdy German and Scandinavian peasant farmers attracted to the Southwest by the prospect of cheap land.

Perhaps more were from the South than from any other section. My two lawyer uncles from the Irish side of the family came to Arizona before 1900 and were both born in California. A great many were of the pioneer strain that left Virginia and North Carolina for Kentucky and Tennessee went from there to Missouri for a generation, and then jumped farther west.

Many of these people had led violent lives. At the time of my earliest memories Indian troubles were fairly recent as history goes. Geronimo, the famous hostile Apache, was not de-fanged and penned up until about the time my grandfather's family moved to Arizona. The last Apache badman, the Apache Kid, was murdering people later than that. About the time I was born Mexicans and Americans of Nogales, Arizona, and Nogales, Sonora, got together and ambushed and slaughtered a band of Yaqui Indians who were planning to raid the city. A traitor in their own ranks had given their plans away.

The Arizona pioneers were tough and violent people. Many men were killed in the Tewkesbury-Graham feud in the Tonto Basin in central Arizona and the last male survivor of the Graham faction was murdered near Tempe when I was a small boy. People were always killing each other, generally with revolvers or shotguns—in disputes over irrigation rights, water holes, cattle, cards, money, and women. It was considered American and sporting to gun a man down with a revolver or to blast him with a shotgun, but killing anyone with a knife was looked down upon as a dirty Mexican trick.

People were touchy about their honor. A man who tolerated an adulterous wife would have been laughed out of the territory. If a man found that his wife was playing around, it was mandatory for him to kill her lover. If he killed the erring wife too, he could be sure of a sympathetic jury. If he killed the wife's lover and took the Jezebel back, it was generally agreed that the husband was a bit odd but a pretty magnanimous guy. But if he only beat the hell out of the other guy and ran him out of the state but took his wife back, he was regarded with suspicion if not outright contempt. Anyone who neither killed his wife's lover nor beat him half to death and moreover forgave his wife would be shunned by all decent and right-thinking men.

Along about 1914 or 1915 a member of a well-known Tempe family, a young married man with a wife and two or three children, was caught in a very compromising position in the back seat of an automobile with another man's pretty wife. The husband pulled out a revolver and shot him dead, then pistol-whipped his wife. The husband was arrested, of course, but he was quickly freed on bail and later acquitted.

The local verdict was about as follows: "Too bad about ole Rex. A lot of folks was a-lookin' for something like that to happen because everybody could see she was a-rubbin' it against him. The poor son of a bitch was playing with fire and he knew it. If he got his ass shot off it was nobody's fault but his own. Of course that woman started it, and her old man should have put the rest of them bullets from that six-shooter in that ornery little bitch. But that ain't excusing ole Rex. He knew what he was getting into!"

You didn't monkey with other men's women lightly in Arizona in 1900–20!

Fist fights between grown men were common. Local option made Tempe dry about 1912, but when there were two saloons on Mill Avenue a couple of knock-down-and-drag-outs in each saloon every day was about par. When I was six or seven I was conned by an advertisement in some magazine into peddling throughout town a journal called *The Saturday Blade and Chicago Ledger.* If I sold enough copies at ten cents each I got an air rifle. The paper was full of handsomely illustrated tales of illicit love, buried treasure, and the wonder of science. I discovered that my best market was in the two saloons. I must have looked like a timid little waif because on two or three occasions some half-tight farmer or ranch hand would say: "How many papers you got, son? Five? Here's four bits. I'll take the whole shebang!"

Once when I was in a saloon a quarrel broke out between two gigantic men who fell to pummeling each other. Tables and chairs were overturned. Fists thudded against flesh. Blood ran. It was a terrifying experience, as ghastly as an encounter between a grizzly bear and a bull which I saw many years later in Mexico. I dropped my papers and fled.

Today, at least in schools where most of the children are of middle-class origin, there are few fights. When I was going through the grades in Tempe there were two or three tentative passages at arms every recess and a serious fight-to-the-finish battle after school once or twice a week. My own sons had few if any fights when they were in grade school, but when I was in the grades and in the first couple of years of high school I went around about half the time with black eyes, puffy lips, and skinned knuckles.

Males young and old tried to work off their frustrations with their fists. When I was not quite thirteen and a freshman in the academic department of the normal, which was the same as being a freshman in high school, I sat next to a girl in English composition and history whose nickname was Johnny. As I have said elsewhere there were but few high schools in Arizona at the time and parents in the back country sent children to the normal for their high-school work. Johnny was sixteen or seventeen and a rather attractive brown-eyed girl in a bovine sort of way, but she didn't know the difference between Austria and Australia and she was almost illiterate. She discovered that she could get through history examinations by copying my answers and through English by copying off in her own laborious handwriting the themes I facilely dashed off for her.

Johnny had a steady boy friend and from rumors I heard I suspect that his relationship with Johnny was something more than casual. He was a large, powerful lad who played tackle on the normal football team and who came from some forlorn little cow town in southeastern Arizona. I can still remember that he had a shock of greasy light brown hair and a pimply face. He was in the normal school proper and must have been eighteen or nineteen. At any rate, he flew at me one day completely without warning, knocked me down, and started kicking me. One of the other boys stopped him and wanted to know what was going on. He screamed that I had been fooling with his girl. Apparently Johnny had told him that I was good in English and history and he felt frustrated because he wasn't. I doubt if the virtue of a full-blown and voluptuous houri of sixteen was gravely menaced by the fact that a skinny-legged boy of thirteen who wore knickerbockers and whose voice had not yet finished changing was writing some themes for her.

When I was in grade school I probably got into more fights than most. For one thing I had a quick temper and when I was angry I would fly at anyone. For another I had always done a lot of reading. I had a considerable fund of worthless information, and since I have always been articulate I loved to show off my staggering wisdom in class. Some of my classmates resented me because of this habit, particularly since I was one to three years younger than most of them.

Soon after I started to school I resolved to learn something about handling my fists, as I quickly became aware that anyone who couldn't or wouldn't fight was on the very bottom of the pecking order. Somewhere I got a book on boxing, and from it I learned some of the fundamentals. I also worked out some sneaky tactics on my own. I always tried to maneuver so that the other guy had the sun in his eyes. I used to try to get my opponents facing me with their backs toward something they would fall over—a ditch bank, a curb, a garbage can, a bicycle lying on the ground. While I was maneuvering my victim into the proper position I would try to keep him off balance with left jabs but otherwise I simply blocked or ducked his blows. Then when he was least expecting it I would rush him, swinging with both hands, and when he backed up he would fall over whatever was behind him. The crash to the ground usually took the fight out of him.

It is the habit of most males of whatever species to huff and puff awhile before they actually engage in combat. Often neither of two boys would actually want to fight, but the other boys would gather in a circle and egg them on. Then they would lose face if a fight didn't come off. While the huffing and puffing was going on the boys were working themselves up for the moment of truth, just as bulls bellow and paw the ground before they lock horns. I discovered that if someone was trying to pick a fight with me it was to my distinct advantage to hit him first, land a damaging blow, and follow it up before he got himself worked up.

I cannot remember ever picking a fight. If someone picked one with me I generally had butterflies in my stomach until the fisticuffs actually started, but from then on I enjoyed fighting immensely. I think conflict is instinctive with the human male. I also think that fighting with one's kind, learning to give and receive hard blows, is probably important to the emotional development of the normal male.

I had a wild temper which sometimes got me into trouble. I remember one occasion when I was in seventh grade. I was a passionate baseball player and I used to fasten my first baseman's mitt to my desk by putting the strap that went around the wrist to the cast-iron fancy work of the desk. Seeing that I was absorbed in a book, the boy across the aisle unbuckled the mitt and passed it to someone else. I remained oblivious to the theft and my classmates considered this very funny. The glove was passed from hand to hand until it came into the possession of a lad a couple of aisles over. He thought it would be even funnier to throw it at me.

The mitt hit me in the head, startled me, and hurt like the devil where the buckle struck my right ear. I turned to my right and I could tell who had thrown the mitt from the look of triumph on the face of one of the boys. Instantly in a red rage I vaulted over a row of seats, grabbed the boy by the hair, forced his head back on the desk behind him, and while the girl sitting at the desk was screaming I was doing my best with my right fist to spread the boy's nose all over his face. The poor frightened twenty-year-old student teacher finally pried me off and sent me to the principal.

A big, good-natured, dumb Negro boy went to my school. He must have weighed 180 pounds and was bull-strong. One day at recess he blocked me when I was trying to steal a base. Running into him was like running into a brick wall. It hurt me and made me furious. I jumped up, flew at him with flailing fists. He swung just once, hit me on the cheekbone, and I took off like a golf ball. Just then the bell rang and we all started filing in.

My cheekbone swelled within seconds into a really surprising lump as large as a walnut. The principal of the school noticed it as I went past. "Where did you get that bump?" he asked. "Jim Green hit me." "Why did he hit you?" "I guess because I hit him first." "You had it coming then!" "Yes, sir!"

After school good-natured old Jim came up. "Hell, Jack, boy, I don' wanna hit you. You're littler than I am. You just come a-foggin' into me like you was crazy. I hope that ole cheek don' turn that there eye black."

# 6 · School Days

I STARTED to school in the fall of 1910 in a red-brick building at the corner of Mill Avenue and what was then called Eighth Street in Tempe. Now that the humble little Tempe Normal has become big Arizona State University, Eighth Street is called University Way. A drive-in hamburger joint, a supermarket or some such monument to Lower Slobovia now occupies the site where that old grade school stood.

It was only about a walk of three blocks from Grandfather's place to the school. Mother taught in an adjacent building which had been the Baptist Church until Grandfather gave the Baptists ten thousand dollars toward a new one. She told the principal, an austere dark-haired man, that here I was ready for school and that I read very well. The principal said I'd start in first grade where I should have started two years before, that as a teacher she should have known better than to let me stay out as it would ruin my social adjustment.

She left me with the first-grade teacher. As I had anticipated three fourths of the children were bawling and the rest were fighting. A little Mexican girl with long, greasy black pigtails sat in the seat in front of me. I thought that if I put the end of one of her pigtails in the ink bottle on my desk and then put the cork back in, the effect when she got up might be interesting.

I had expected to be bored, so before I left Grandfather's house I had picked up a copy of a now defunct news magazine, *The Literary Digest.* I was reading it when the teacher noticed what I was doing.

"What is that you have, Jack?" she asked.

"*The Literary Digest.*"

"What are you doing with it?"

I was tempted to ask her what the hell she thought I was doing with it, but I answered with polite manners: "Reading it."

"What are you reading?"

"It's about radium," I said. In explanation I added: "It's an active metal."

"Oh, dear," the teacher said. She left the room and presently returned with the principal. I was promoted to second grade. Two days later, after I had corrected the teacher's grammar, I was promoted to third. Within a month I wound up in fourth—and my troubles began.

I read very well, but my spelling was almost as erratic as Shakespeare's. Maps and the very thought of faraway places fascinated me, and I had gone through an old geography text my mother had around. The teacher taught the Palmer method, which has done so much to make the handwriting of two generations of Americans completely without character, and I did everything wrong. I wrote "with my fingers" (primary sin in the Palmer book; you were supposed to grasp the pen loosely and write with the whole arm). My exercises of slanting lines and successions of overlapping loops (push-pull-push-pull, one, two, three, four) were too small, were messy, ink-splattered, and in general looked like hell.

The teacher was Miss McComas. She was red-haired and fat. She wore pince-nez glasses, white shirtwaists with high collars, a small watch affixed to her shirtwaist with a gold fleur-de-lis pin. She always wore dark skirts that almost swept the floor, and her corset made her waist small but gave her big hips and a belly. She wore her red hair piled high on her head, and like many women with dark red hair she had a beautiful complexion. I never thought of Miss McComas as having legs. Maybe she didn't.

She was horrified when I wrote a theme in which I spelled goat not only the orthodox way but "got," "gote," and "gout"; and also when she found out that although I knew the capital of South Dakota and could bound Iowa, I added poorly and hadn't the faintest idea of subtraction, a subject generally mastered by third-graders.

That first day in fourth grade I stole the show during the geography period when I explained how the Grand Canyon was formed. During the civics period the subject of political parties came up and I modestly let it be known that my Grandfather Woolf was the Democratic national committeeman for the territory of Arizona.

I felt that I had made a rather good impression among my peers that first day, and when school was over at three o'clock I walked out with what I fancied was a proud and jaunty air.

In the school yard a boy a head taller than I was, a lad with small eyes set close together, cottony hair, and buck teeth, fell in beside me. I had seen him playing baseball at recess and I had rather admired the guy.

As I headed homeward he walked beside me, saying nothing.

I felt the silence was a bit awkward, so I said: "I like the fourth grade. I like the kids in it. I don't think it is going to be hard."

The big boy stopped, scowled, then suddenly yelled: "Oh, ain't you the stuck-up smart little bastard!"

I was stunned with surprise.

Then he clouted me on the ear with his fist. Then his other fist took me in the mouth and cut my lip.

I fled bawling. He chased me, yelling: "Think you're smart, you little son of a bitch!" My terror and my long legs gave me a fair turn of speed and my tormentor was unable to catch me. Howling loudly, I made it to Grandfather's front gate. As I shot in I saw Grandfather open the door to his study and look out. He said nothing.

I went upstairs and lay down on my bed, shaking with rage and humiliation. I knew I was a coward. I felt degraded and unclean.

That night at supper my mother asked me how the fourth grade had gone. I said: "All right, I guess." My grandfather looked at me sharply but said nothing.

The next day was pretty bad. My enemy, whose name was Howard Potts, kept watching me with a meaningful leer. At recess I didn't join in any of the impromptu games. Instead I stayed near Miss McComas. At noon I ate my lunch at my desk.

I dreaded the dismissal of the class that afternoon as a condemned man must dread his approaching electrocution, but inevitably it came. I stayed at my desk, pretending to straighten the books and papers it held and hoping that Howard would leave. But when I ventured out he was waiting for me. Again I fled howling.

As I covered the last fifty yards toward the safety of my grandfather's front gate, I could see Grandfather watching the chase by the door of his study. I tried to creep upstairs to wallow in my shame and degradation, to quiver in futile rage, but he called me over to him and led me inside.

He put his arm around me briefly and patted my shoulder. He was not a demonstrative man, and this was the only overt sign of tenderness on his part that I can remember. It was too much for me and I began to blubber.

"Boy," he said, "what's the matter?"

"Howard Potts chased me home."

"Yes, I noticed. Why did you let him chase you? If you hadn't run he wouldn't have chased you."

"I was afraid he'd hurt me. Yesterday he hurt me and he's bigger than I am."

"I thought your lip was cut and swollen last night, but you're still alive, aren't you?"

I admitted I was.

"Boy," he said, "this fellow Howard is bigger than you are. He is a coward or he wouldn't pick on you. Why is he picking on you?"

"I think he's mad because I told the class how the Colorado River made the Grand Canyon." I thought I noticed a glint of amusement in the brilliant blue eyes behind the steel-rim glasses and a twitch of the lips surrounded by white beard and mustache.

"Son," he said, "you started out in the fourth grade by making two mistakes. One you can't do much about. The other you can do something about."

"What's that, Grandfather?"

"Well, you showed those other children you knew more than they did. I am quite sure that Howard Potts isn't the only one who hated you for it. But Howard is stupid. Howard is older than you. From the looks of the boy I'd say he's twelve or thirteen. It has taken him six or seven years to get into fourth grade. He knows you just started to school this year. Then you showed off how much you knew. You made Howard feel inferior and stupid. That's why he hates you.

"Most people hate those who make them feel unimportant and ignorant. All men hate other men who are smarter and more successful. Mostly they don't let on, but they do. That's why politicians talk about being born poor and in log cabins and that's why many of them deliberately use bad English. Women hate beautiful women. Great beauties make all other women feel plain and inferior. That's why beautiful women are always gossiped about. That's why beautiful women who are smart pay great attention at parties to the homeliest women there. You're smarter than many. You can't help it any more than a beautiful woman can help it, but don't show off too much.

"And remember something else, boy. As long as you'll run, somebody's going to chase you. Don't run!"

"But he'll hurt me!" I said.

"There are two kinds of hurts," Grandfather said. "The hurt of the body and the hurt of the spirit. Which really hurt you worse, your cut lip or your running? Which made you feel worse?"

"Running," I said.

"All right," Grandfather said. "Don't run. Stand up to him. He won't kill you. I could call up the school superintendent and he'd call that boy in and whip him. If I told him to expel that boy he'd do it. I know the boy's father. He's stupid. He's a nobody. But if I did that it wouldn't do *you* any good. Next time don't run. Fight him!"

"He's bigger than I am," I said.

"Pick up a stick. Pick up a rock. Go after him with a knife. Do anything you want to but don't run. If you run tomorrow you'll run the day after that and the day after that. Then other boys will chase you. You'll never get through running. The time comes when any man has to fight. I've had to kill a few people. I don't talk about it and I am sorry I had to do it but there was nothing else I could do.

"Once some drad-blasted reservation Indians were stealing my cattle. I tracked the cattle right back to the reservation and I found the hides with my brand on them. I told the Indian agent and I told the chief. They didn't do a single thing. Those young Indians kept stealing my cattle. I had to do something or they'd ruin me. I told the agent and the chief that if any more of my cattle were stolen I'd go over to the reservation and shoot one buck Indian for every cow they stole. They stole three cows and I went over and shot three Indians. I then rode over and told the Indian agent what I'd done. I told him that if he made any trouble for me I'd beat him within an inch of his life and I'd report him to the Indian bureau as a crook, a booze hound, and a gross incompetent. All of that was true. I have influence and I could have got him fired. I never heard one dratted word about it.

"Another time, a big outfit that had title to our land by an old Spanish grant was trying to run the small cattlemen off. I offered to leave if they'd pay me a fair price for my cattle and improvements. They offered me about a fifth of what they were worth. They'd killed one rancher and beaten up a couple of others and burned their barns and houses down. They sent three mean Texas cowboys after me." His grin became wide then. "I bushwhacked the rascals. I hid up in the rocks above a trail, and when they rode up I just opened up and killed every dratted one of their horses. I yelled down that if they ever came that close to my place again I wouldn't shoot at the horses. I never did any better shooting with a rifle in my life. Bang, bang, bang, and every one of those horses was down. Those Texicans had to walk twenty miles, and if there is anything a Texican hates it's to walk. Anyway, next week a lawyer rode out from Trinidad and offered me exactly what I asked for my cattle and improvements. If I hadn't fought they'd have robbed and maybe killed me."

ALL THE NEXT DAY at school my humiliation, my hatred of my tormentor, and my grandfather's advice all whirled around in my head. I was alternately seething with rage and trembling with terror. I had fantasies of choking Howard to death, of cutting his throat, of gouging his eyes out. I hardly heard Miss McComas. I recited poorly and haltingly.

By the time school was ready to let out I was as worked up as a Viking about to go berserk or a Moslem warrior about to throw himself on the spears of the infidels for the glory of Allah.

At the entrance to the schoolroom there was a hallway with rows of hooks for the children to hang their coats on. The coal box for the pot-bellied stove that kept the schoolroom warm was there, and when it was raining and muddy this was where the children parked their rubbers. It was here that they also left their baseball bats.

I had no particular plan except to fly at Howard if he bothered me. He was right behind, grinning at me. "Just wait till I get you outside, you little bastard," he said.

Suddenly I went into a red rage, the first but by no means the last of my life. It was a curious experience. I saw everything through a sort of a pink haze. I was light on my feet. I was prodigiously quick and strong. I had no fear. I had but one desire—to destroy this creature. I picked up a bat, and more by luck than good management I dealt him a terrific clout across the bridge of the nose. He staggered back with the blood spurting. The bat seemed no heavier than a small twig. I brought it down on his head.

He turned and fled into the classroom. I hit him again with the bat as he ran. He tripped and fell over a desk and as he lay there I got in a good solid one.

Miss McComas was in her private cloakroom doing whatever she did in her private cloakroom after school. She rushed out, and when she saw what was happening she screamed. "You horrible child, what are you doing?" She grabbed my bat. Howard scrambled to his feet, the blood cascading from his broken nose. He started to bawl. "He didn't fight fair," he said. "He hit me with a baseball bat. He's crazy."

Most of the children had rushed back in to see the fireworks.

"Howard got what was coming to him. He beat up on Jack and chased him home," one of the boys said. My heart was flooded with love for my defender. I had secretly admired this boy. His name was Bert Higgins. He had dark red hair and was so freckled you couldn't put the eraser end of a lead pencil down anywhere on his face and hands without hitting a freckle. He was the best marble player in the grade and one of the best in the Eighth Street school. He was two years older than I but an inch or so shorter.

Suddenly my rage left me. I felt shaky and weak, but *good.*

Miss McComas went to her mysterious private cloakroom, returned with a wet rag. She wiped the blood off Howard's face, bathed his nose, examined the abrasions and contusions on his head. "You go on home now, Howard," she said. "I'm going to take this young man over to pay a visit to the principal." As she led me off. Bert Higgins whispered that he'd wait for me.

I was limp, numb, drained by emotional exhaustion. I listened to Miss McComas describe what had happened. She shuddered and wept a little when she told the principal that I was trying to kill the boy. "A murderer, a potential murderer!" she said.

"Thank you, Miss McComas," the principal said. "You may go now. I'll attend to this young man." I had heard how the principal kept a rubber hose in his office and beat bad and defiant boys with it. I expected to be thrashed but somehow I didn't much care.

Miss McComas left. The principal swiveled his chair around and looked me full in the face. I tried not to cry out but tears came in my eyes.

Finally he said: "How are you doing in fourth grade? Is it hard?"

"Arithmetic is kind of hard," I said, "but the rest is easy."

"I never knew your father," he said, "but I hear he's a fine trap shot. I do some trap shooting myself."

I said nothing.

"I've known J. W. Woolf, your grandfather, for years," he went on. "I can see something of him in you. You've got the Woolf eyes and your grandfather's hair and mouth." Then he cleared his throat. "Just how did all this come about?"

"He hit me the first day and chased me home. He chased me home the next day too."

"Did your grandfather talk to you?"

"Yes."

"I presume you followed his advice."

"Yes, sort of."

"I think it was probably pretty good advice. J. W. Woolf is a very wise man. Miss McComas was a bit overwrought, I'm afraid. Women don't understand these things. Oh, well, when you get home give J. W. my regards."

Bert Higgins was waiting for me outside the principal's office and walked home with me. Grandfather let me show him his guns and even showed us the tooth marks made in the stock of the Model 76 Winchester where a dying grizzly had bitten it. I showed him the walk-in refrigerator that held 1,200 pounds ice and the faucet on the outside that always ran ice water. I showed him the hot-air registers over the house and furnace in the basement. "Gee," he said, "your grandfather must be rich!"

When Bert had left just before supper Grandfather called me into his study. "Well," he said, "I hear you had to see the principal today. What happened?"

I could see that those bright blue eyes were twinkling.

"I beat up on Howard Potts."

"What did you use?"

"A baseball bat."

"Well, well," he said. "Not a bad choice!" He cleared his throat. "Boy, you are eight years old and you'll be nine in January. I think you're about old enough to have a shotgun, and I've been noticing a little single-barrel 20-gauge down at Curry's hardware. I think you might do pretty well on quail with that. Now, don't thank me, dad-drat it! With all the retrieving you've done for me you've earned it. Shucks, you're almost as good a retriever as a good bird dog, and a dang sight better company!"

# 7 · Fun and Games

THE picture that remains in my memory of the playground of the Eighth Street school in Tempe from the fall of 1910 until the spring of 1912 is rather like a Brueghel painting—hundreds of little figures in violent action, all shouting and yelling. There was no playground equipment—no slides, no swings, teeter-totters, or monkey bars. The only contribution of the taxpayers of the Tempe school district to the recreation of the young was the vague supervision of a couple of teachers who watched from steps like biologists overseeing a seal rookery. Just so long as the pupils did not strangle each other, brain each other with baseball bats, or carve each other up with knives, everything went.

The grounds were as bare as the Gobi Desert. The boys played on one side, the girls on a smaller area on the other. The girls giggled, gossiped, jumped rope, played innocuous games like jacks and hopscotch. The boys played baseball, marbles, shinny, various games with tops. When girls quarreled they wept, pulled hair, sometimes scratched each other's faces. Boys stood on their hind legs, fought like men. The boys had a rough and imperfect code of chivalry. It was not considered cricket to beat up on boys a great deal smaller, to gouge eyes, to kick anyone who was down. Nor was it considered ethical to use a club or a rock on someone your own size; but if someone bigger picked on you, anything went.

The games of the boys ran in "seasons." One week everyone would be spinning tops, the next week they would all be playing shinny, a violent game that was a sort of hockey played with sticks and tin cans. Baseball games played at noon and recess were generally of the informal variety, such as One-Eyed Cat, with only a pitcher, a catcher, and a first baseman, and where the batter could continue to bat as long as he could hit the ball far enough so that he could make it to first base and back to home plate before he was thrown out.

After school formal baseball games were organized with nine men to a side. On the teams, the pitcher had the most status and the catcher was next. The low men on the totem pole were the outfielders. These were usually the smallest, weakest, youngest, and most inept boys. Playing in the outfield was considered only slightly better than not playing at all. Since little boys learn to bat long before they learn to pitch well, the scores were like those of basketball games—62 to 47, 39 to 28, and so on. By the time I was in sixth grade I was generally a catcher, partly because I was a fair-enough catcher, I suppose, but partly also because my father, in a spasm of paternal solicitude, had sent me a catcher's mitt, mask, and chest protector. He had been a catcher himself in his youth.

As I look back on the games played by the grade-school boys of those days I think the one that required the most astonishing skill was marbles. There were several varieties, but the principal one was called Bull Ring. The ring was casually drawn on the ground and could be as large or as small as desired. It was always a gambling game in that it was played for keeps, not for funs. Each player put in an agreed number of marbles in the center of the ring and he kept all he shot out of the ring legally. Contestants tossed marbles to a line and took their turns in the order of their nearness. The boy closest could shoot his "taw" down into the mass of marbles. If he knocked one or more out of the ring and his taw stayed in he could shoot again and again, as long as he shot a marble out and his taw stayed in. Some of the more skillful boys accumulated enormous hoards of marbles. Daring and reckless lads, the cream of the marble elite, gambled with precious agates, glassies, and snot agates. Ordinary players like me used cheap marbles of baked clay with glazed surfaces. Those we called "dobies," probably because they were of clay—"adobe." Ball bearings were in great demand as taws, but I liked "steelies," marbles of hollow steel marked with a cross. If a steelie was struck just right with a hammer, the cross was opened slightly and from that time on it gave out a most satisfactory ring. The possession of a melodious steelie for a taw was the mark of an urbane and sophisticated marble player.

The skill of the better bull-ring experts was something to contemplate with awe and wonder. They could hit another marble most of the time at two and a half or three feet, a good part of the time at four feet, every time at two feet. They could play "position" with their taws as a pool player does with his cue ball.

I became a fair marble player, perhaps better than most, but not nearly as good as the best. Such skill as I had is responsible for the fact that my nose is slightly crooked. I was playing bull ring with a lad named Tom Baker one day. I was beating him and pocketing his marbles. He became more and more frustrated. Finally when a marble I had shot from the ring went into an irrigation ditch he made up a rule that I had lost my turn because I had not recovered the marble. My sense of justice was outraged. I beat him up, picked up the marbles in the ring, and marched grandly off. When I was in the middle of the street a large stone whizzed past my head. I turned, and as I did so another large stone crashed into my nose. I fell like a brain-shot elephant. Tom Baker was a far better rock thrower than he was a marble player.

When my poor hard-working mother got back from school to cook dinner she found me lying on my bed in a pool of blood with my nose spread over half my face. This happened on a Friday. Except for a visit to the office of Dr. B. B. Moeur I lay low Saturday and Sunday. I was back at school on Monday. Both of my eyes were hideously black. My nose was still swollen and had a great gash in it. I grabbed the Baker kid and belted him a couple of times, but each time I hit him I am sure it hurt me worse than it did him as excruciating pain stabbed through my wounded nose.

Some of the feats performed with tops required great skill. Tops could be bought at any general store, but the "boughten" top was a joke and no self-respecting grade-school boy would be caught dead with one that was unaltered. Store tops were turned on a lathe and came with little round knobs on top and very flimsy pegs. Aficionados always cut the knob off and then cut a ledge around the top to hold the string. Then the peg that was factory equipment was removed and a stout nail driven in to replace it. The nail was then sharpened with a file. Top string furnished by the stores was likewise held in low repute. The best was obtained by moonlight requisition from building sites where it was used to mark off foundations. It was stout, stiff, just the right size. I found a cache of this heavy string at my grandfather's place, where it had been used in the construction of his house. To save face I always pretended I had stolen it.

Almost anyone can learn to spin a top. Most people can learn to pick a spinning top up in the hand. But only the chosen can learn to spin a top so as to hit and split an opponent's top, or to knock other tops out of a ring. A game requiring great skill was Chip-Cheeny (spelling my own). The players drew two lines about fifty yards apart, placed a large marble directly between the two lines. The idea was to spin a top, pick it up on the hand, bring the hand down so the spinning top would strike the marble and send it sailing off in the direction of the spin. The first player who got the marble across his goal line was the winner.

BICYCLES GAVE THOSE of us in grade school great freedom of movement. We all had bicycles. I got my first at ten. I know now that my mother bought it at considerable sacrifice, as it cost $35, about one third of her monthly salary. It was red, had front and rear fenders, and a "motorcycle" frame. It was fashionable for youthful bicycle owners to take their coaster brakes apart every two weeks, wash the parts in gasoline, reassemble them, and pack the works in cup grease. Machinery and I hate each other. I could never get the coaster brake together again so it would work and I always had to sneak it down to a garage to have some mechanical genius assemble it properly.

We rode long distances on our bicycles. We had races. Across the river in the caliche hills and arroyos we had an up-and-down-hill course of about a half mile, where we ran against time as taken on an Ingersoll pocket watch costing a dollar.

On foot we explored the country around. We climbed all the cave-pocked red sandstone hills to the north of the Salt River in what was later Papago Park. We wandered far up the channel of the Salt River across bars of clean white sand and through willow thickets. We felt it our duty to kill every rattlesnake and every Gila monster we saw.

Once in a cave in one of the red sandstone hills I found the weathered skull and horns of a fine old desert bighorn ram. I lugged it laboriously home and for many years it reposed in our woodshed. Another boy and I discovered the body of a Chinese cook who had worked in Joe Holland's restaurant. It was in a cave high in the rocks and hard to get to. Because the body was out of sight the buzzards had not devoured it. At the time we found the body the Chinaman had been dead at least two months. He had shot himself with a pearl-handled, nickel-plated revolver. I didn't want the revolver, but my companion did. He had more guts than I had, as he braved the stench and took the revolver out of the dead, desiccated hand.

Joe Holland, who was half Chinese himself, had reported that his cook was missing. The old Chinese had been depressed and had been badly taken by Chinese friends at fan-tan in Phoenix. He was a bit nuts anyway, the people of Tempe thought. We boys used to go to the back door of the restaurant, stick our heads in, and yell "cheely-moka-hilo" at him. This was believed to be an insulting term in Chinese, but what it meant, if anything, I have no idea. The old Chinaman always rushed to the door with a knife or cleaver and chased us down the alley.

When nothing was heard of the old cook the law officers decided he had somehow got to San Francisco and had either found work there or had gone back to China. My friend and I never told anyone we had found the body. We kept it a secret, and every now and then we would go back, climb up to the cave, and inspect the carcass. Eventually, it became completely mummified and did not smell at all. When we tossed stones at it, it sounded as hollow as a gourd. For all I know it is still there.

WE SCROUNGED THROUGH the trash and garbage back of the stores and pool halls for YB cigar bands and coupons from Fatima cigarette packages. It was generally believed that the bands and the coupons were immensely valuable and if enough of them were collected wonderful premiums like saxophones, motorcycles, and shotguns could be obtained. However, I cannot remember that anyone ever sent the coupons or cigar bands away for the premiums. The possession of a cigar box full of bands or a thick wad of coupons conferred far more status than anything they could have been exchanged for. We became cigar-band and cigarette-coupon misers, gloating over our hoards with deep satisfaction like Texas millionaires counting oil wells.

Among other strange status symbols cherished by the preadolescent males of Tempe for a time were human skulls. Some of the more observant among us had noted that between the two buttes that stood between the town and the Salt River was a collection of mounds that looked as if they might be graves. What genius first decided to dig into them I cannot remember, but whoever he was discovered that they actually were graves and that they were full of human bones and skulls of all sizes. The graves were shallow, since the ground was very rocky. We used to go at night carrying picks, shovels, and old barn lanterns to dig into them. The only things we saved were the skulls. These we soaked in water, scrubbed with brushes and Old Dutch Cleanser until they were clean and sometimes white. I kept a very good one and displayed it on a bookcase in my room until my mother told me it gave her the creeps and to get rid of it. I gave it to a friend and his mother threw it away. What the garbage man thought when he found a human skull in with the ashes, broken dishes, and bent curtain rods I do not know.

We amateur archaeologists had various theories about the graves. Most thought they were Indian. The most romantic theory was that they were the graves of Aztecs who had fled from the Spaniards under Cortez. I believe that they were the graves of early Mexican settlers because I once found a metal crucifix among the bones. The graves were not far from Mexican Town, and possibly Mexican laborers buried their dead there along in the 1870's before there was a Catholic church and cemetery. I made discreet inquiries among the older adults but none of them had ever heard of such a cemetery.

I traded one skull for a single-shot Hopkins & Allen .22 rifle that I could never hit anything with, others for steelies and snot agates. One day I was walking through the normal-school campus with a nicely cleaned skull in my hand when one of the students saw it. He offered me five dollars for it. When I showed my mother the five-dollar bill she took it away from me and bought me a new pair of shoes. I told my friends about the sale and within a week all the remaining graves were opened and looted and the skulls offered to students who lived at the boys' dormitory. The flood of skulls was so great that the price fell to a dollar, except for good skulls of children. These went for two-fifty.

TEMPE'S PRINCIPAL CONTACT with culture in those days before World War I was the Lyceum Course at the normal school. A committee of normal-school faculty members selected the entertainment that was to be presented, and the events, as I recall, were held about six weeks apart throughout the winter. I can remember lecturers (serious) and lecturers (humorous); clean, inspiring plays direct from Broadway with genuine New York actors; magicians who did tricks with cards, took fluttering white pigeons out of hats, pulled endless silk scarves of various colors out of people's pockets, poured grape juice out of empty pitchers, and even sawed pretty girls with nice legs in two.

Everybody who was anybody in Tempe bought season tickets to the Lyceum. The entertainment was held upstairs in the red-brick auditorium. The basement in the same building was the girls' gymnasium, where the young ladies improved their muscle tone by marching and doing exercises with dumbbells and where the dances of the Wallflower Club were held. The small boys all flocked to the balcony of the auditorium, and until the entertainment started they wrestled, goosed each other, and filled the air with paper airplanes made from folded programs.

I believe I enjoyed the magicians more than anything, the humorous lecturers least. I found most of these about as unfunny as I find most stand-up comedians today. I generally liked the lecturers (serious). I worried about the Yellow Menace, Companionate Marriage, and Race Suicide. I was thrilled about Twilight Sleep and the Coming Wonders of Science, and I was happy to learn that if worse came to worse the human race could exist indefinitely on the Bounty of the Sea.

WHEN MY MOTHER OBTAINED her position as critic-teacher at the normal school, I entered the sixth grade at the "training school," where the student teachers learned their craft. The first year, my poor mother was in charge of all the instruction in music. She was an excellent teacher but she was even less musical than I am. I remember feeling sorry for her when she led the training-school student body every day in singing "Flow Gently, Sweet Afton," "Columbia, the Gem of the Ocean," and "Drink to Me Only with Thine Eyes." It embarrassed me no end that my mother was generally a little flat when she led off with the songs. Fortunately she had to suffer as the music critic only one year. The next year she was replaced by a real musician and went back to teaching things she was more suited for.

My first year in the training school was 1912, and I remember turning in a paper dated 12–12–12 and thinking romantically that the next time a paper could be so dated would be a hundred years from that time and that I would long since have been moldering in my grave.

In the sixth grade we were for the most part good little children in class. We listened politely to our student teachers, mostly ranch and farm girls from nineteen to twenty-one years old. It is true that we put straight pins between the uppers and soles at the toes of our shoes and jabbed them into each other's bottoms through the crack in the seats. We held contests in the boys' toilet to see who could pee over the partition that separated the boys' toilet from the girls' toilet. But for the most part we were quiet, orderly, and decent little boys.

The next year in seventh grade we were fiends. It is a wonder that someone did not beat us to death, drown us, or take us out and shoot us. I am quite sure that the reason for our disorderly and antisocial conduct was that the mysterious glands that were to make functioning males out of us were beginning to secrete their disturbing elixirs. One of the girls in the class was a boarding student who lived at the girls' dormitory and whose father was a mining engineer. She had been able to go to school very little. She must have been about fifteen, a pretty dark-haired girl with well-developed breasts, lovely round arms, and in general the curves and contours of sexual maturity. All the boys in seventh grade were mad about her and to show their devotion they made her life hell. They put grasshoppers down her neck. They dumped toads and large spiders on her desk. They put glue on her seat so that she was unable to get up when recess came. They sneaked in and stacked the books in her desk in such a way that when she touched anything all her books tumbled out.

Our student teachers were young and many of them were pretty. We were excited by the white, soft arms seen through peek-a-boo waists, by their round white necks, by the bulges in their shirt-waists we knew were caused by breasts. We adored them and we almost drove them mad. We cut up. We showed off. We sassed them. All of us brought rubber bands and tinfoil to school. We folded pieces of tinfoil into tight strips, bent them so they could be shot with rubber bands. We pelted each other with these dangerous missiles. They hit so hard that they raised white welts. I became very expert, so good that I could hit a fellow student on the side of the face clear across the classroom.

Once we had a lovely young girl as an arithmetic teacher, a lass so pretty that she sent our young hearts to pounding and filled our young brains with turbulent and voluptuous thoughts. We were all madly in love with her. One day she wore an especially provocative blouse to class. When she turned to put problems on the board we could see through the diaphanous blouse a considerable expanse of delicate and tempting skin. Someone gave a signal. A dozen of us aimed those wicked tinfoil missiles at the lovely back that had so inflamed us. We all cut loose at once and every missile found the mark.

If the object of our affection had become angry we would have been delighted. Instead she sat down at her desk, put her head in her hands, and sobbed uncontrollably. We all cringed in shame. Presently I went to her, put my hand on her shoulder, and told her we were sorry. All the other boys came up and apologized. Some of them wept. She became our favorite teacher and we never pelted another girl with those stinging missiles.

Most of us had Daisy air rifles. Many of us also had .22 rimfire rifles and even shotguns, but we liked to play with the BB guns because they made less noise and were somewhat less lethal. When I was in seventh grade I had one that cocked with a slide handle instead of a lever. I believed it was the most powerful air rifle in town. I killed many blackbirds, sparrows, and even mourning doves with it.

About a dozen of us used to go out to "Chicken" Alexander's place to play soldiers and Indians with our air guns. "Chicken" was so called because his father had a chicken farm. It was ideal for our purposes since it contained many small buildings we could use for cover while we ambushed each other. One day, Chicken and I were stalking each other to see who would get in the first shot. I got the drop on him. He was looking in another direction. His shirt was unbuttoned and a nice expanse of bare, white, plump belly was revealed. I put a BB right in the middle of it at a range of about thirty feet. Generally a BB simply stung and raised a white welt. But this one penetrated about a quarter of an inch into Chicken's tender belly and *stuck*. He let out a yelp, took one look at the black BB imbedded in his white hide, and fell to the ground writhing and bawling. I ran over, saw what I had done, jumped on my bicycle, and fled. Chicken's father called my mother up and told her that if he caught that damned kid of hers on his place with that goddam powerful BB gun of his again he'd take it away from him, turn him over his knee, and tan the little bastard's ass.

My mother told him she'd give him to understand that he was talking to a lady and she was not used to having people curse and threaten, and anyway if he so much as laid a hand on me she'd get her brother Charles to have the law on him. The whole soldier and Indian idea, she said, had been hatched by his kid anyway. But she took the BB gun away from me for two weeks and told me that if she ever heard of me shooting another boy with it, she'd take it away for good.

Such is the mystery of the ductless glands that when we entered eighth grade the next fall we were all quiet, decent, orderly boys. I still don't know why.

# 8 · Horse and Buggy Town

EXACTLY how large my home town of Tempe was in 1910 I cannot say and actually for the purposes of this history it makes little difference. The population may have been 1,800 or it may have been only 1,200. Even then it was overshadowed by its larger neighbor, Phoenix, which according to the 1910 census had only a little over 10,000 people. However, Phoenix always had a tendency to sprawl and to lap over the city limits so in 1910 what was actually Phoenix must have contained around 15,000 people—possibly more.

Tempe was upstream from Phoenix on the Salt River, on the south bank, whereas Phoenix began on the north. It was nine miles from the center of Tempe to the center of Phoenix. I can remember making the trip with my mother and grandfather behind my grandfather's mare Pet about 1907 or 1908. My grandfather wanted to see someone at the territorial capital. My mother wanted to go to the dentist and also to do some shopping. I remember splashing across the ford with the buggy wheels clacking against the boulders; the boring, interminable wait in the dentist's office; my panic at getting separated from my mother in a department store; lunch in a hot, crowded, noisy restaurant full of strange smells; getting back home after dark. My mother must have taken me with her to buy me some clothes but I have no recollection of it. The journey from Tempe to Phoenix was not one to be undertaken lightly. A horse pulling a buggy with two people in it will average about

three miles an hour—and the trip between Tempe and Phoenix took three hours each way. People who didn't have buggies went by train.

I remember Tempe just as the horse-and-buggy age was coming to an end. None of the streets in town was paved and neither was any of the country roads. In wet winters Mill Avenue (Tempe's main street) was a foot-deep mass of mud mixed with manure and urine from the horses. The soil in the valley was locally called "adobe" and the longer it rained the deeper the mud got. Valley soil had no bottom.

In 1910 the automobile was fairly common, but one still saw more wagons and buggies than automobiles on the streets of Tempe. The modern motor car has its faults. It is noisy, smelly, unsafe. But the horse was no paragon of virtue, safety, or sanitation. Wherever the horse went he urinated and dropped road apples. Hordes of flies bred in his droppings. Until fairly recently automobiles were housed in garages built as far as possible from the house because that was where the stable had always been built—and the stables were there because the smell of horses attracted flies.

Anyone born in the automobile age has no notion of the vast number of flies that used to haunt every house during the warm months. They were so numerous that every time a door was opened scores darted in. As a child I swatted flies until I was musclebound. Every household had sheets of sticky flypaper called Tanglefoot lying around black with dead, dying, and suffering flies. Butcher shops and grocery stores swarmed with flies. I can remember strips of flypaper six and eight feet long and black with struggling flies hanging from lighting fixtures in grocery stores.

The flies carried all kinds of diseases, as most of the houses in Tempe had outdoor privies. In Mexican Town there were very few of even these monuments to civilization. The Mexicans simply used their back yards, or at night the street. Actually this was not such a bad arrangement. Human droppings were always promptly devoured by foraging dogs and chickens, just as in India today.

This is a natural process known to scientists as the reutilization of essential nutrients. This system actually worked very well in the Mexican sections of Arizona towns then, but when the Mexicans began to put up privies (to keep up with the gringo Joneses or through pressure by unthinking Anglo-Saxons) their sections were actually less sanitary than before. Everyone was less well off. The dogs were less well fed and were even noisier and surlier than before. The chickens laid fewer and less nutritious eggs. There were more flies and more dangerous material for them to breed in and walk upon. More flies contaminated more food and more babies died. The outdoor privy almost ruined Mexican Town.

One of my earliest memories is of the characteristic smell of Tempe's Mexican Town—a mixture of damp earth (none of the adobe houses had wood or cement floors, and good Mexican housekeepers sprinkled the dirt floors and swept them every day), garlic, onions, and chili, faint overtones of human droppings, and woodsmoke—a spicy, delicious, characteristic smell found nowhere but in Mexican villages. In the Mexican state of Sonora the villages still have that wonderful smell. Many years later in a fit of nostalgia I walked through Tempe's Mexican Town. The houses now had glass windows and wood and cement floors. Most had indoor plumbing. Instead of bony horses and burros starving quietly in vacant lots there were scabrous old jalopies. But the place didn't smell the same. I could detect the odor of chili and onions and garlic. Some of the older women still watered down and swept the dirt in front of their houses. Some still burned wood, but the smell was not the same. I was puzzled.

Inadvertently I later found the answer. I was hunting deer from a Sonora cattle ranch. There were about a dozen men there who worked as vaqueros and did other chores around the ranch. Each vaquero had a family and all the families lived in little one-room huts made of ocotillo stalks and mud. All the families burned wood, and whenever the woodpile started running low the vaquero head of the family would tie his riata on some dead branches of mesquite or ironwood and drag them back with his saddle horse to the woodpile by his hut. There were few people and plenty of trees, so there was never a lack of fuel. One nippy November night I decided to move my cot and my light eiderdown out of the little adobe house where I was living and sleep outdoors. It was a

night of brilliant desert moonlight. I had shot a beautiful big desert mule deer that day. I was tired, well fed. I had a little tequila in me and I was happy to be in Mexico and happy to be alive.

I could hear the Mexicans talking softly in their little huts. Three of the men were gossiping around a fire. In one hut I could see the dull orange glow of a kerosene lantern and someone was singing a sad Mexican song of horses, unrequited love, and death. I couldn't understand the words very well and what the horses had to do with unrequited love I could not figure out. Then the gossipers around the fire got up and went to their huts to turn in. Every one of them went to his woodpile and peed on it. Then the man who had been singing by lantern light came out of his hut and peed on *his* woodpile. I had solved the mystery of the characteristic smell of woodsmoke in Mexican villages. Male Mexicans pee on woodpiles as naturally as male dogs pee on lampposts, and when the wood is burned it gives off that Mexican-village smell.

And never let it be said that the horse-and-buggy age was without dangers. The horse is a large, powerful, stupid beast given to strange fantasies and sudden panics. An unfamiliar noise, a piece of newspaper blown by the wind, a fluttering garment—almost anything can throw a horse into a panic. Every year several people were killed by runaway horses. Mill Avenue in Tempe must have averaged one runaway a week. It was a characteristic sound of the horse-and-buggy age. There is a sudden frantic pounding of hoofs. Shouts of "Whoa, whoa, whoa! Stop, you crazy son of a bitch!" People on sidewalks halt. Those in stores rush out to see the fun and excitement. The owner of the rig is standing up in the wagon and sawing desperately on the reins or is running frantically and futilely after it. Someone on a sidewalk runs after the team and tries to grab the reins. Then there is a crash. The horses have run into another buggy, have got tangled up with a hitching post, or something. Often they tore buggies up. Sometimes a horse broke a leg and had to be shot. Once a team came barreling through a big glass window right into Shorty Hogan's barbershop. A drummer, or *traveling salesman,* was in the chair getting a shave. Shorty had shaved off the whiskers, and had put another hot towel on the salesman's face to soften it. Then he was planning to squeeze a few blackheads he had noticed. This was a service offered only by Shorty and he did not charge extra for it. He always put bay rum on his hands and rubbed it on the customer's face after the last hot towel. He next massaged it briefly with a soothing and pleasant-smelling cold cream. Finally he splashed on some more bay rum and dusted on talcum powder. Shorty was the best barber in town and his shaves were worth every cent of the twenty-five they cost. On this particular day the traveling salesman had dozed off under Shorty's deft ministrations and the next thing he knew there was a hell of a crash and two horses plunged into the barbershop, one with its head within six inches of the customer's face. He scrambled out of that chair, tossed Shorty a four-bit piece, and left by the back door.

THERE WERE TWO grocery stores on Mill Avenue—the Tempe Mercantile Company and Birchett Brothers. Tempe went dry under local option about 1912 but until then there were two saloons. There were two hardware stores, a blacksmith shop, a dentist, two lumber yards, two drug stores, two barbershops, a pool hall, old Joe Holland's restaurant, a men's clothing store run by a Turk, a livery stable, and a place that was a furniture store in front and an undertaking establishment in the rear. Once when I was about twelve my mother sent me to the furniture store–undertaking parlor on an errand. It was a one-man operation and the proprietor had a bell on the door of the furniture store that rang when anyone opened it. He came out of his embalming room with his sleeves rolled up when he heard me come in. He forgot to close the door to the back room and I could see old Mrs. Hankins, who had died the night before, laid out stark naked on a marble slab. It scared the hell out of me and I dreamed about it for weeks.

There were two hotels. One was the Casa Loma, where the traveling salesmen usually stayed. It was a fairly large two-story building and sometimes it ran a restaurant. The other hotel, the Olive Rooms, would take transients but it was more of a roominghouse for permanent residents than a hotel. The bus from Buck's stable met all the trains. It was drawn by two beautiful big black horses. A long padded bench ran along each side of the bus and there were steps in the rear. Buck charged twenty-five cents to deliver passengers anywhere they wanted to go—to the Casa Loma, to the normal school, or to private houses, just so long as it wasn't out in the country. In the fall, when the normal school opened, the bus would be full of pretty, brightly dressed, giggling girls. They gave Buck their baggage checks and he or one of his men picked up their baggage later and delivered it to their dormitories. For this service he charged fifty cents.

Buck's livery stable was one of the most interesting businesses in Tempe. He had an enormous stable redolent of manure and hay; stalls filled with sleek, handsome horses; a big storage space crowded with shiny buggies. When there was a funeral Buck took his fine black team off the depot bus and hitched it to a black rubber-tired hearse with glass sides so the coffin inside could be seen. Sports used to like to gather in Buck's office and talk about women, booze, race horses, and to tell jokes about buggies that came from rentals to amorous couples with upside-down footprints on the dashboard.

When the motor age came on with a rush, it killed Buck's business—dead. Nobody wanted to rent a horse and buggy for three or four dollars when you could accomplish the same purpose and get farther from town and be more comfortable in a flivver with twenty-five cents worth of gas. In order to use his fine horses he had to hitch them to wagons and haul sand and gravel for contractors to sites where buildings were going up. When I was in my teens I worked for him one summer. I'd go down to the river, fill the wagon bed full of sand shovelful by shovelful. Then I'd toil slowly to the building site, drive my team up to the sand pile, move the boards in the wagon bed so the sand would run out. That was one of the best jobs I ever had. Shoveling sand was hard work but I did it in the open in the pleasant river bottom. I spent more time driving the wagon than I did in shoveling and I had plenty of time to think.

Buck finally had to sell or give away all his horses and his fine shiny buggies—even his wagons, since he couldn't compete with trucks. He bought a Buick touring car to meet the trains in and a truck to pick up merchandise at the wholesalers in Phoenix and deliver it to the local merchants.

Another casualty of the automobile age on Mill Avenue was the blacksmith shop. Just when it disappeared I cannot say, but it must have been somewhere between 1912 and 1914. I used to hang around the shop and watch the blacksmith perform all manner of wonders with his forge and anvil. Winter and summer he worked in a leather apron and a wool undershirt with the sleeves cut off almost to his shoulders. He was a large, dark man with tremendous shoulders and arms. He spoke only to give an occasional order to his young helper. He never spoke to me or the other little boys who came to gape. He nodded to acknowledge our presence, motioned us back if he thought we might get burned by the sparks from his anvil.

He could forge and temper springs and knives, and make axheads and all sorts of iron and steel objects that are mass-produced today, but his major business was shoeing horses. I can still remember the roar of the forge, the smell of coal smoke and of burning hoofs, the showering white-hot sparks. The blacksmith worked swiftly and efficiently. The big horses stood patiently while he shod them. He tied up the hoof he was working on, pared it down with a draw knife, shaped it up with a rasp. Then he forged a horseshoe to fit and hammered down the caulks on his anvil. He burned the red-hot shoe to a perfect fit with the hoof.

What happened to this man so skilled in his ancient craft,

where he went when his village smithy folded up, what he turned his hand to, I have no idea.

Jeeter's Meat Market was the only one in town, but there was a small meat department at Birchett Brothers and one at Moe Levitsky's store out on Eighth Street. Old Man Jeeter sold good meat. He always had the big cream-colored carcasses of fat steers hanging in his cooling room and quarters out in front. He also hung up the carcasses of pigs, sheep, and chickens, and in the spring those of pathetic little lambs. He had a showcase cooled by brine solution to display choice bits of flesh. The floor was covered with sawdust. The shop was always cool and clean and over it hung the faintly repugnant, faintly stimulating smell of raw flesh and blood.

They said of Jeeter, who was a poor white from Tennessee, that he had got the money to start his business by selling a pretty sixteen-year-old daughter to a Chinaman. The way I heard the story from my Uncle John Woolf was that the Chinaman, who called himself Pete Lee and who owned a very profitable store in the Mexican section of Phoenix, had become enamored of the girl and had offered old Jeeter two thousand dollars for her. Jeeter said he wouldn't think of selling her for less than five thousand dollars. The Chinaman didn't try to haggle. He just went to the bank and drew out five thousand dollars, handed it to old Jeeter and walked off with the girl. As far as anyone knew she was happy. She used to come to see the old folks with her five half-Chinese kids. A couple of them looked pretty much Chinese, but two of them were blond. It must be pretty easy to breed out Mongolian genes because none of Pete Lee's grandchildren looked as if he had any Chinese blood at all.

Many years later I met one of Pete Lee's granddaughters in Phoenix at a party and danced with her several times. She didn't look any more Chinese than I do. I said that Lee was a grand name and she said she was very proud of it. I asked her if she was from Virginia. She said her parents were. Was she related to Robert E. Lee? Well, not directly, she said.

My favorite store on Mill Avenue was Laird & Dines drug store, which I can remember as far back as 1907. It was owned by a pharmacist, "Doctor" Dines, and the Laird brothers. For years it displayed big, fancy glass jars full of colored liquids in the windows. It had a soda fountain, a magazine rack, a cigar counter, the turn-of-the-century tables and chairs used in those days in ice-cream parlors. When I was small there was nearly always a life-size cardboard cut-out of a pretty girl sitting at a table drinking Coca-Cola. In the summer the place hummed with electric fans, smelled of drugs, green soap, vanilla ice cream, Coca-Cola, and fruit syrup.

In the fifty years I knew the drug store it changed almost not at all. The fancy jars full of colored liquids were eventually taken out of the window. A less fancy, more utilitarian soda fountain was installed, but in the same location, the ice-cream-parlor tables and chairs were replaced. Old Dr. Dines grew more and more feeble, retired, and died. The Laird boys grew older. I would be away from Tempe for years at a time but whenever I went back Bill Laird would be standing behind the cigar counter with a little less hair, a little more belly, but otherwise unchanged. Hugh would be behind a counter on the other side. Once, after I had moved away from Arizona for good and was back in Tempe to see my mother, Hugh Laird called to me when I came in. "Oh, Jack," he said as if he had seen me the day before, "you left something here!" I wondered what in the world it could be. He went into the back of the store and came out with a normal-school annual I had left there thirty years before.

I moved away from Arizona in 1948. Some years later I was back for a brief visit with my mother. I had written books, had shot lions and tigers, had visited in far places, but to Bill I was still the barefoot, towheaded kid that used to come in with a dime and linger a long time at the fountain with a pineapple ice-cream soda.

"What are you doing now?" Bill asked. "Are you still down at the university?" To Bill I was the Local Kid Who Made Good because I had been a professor at the University of Arizona. I believe it was on that visit that I told Bill that if I ever came back to Tempe and did not find him behind his cigar counter that I would know my world was coming to an end.

Now, alas, the drug store is closed, a victim of urban sprawl and shopping centers, and Bill is dead.

The Tempe National Bank was also on Mill Avenue, a sort of a pseudo-Classical structure with white pillars. The building still houses a bank but the Tempe National was sold down the river when Uncle Charles was getting old and no longer wanted the responsibility of being president. As long as I can remember, his Tempe law office was upstairs in the bank building, and he also maintained an office in Phoenix. American irrigation law grew up in the Salt River valley as the Roosevelt Dam was the first big irrigation project, and Uncle Charles was an authority on the subject.

Before World War I there were two doctors in town—Dr. B. B. Moeur, whose office was in the Tempe National Bank building, and Dr. Brecken, whose wife was a nurse and whose office was in his residence. There was no hospital in Tempe and no surgeon. If someone had to go to a hospital or be cut into he went to Phoenix.

Dr. Moeur was one of Tempe's first citizens, and during the depression many years later he was the governor of the state. Like many small-town doctors he took pride in being a character. He was bluff, profane, ribald, and everyone loved him. He had taken the full two-year course at the University of Arkansas medical school, but by today's standards he wouldn't even be a good horse doctor. He removed my adenoids by simply painting my throat with some mildly anesthetic solution, promising me a dime for an ice-cream soda if I didn't howl too loud, putting a knee against my chest and his left arm around my head to hold me immobile, and then cutting out the growth with a scalpel in his free right hand.

But he had a fine bedside manner, and anyone who was sick knew that with this big, blustering, bald-headed fat man on his side he could not lose. He always prescribed a vast number of pills, powders, and liquids, all of which tasted horrible and none of which did any good. When my sister and I were sick he made us live at considerable expense on Horlick's malted milk and an evil-tasting tonic known as Panopeptin, which evidently contained some beef extract. If we so much as had a sniffle he prescribed castor oil or an enema. He believed that a sluggish colon or a torpid liver was the root of all evil. In 1928 when my wife and I had been married less than a year we visited at my mother's home in Tempe. My wife had not felt well, was losing weight, and was running a slight temperature. I suspected tuberculosis and took her to Dr. Moeur for an examination. He diagnosed her ailment as a torpid liver, prescribed a massive doze of calomel, and sent me a bill for fifteen dollars. Actually she did have tuberculosis and spent a year in a sanatorium in El Paso, Texas. She returned to her wifely duties completely cured.

Tempe's one dentist lived behind his office on Mill Avenue. He was a gay blade but a rough-and-ready dentist. He was one of the first people in Tempe to have an automobile and he used to spend a good deal of time in Phoenix. It was rumored that he sometimes gave attractive women gas and took certain liberties with them. But one pretty Mormon girl who was going to the normal remembered what had happened, told her father, and the dentist was badly beaten.

When the poor came down with some contagious disease like smallpox or diphtheria they were taken about a mile south of town to the pest house, a dismal wooden building painted red. There they stayed until they died or got well, with relatives who cooked for them and nursed them. Dr. Moeur went out now and then to see how they were getting along.

The infant death rate was high in those days. Almost every Tempe family had lost a child. It seemed to me that during the summer at least once a week there was a funeral procession bearing through Mexican town a small child's coffin on the shoulders of pallbearers. The children were killed by "summer complaint"—diseases that were the result of myriad flies and of poorly handled food and milk. I almost died when I was about eighteen months old of what was called "cholera infantum." I probably saved myself by drinking the water out of a goldfish bowl. Since the little victims died because constant diarrhea removed all moisture from their bodies, the treatment in those days was to withhold all liquids. My mother was following the doctor's orders to let me have no liquid but a piece of ice sucked through cloth. She went into another room for a moment and when she came back I was finishing off the last of the water in a small goldfish bowl. The two little goldfish were never seen again. She expected me to die within minutes, but instead my fever went down, I began to sweat, and the next morning I was just about well. My mother told me the story many times. For years I thought the name of the ailment that had almost done me in was "collar and fantum."

There was a jewelry store on Mill Avenue beside the Tempe National Bank. My grandfather owned a piece of the bank, was the president one time, and was on the board of directors as long as he lived. When he died my Uncle Charles Woolf became president. Catty-cornered and a block away was the Ranchers & Miners Bank. The Pillsons, who owned it, lived in the biggest house in town. They had a cook, a maid, a laundress, a gardener. Mr. Pillson had gray hair and a potbelly. He looked like someone's idea of a Wall Street financier. Mrs. Pillson was slender and willowy, and I thought she was beautiful. She always smelled sweet and she wore big hats and spectacular clothes. Once, when I was about ten and went to Buddy Pillson's birthday party, she kissed me. Mother said she dyed her hair and painted her face and a woman of her age should know better than to try to dress like a young girl. The Pillsons had rich friends from the East who came in private railway cars that were left on the siding near the depot. It was rumored that all these people were *fast,* that they drank quantities of wine, danced madly through the night to fiddle music, and were too familiar with each other's wives.

A lot of the kids thought Buddy Pillson was a stuck-up little prick. Everything the Pillsons did had to be classy, so they sent Buddy to some military school in the Middle West. Later he went to St. Mark's. He was in his sophomore year in Princeton when his father called in the state bank examiner, told him he had lost a half million dollars of his depositors' money gambling on cotton and playing the stock market. Then he walked into his private office at the bank and shot himself.

But that's getting ahead of my story. Mrs. Pillson always asked me to Buddy's parties because I was old J. W. Woolf's grandson and Charlie Woolf's and Jim O'Connor's nephew. She knew Buddy was lonely so she encouraged me to go up there and play. I learned to play tennis on the clay court behind the Pillson house. At first we just patted the ball around, but I found a book on tennis in the Pillson library. I used old Buddy to practice on. By the time I was eleven I could cut loose with a pretty good topspin serve and my forehand and backhand drives were shaping up. Buddy was a goodlooking kid with his mother's blue eyes and fair hair, but like his father he was too fat and he was lazy. Pretty soon I was beating the tail off of him any time I felt like it, but I took care to let him beat me quite often because I was afraid that if I didn't he'd get sore and not invite me up.

I liked being around the Pillson house and I liked the Pillsons—particularly Mrs. Pillson. I was at their house mostly in the summers when Buddy was home from school. Somehow it always seemed cooler in that house than in any other in town. Maybe it was because of the big yard with the grass and the tall trees. That might have been the reason. Late in the afternoons all summer the Mexican gardener came and watered everything. Most of the houses in Tempe at that time were made of lumber. A few were brick and some, like my grandfather's place, were made of concrete blocks. Most people looked down on adobe bricks as being material fit only for Mexicans. But the Pillson house was adobe and the walls were three feet thick. The ceilings must have been at least fifteen feet high and the living room was just about long enough to play basketball in. Before I started going up to the Pillsons' house I thought Grandfather's house had a big living room, but after being at the Pillsons' I thought of it as being small and crowded with furniture. With six or seven people in it in the summer you could just about feel them sweat.

At my grandfather's house we always ate in the dining room at night, but at noon everybody just sort of gobbled on the oilcloth in the kitchen. Sometimes at noon Grandfather would come in without a collar and tie, just his shirt with a collar button in front. But the Pillsons always ate in style. Buddy wouldn't think of sitting down to a meal unless his hair was combed and his face washed. Mr. Pillson always wore a coat at mealtimes, even in the summer, and Mrs. Pillson always had her rouge on and every hair in place. She had a little silver bell beside her place and when she banged it the maid would come out, take dishes away, and bring the next course.

The Pillsons had an enormous bookcase along the inside wall of the living room, and Mrs. Pillson used to see me eying it. Now and then I'd take a book down and peek in it. One day she said to me, "Jack, you like to read, don't you?" I said I did and she told me to feel free to come over and read any time I wanted to. Buddy and I used to play tennis late in the afternoon when it had started to cool off a little, so I formed the habit of coming over an hour or two early and reading. Sometimes Mrs. Pillson took a nap in the afternoon, as Buddy always did. I'd knock softly and the maid would let me in. Sometimes I'd find a chair by a window and read. Sometimes I'd just lie down on my belly with the book in front of me. Now and then Mrs. Pillson would come out, sit in a big wicker chair, and read with her legs curled under her like a little girl. Until recently I'd thought of legs only as something to get around on, but the older boys at school were always talking about women's legs. Sometimes they would see some stocking above a woman's shoe tops. Then they would punch each other and giggle. Because the boys talked about legs, I made something of a study of them. Some, I noted, had smooth, swelling calves and trim pretty ankles. Some legs were thin all the way up, some were too heavy. Often I saw a good deal of leg when Mrs. Pillson sat reading in the big wicker chair. I could see that her legs were very pretty. I was also aware somehow that Mrs. Pillson was female and I was male, and this awareness made me a little shy around her. She treated me as if I were grown up. Sometimes she would ask me what I thought of the book I was reading, and she'd listen as gravely to what I said as if I were a professor. Many years later when I was in college I had to read *Madame Bovary.* As I got into it the story grew more and more familiar and presently I remembered that I had read it one summer in the Pillson living room when I was about ten years old. Of course there was a lot about the book I didn't understand, but when I told the beautiful Mrs. Pillson about it she sat in her big wicker chair and listened. I can see her now. She was wearing something soft and cool and blue and she wore a blue ribbon in her yellow hair. At the time I thought of her as being very old. She must have been around thirty-seven.

With their big house, their servants, their Pierce-Arrow, the pony cart that the cook used for shopping and Buddy drove occasionally, and with the rich friends that came to visit them in private railway cars with Negro cooks, the Pillsons lived a different sort of a life from any other family in town, but Uncle Charles used to say they were living beyond their means. "Hell," he said, "Old Man Pillson and his fancy wife like to live rich, but they aren't. They're pretty well off but they surer than hell are not rich. Pillson makes some pretty risky loans and some investments that I wouldn't touch with a ten-foot pole. One of these days he's going to get burned."

There were no rich in Tempe, but several families who were "well-to-do." Nearly all of these were ranchers or farmers who had operated on a large scale, were worth from $100,000 to perhaps $250,000 and who had moved to town to take it a little easier or to have it so their children could go to the normal.

Those of the next economic grade were "comfortably fixed." These were merchants with good businesses, professional men like doctors and lawyers with good incomes, farmers who had retired with enough income from mortgages or leases of land so they didn't need to scrimp and could go to the mountains or the Coast during the worst part of the summer. The comfortably fixed generally had some sort of conveyance—a horse and buggy, perhaps a team and a surrey; but by 1910 or 1912 some were getting automobiles. A. J. Matthews, the president of the normal school, would have been in the ranks of the comfortably fixed, for the state paid him well, gave him a good brick house, and kept up an automobile for him.

Most of the citizens were in moderate circumstances. If they owned their own houses they were not pretentious. If they had money laid away it didn't amount to much. They were clerks in stores or banks. They taught school. More often than not they kept their own cows and had a flock of chickens. Many had gardens, and in the Salt River valley it was possible in the winter to raise the hardier vegetables like onions, radishes, lettuce. They usually had fruit trees. The valley was too hot for apples and cherries, but grapes, peaches, and apricots did well and the enormous old fig trees produced tons of fruit. The thrifty wives of those in moderate circumstances worked long hours every day when the fruit was ripe. One woman would put up dozens of quarts of jams, jellies, preserved peach and apricot halves. Most of the cooking and preserving was done on wood stoves and in the hottest months of the year. Since a day when the thermometer did not go over 100 was considered pleasant and the mercury sometimes climbed to 118 or 120 degrees in the shade, it can be seen that preserving time had its problems.

The town teemed with domestic birds and animals. Cows bawled. Hundreds of dogs barked. Chickens crowed and cackled. Ducks and geese waddled around. Cats screamed and caterwauled on fences and in back yards. Horses neighed. Great flocks of blackbirds, some with red spots on their wings and some with yellow, swept through town and perched noisily in the trees. In the summer the trees were filled with nesting mourning and whitewing doves and their melodious somnolent cooing filled the warm, moist, caressing summer air.

It must have been against either law or custom to keep hogs in town, but I knew families on the outskirts who owned a few acres; many of them had hogs. When the pigs had been fattened on "slop" and "swill" they were shot in the head with .22-caliber rifles, dunked in a barrel of scalding hot water, scraped, skinned, cut up. The intestines were cleaned. The hams and side meat for bacon were pickled and smoked; meat was ground up, mixed with salt and spices to make sausage. The whole family worked madly at hog-butchering time. The term "living high on the hog" does not have much meaning for those who have never seen hogs butchered and hog meat preserved.

Not many of these thrifty folk in moderate circumstances kept horses and buggies. None of them had automobiles. Sometimes if they had old horses they used to plow a few acres with them. They would also ride them or hitch them to light wagons. The common means of transportation for the men was the bicycle, and many women also had bicycles. Bicycles for adults usually had wire baskets hung on the handlebars above the front wheel to carry things in and some also had baskets or little platforms over the rear wheels. Bicycles had lights for night riding and little bells on the handlebars that went *ding-a-ling* to warn pedestrians. Many women rode bicycles downtown to buy their groceries and dry goods. Men rode their bicycles to the stores and offices where they worked. They did so with no loss of dignity, since they sat upright, pedaled slowly and deliberately. The men wore "bicycle clips" over the cuffs of their trousers so they would not rub them against the greasy chain. Many of these older people called their bicycles "wheels," an atavistic memory of the time when bicycles had one enormous wheel with a very small one behind. Those they rode in 1908–12 were "safety bicycles."

The young boys, on the other hand, rode bicycles that they tried to make look like motorcycles. They turned the post that held the seat around backward so the seat would sit low over the rear wheel like the seat on a motorcycle. They bought bicycles with "motorcycle handlebars." The result was that the boys sat hunched up and uncomfortable and strained their back muscles while pedaling. But like the Chinese women who bound their feet, and women who wore corsets so tight that they displaced their internal organs and could breathe with difficulty, they were in fashion.

The next step below the people in moderate circumstances were those in "reduced circumstances." These were people who were respectable, had seen better days, and who might see them again. These were families who had been through a severe illness, families whose breadwinner was out of a job, young widows whose husbands had left them little but debts and children. More affluent people helped those in reduced circumstances in tactful ways: "Mrs. Jones, I don't know what in the world is the matter with Sam. He went down and bought two fifty-pound sacks of flour. He should have known that with only two of us at home now the weevils will get into the other sack before I can use it up. I was wondering if you could make use of it. I'd be very grateful if you could!"

Those in reduced circumstances made over garments for children. They were grateful for cast-off clothes that could be altered. When my father took it on the lam he left, among other things, his two-piece bathing suit. I'll never forget my shame and humiliation when at the age of seven or eight I had to go swimming in the damned thing. It was thick wool, and when it was soaked with salt water the shirt portion hung down a full eight inches below my bony little knees.

I was with my grandfather a couple of times when he was helping the young widow of a man who had once worked for him.

"Oh, Mrs. Simpson, I was going over my books the other day and I was shocked to discover that I still owed your late husband two hundred dollars at the time of his unfortunate demise. I have the money in the envelope here. Please accept my apologies and my sincere wish that my negligence has not caused you any embarrassment or inconvenience."

And later: "Mrs. Simpson, I have been noticing that handsome little cart behind your house. I have been looking for something exactly like that and if you could spare it I should like to offer you two hundred and fifty dollars for it if you deem that sum adequate."

Grandfather was always very formal in his relations with women outside the family, particularly with pretty young women. I noticed that he always took me with him when he called to see how Mrs. Simpson was doing.

Mrs. Simpson knew, of course, that Grandfather didn't owe her husband a damned cent when Joe Bowers, another ranch hand, shot him in an argument over a Mexican floosie in Prescott. She also knew that Grandfather had about as much use for that cart as he had for a performing seal. She appreciated his tactfulness. When Grandfather heard Mrs. Simpson had married again he breathed a sigh of relief.

"I just hope that young woman has found a good steady man this time," he said, "and not some wild man that will go gallivanting around where he has no business being and get himself shot."

And below those respectable and unfortunate people in reduced circumstances were the poor. The Mexicans were poor but they were not considered poor. They were just considered Mexicans and in another category. As my Uncle John Woolf always said: "Hell, a greaser don't need much. Give him some coffee, a tortilla, and a handful of frijoles a day, a shot of tequila now and then, a shirt and a pair of pants, and he's happy."

The poor white people were the feckless, the ne'er-do-wells. Often the head of the family was a drunkard. Sometimes he was sick but generally he was lazy. Often the poor were Southern hillbillies. The church people gave them cast-off clothing, cheap and bulky food. When they died the county buried them.

# 9 · My Uncle Jim O'Connor

It would seem that because I grew up with no father to guide me and for me to emulate I should have turned out to be on the odd side. Actually I am now aware that I was not so badly off, as there were two father figures in my life. One was my Grandfather Woolf. The other was Jim O'Connor, one of my father's brothers. Both were named James. My Irish uncle was Jim O'Connor to everyone, but I never heard anyone dare to call my Grandfather Woolf "Jim." To most people, even to those who had known him for years, he was Mr. Woolf or the Hon. J. W. Woolf, but a few intimate friends dared call him "J. W." He was a man of enormous dignity and of cold blue eye.

My Uncle Jim O'Connor, on the other hand, was friendly, affable, approachable. He was Jim to everyone in Arizona from the governor to little Mexican waifs on the streets of Florence, who pronounced his name "Jeem." In his youth his hair had been ash-blond, but as I remember him he was a tall man wide of girth and ponderous of movement with blue eyes, thick, wavy, snow-white hair, and a large white mustache with ends curled up like the tails of mallard drakes. He looked like a Santa Claus who had shaved off his beard but had kept his mustache.

I loved and admired both Jim and my grandfather. Both went

out of their way to be kind to me. My grandfather was taciturn and undemonstrative. Simply to call a boy of my age by his first name seemed to him to be an obscene and exhibitionistic show of sentimentality. Generally he simply called me "boy." In the years I knew him I can recall only a couple of tentative hugs and a few pats on the head. He seldom talked to me and never talked idly.

My Uncle Jim O'Connor, on the other hand, was affectionate, articulate, a teller of tales and jokes, a man who liked an icy glass of

beer with his lunch, good cigars, good food, fine bourbon whiskey, pretty women. He had a gallant way with the ladies, often kissed their hands, sometimes to their shocked surprise, but he was a faithful husband and a kind and affectionate father. My Grandfather Woolf and my Uncle Jim O'Connor both died while I was young, my grandfather when I was thirteen, Jim O'Connor when I was fifteen. I am aware that there is plenty of O'Connor and plenty of Woolf in me, perhaps a little more California Irish than Kentucky Anglo-Saxon.

My Uncle Jim O'Connor was, I believe, that rare creature—a truly kind man. Many are kind if they can inflate their own egos by being so or if they feel their good deeds will be returned with six per cent interest compounded semiannually. Uncle Jim went out of his way to be kind to me although there was no way I could return his kindness and there were few to observe his deeds. One reason for his interest in my welfare was possibly a feeling that my father had been less than responsible in his relation to his wife and family. When it became apparent that the separation of my mother and father was permanent, it was my Uncle Jim O'Connor who acted as my mother's attorney to obtain the divorce.

As a young lawyer, Jim O'Connor had settled in Florence, a desert town of windmills and adobe houses near the Gila River, when he moved over from California. The town has lived because it is the seat of Pinal County and it has not grown much or changed a great deal since the days of which I write—over fifty years ago.

I was in Florence the last time in 1965, when my wife and I went back to Arizona for a few days of quail hunting. We pulled up in front of a hardware store run by an ancient, palsied man to buy our nonresident hunting licenses and some shotgun shells.

I asked if he would take a check. My name was O'Connor, I said, and I at one time had an uncle who had lived in Florence. Hell yes, he'd take my check, he said. I must be Jim O'Connor's nephew, Andy's son. The check was on an Idaho bank in a town he'd never heard of but he wouldn't even look at the identification I offered because I was Jim O'Connor's nephew. "Why, goddammit," he said, "I remember you when you used to hang around Florence in the summers!" I felt about twelve years old.

Florence in 1965 wasn't too different from what it was in 1912 and 1913. There was one main street with some ramshackle stores. Most of the buildings were adobe but more worn and woebegone than they were a half century before. The old two-story hotel where Uncle Jim and I used to eat lunch was closed, as traveling salesmen that hit Florence and are unfortunate enough to have to stay overnight hole up in motels on the Tucson highway. The Pinal County courthouse is still the most impressive building in town, but its tin dome looks rusty and unkempt. The state prison looks today from a distance much as it looked fifty years ago. Actually Florence is probably a poorer business town now than it was in 1913. Half the store buildings are empty and those that remain are no buzzing hives of commerce. Phoenix and Tucson are now great cities but Florence, which is directly between them, is a backwater.

My Uncle Jim must have come to Florence around 1895. He quickly established a successful law practice, and when I used to visit him he had a 400-acre irrigated farm on the edge of town and a cattle ranch on the desert about twenty miles from Florence. He had made his stake and had got himself elected superior judge of Pinal County. This was a position of great honor and prestige. How much it paid in those days I have no idea.

Like my uncle, his wife, Lily, was a Californian, but unlike Jim, Lily had never grown fond of the Arizona desert. As soon as school was out every spring Lily fled to California with her brood to escape the broiling heat. Jim had bought a summer cottage at Venice on the California coast about twenty-five miles from Los Angeles. There my Aunt Lily spent every summer amid a vast disorder of bathing suits, sand, dirty towels, unwashed dishes, shouting children. Lily was the sort of person for whom life is simply too complicated, too full of too many things, too much noise, and too many people. She and Jim had five children when I used to spend the summers in Florence—four girls and one boy. Another boy came along later.

Jim, I believe, was genuinely sorry for me because I was a small boy without a father. I think he also found me pretty good company—or at least far better than no company at all. My father and both of his brothers were prodigious readers, particularly of history, biography, travel, anthropology. Their Irish father likewise.

My cousins, Jim's children, were exposed to Jim's reading habits to a far greater extent than I was, but none of them inherited the O'Connor history-reading genes, whereas for some reason I did.

When Aunt Lily and the children were in residence at the farm home on the outskirts of Florence the big, sprawling part-lumber, part-adobe house was almost as bad a shambles as the beach cottage. My aunt had two Mexican girls to help her but outside of doing the laundry and washing the dishes they seemed of little help. Aunt Lily screamed at them as loudly as she did at her children.

Jim's real refuge was the judge's chambers at the courthouse. It was a big room paneled in oak, lined with bookcases. Most were lawbooks but some were of a general nature. There was a leather couch, a couple of leather chairs, two buzzing, somnolent electric fans. Here, sprawled in a leather chair during hot summer afternoons, I read *Les Misérables, Huckleberry Finn, Tom Sawyer, Life on the Mississippi, Roughing It, Jude the Obscure, Far from the Madding Crowd.*

At noon Uncle Jim and I always had lunch at the hotel. But it was then called dinner—soup, salad, beef of some sort, potatoes, pie, tea or coffee. Used as I was to my mother's mild and wholesome cooking, these meals at the hotel seemed exotic viands of incredible sophistication.

Jim O'Connor was a widely respected scholar of the law, a wit, a shrewd practicing attorney, a raconteur of no mean ability. Of him a friend once said: "There's an hombre who is all man—and two yards wide, by God!" When he left the office in late afternoon he always went into a saloon, had two bourbon Old-Fashioneds, chatted with a few cronies. Then he climbed ponderously into his Cadillac and drove home. If I were with him at the saloon he always ordered me a grape juice with ice and seltzer water. At home he always gave me a small glass of beer with my dinner. He told me beer was a natural drink and far better for a growing boy than the soda pop I preferred. Once he poured the contents of a bottle of strawberry pop over a white handkerchief. It dyed the handkerchief pink. "See how it is!" he said. "Drink enough of that damned stuff and you'll go through life with pink guts!"

Generally we had enough time to shoot a dozen or so whitewing doves out of the flight that went over the house when we got home —Jim with one of several shotguns he owned, me with the 20-gauge Iver-Johnson my Grandfather Woolf had given me. With these Jim made delicious and complicated stews on a kerosene stove. He loved to cook.

A Mexican girl fresh from Sonora, silent and frightened, certain she was at least to be raped if not horribly murdered, used to slip into the house every morning. When we returned at night our clothes were all washed, ironed, and put away, our beds made, the dishes washed, the house swept and tidied up. If Jim was still there when Luz, the maid, arrived she was so frightened of the big fat gringo with the white hair that she trembled and tears came into her eyes whenever he spoke to her.

"Jack," he said one day as we drove off in the Cadillac for the courthouse, "that poor girl must think I intend to rape her."

"Uncle Jim, what's rape?"

"The carnal knowledge of a female without her consent."

"I still don't understand."

"I'll translate that into the vulgar tongue used by boys and ignoramuses—it means screwing a girl when she doesn't want you to. Do you understand now?"

I nodded.

" 'Carnal' comes from a Latin word meaning 'flesh,' " he went on. "It's from the same source as the Spanish word *carne,* meaning 'meat.' "

When I asked him about something he never gave me a brush-off. He always answered my questions with patience and intelligence. Once I ran across the term "illegitimate child" in a law-book. I asked him what it meant. He told me that it was the offspring of a woman by a man to whom she was not legally wed.

I brooded over this for a while and then posed a hypothetical question: "Uncle Jim, if a man and woman had a baby and didn't get married until the child was twenty-one years old, would the child be legitimate?"

"Yes," he said, "—perfectly legitimate, but the whole business would be unconventional to the extreme and would cause everyone concerned no end of embarrassment."

UNCLE JIM was an enthusiastic hunter and a fine trap and bird shot. Before he had got so heavy he had hunted desert bighorn sheep and mule deer with Jim McGee, who like himself was a first-generation American born of Irish parents. When I spent the summers with him he used to shoot whitewing and mourning doves three or four times a week and in the fall and winter he shot ducks along the Gila River and Gambel's quail out on the desert.

He liked guns and enjoyed shooting but he was not a lover of fine guns as I later became. His rifles and shotguns were not fancy. They all showed hard and careless use. But he must have had twenty-five or thirty rifles and shotguns. There were always several cases of shotgun shells sitting on the floor, three or four dozen boxes of rifle cartridges on the shelves. I loved the cluttered gun room. I found cleaning materials, took rust out of bores with light oil and brass brushes, sandpapered scratches out of stocks, finished them with linseed oil.

Uncle Jim had a romantic barn full of hay, a tack room with saddles, bridles, saddle blankets, rifle scabbards, curry combs, a couple of sawbuck pack saddles, pack boxes cleverly contoured on one side to fit the shape of a horse's ribs. Uncle Jim taught me to saddle a horse, how to ride, encouraged me to ride out on the desert with a .25/20 Winchester carbine in a saddle scabbard under my left leg.

Uncle Jim encouraged me to read but in an offhand, man-to-man way which I did not resent. He let me manage my own days. If I wanted to go to the courthouse with him and spend most of my day reading in the judge's chambers, he approved. If I saddled up a horse, took the .25/20 carbine and rode out into the desert, that also met with his approval.

Now and then I would ride the horse over to the prison, call on the warden, who was a friend of Uncle Jim, and spend a couple of hours talking to my friend the prison librarian. Exactly what an eleven- or twelve-year-old boy and a forty-five-year-old murderer had in common I cannot at this moment remember but I enjoyed talking to the librarian and I believe he enjoyed talking to me. His name was Iting and he was a pleasant bald-headed tubercular who within a few years was to die in prison. He had come to Phoenix some years before in an attempt to recover from his illness, and when he ran out of money he invited another "lunger," who had just received and cashed a large check, on a picnic by the Salt River. He then got him drunk and chloroformed him. It was a clumsy crime. Iting was caught and the only reason he was not hanged may have been that there was some doubt as to his intent to kill.

The murderer was obviously a man of some education. He talked well, used good English. Since Harvard was one of the few Eastern universities any Arizonan had ever heard of, Iting was supposed to be a Harvard graduate and the black sheep of a wealthy and distinguished family. He had been a con man and a cardsharp, had fleeced victims on transatlantic liners, and had traveled in Europe. He told me tales of crime and chicanery in a pleasant half-amused voice and made everything sound like a jolly and harmless game.

The warden took me all over the prison—to the condemned row, where the poor wretches who were shortly to be hanged were spending their last days, even to the execution chambers. I saw the trapdoor on which the condemned men stood, the room into which they plummeted. There, pictures of all who had been executed were preserved behind glass, framed by a portion of the rope used to hang them. One rope was still dark with dried blood. It had been used on a murderer so small and light that the hangman had felt his weight was not sufficient to break his neck. To make sure his charge would meet instant and painless death the hangman had tied weights to his feet. But he had overdone it. When the trap was sprung the murderer's neck was not only broken—his head was torn off. Hence the blood on the rope. I thought the pictures of the dull young men framed in the ropes that killed them expressed a very tender and pretty sentiment.

MY UNCLE JIM O'CONNOR'S cattle ranch was about twenty miles southeast of Florence toward the great Santa Catalina Mountains that jutted up high and blue. I was there the first time when I was about five. I remember an interminable ride in a wagon pulled by a four-horse team and swarming with young O'Connors. I also remember a pleasant lunch in a sandy arroyo in the shade of a large mesquite tree, the killing of a rattlesnake found nearby, the rite of watering the sweating horses from a barrel carried on the side of the wagon. I likewise remember the corral made of gnarled and twisted mesquite, the sun-bleached skulls of a desert bighorn ram and a buck desert mule deer nailed above the door of the ranch house.

On that first visit I was excited by the wonders of the ranch—the outdoor privy made of adobe, the bawling cattle in the corral, the little adobe blacksmith shop, the mud and ocotillo huts where the two Mexican cowboys lived with their shy young wives and their little brown children, the grizzled and bowlegged ranch foreman. I remember a wonderful meal of frijoles, beef stew, and biscuits—all cooked in Dutch ovens in the big fireplace.

But when night came on the big room with cots full of O'Connors ranged around the wall was dark. I could hear the breathing of my cousins and of Aunt Lily and Uncle Jim. Outside, coyotes howled and cows bawled mournfully. Suddenly I was frightfully lonely and far, far away from the familiar comforts of home. I began to sob. "What's the matter, Jack?" Uncle Jim asked. "I want my mama," I wept. My cousins—Olive, who was a few months older than I was, and Wallace, who was less than a year younger—teased me about that for a long time.

In later years the ranch was a happy place for me. Sometimes

I used to arise, dress, and get out in the cool gray dawn and ride from Jim's farm out to the ranch, a journey that took me four or five hours. Often I saw coyotes and now and then I managed to kill one with the .25/20. Sometimes I would see gray desert mule deer bounding away through the palo verdes. I shot my first javelina and missed my first deer on those early morning rides.

I used to ride out with the two vaqueros and help them doctor calves for screw worms. When a vaquero would see an infected calf there would be a short, swift, thundering chase. The cowboy would rope and throw the calf, jump off to tie it while his horse kept the rope taut. Then he would pour the medicine into the wound eaten deep into the navel by the screw worms. I can still remember how the evil little creatures who were eating the calves alive would come tumbling out at the hot touch of the medicine. The vaquero then dabbed tar on the gaping wound to keep flies from "blowing" it by depositing more eggs. All this time the mother cow would stand nervously by, sometimes bawling, sometimes threatening. My job was to hold the bottle of worm medicine or the can of tar. Sometimes I threw stones at a threatening cow.

During the summer the days at the ranch were very hot, but at night the foreman and I, and Uncle Jim if he were along, slept on stout Mexican cots under a big mesquite tree far enough from the house to catch the breeze. Since the ranch was fairly high and the air dry it was always deliciously cool not long after the sun went down. I can still recall the creak and the *clunk-clunk-clunk* of the windmill as it caught a sudden breeze and began to turn. Then the water would splash into the tank. When we rode, the vaqueros pointed out the tracks of the desert dwellers—the mule deer, an occasional whitetail or a wandering bighorn ram, the desert pronghorn antelope, the javelina, the quail, the road runner.

I spent two whole summers and parts of others with Jim, and with the erosion of the years these have run together. I remember that for a month or two I worked for Andy Wren, who had married my father's sister Nellie. He had been a Sacramento, California, newspaperman and like many newspapermen he had longed to jump from the frying pan into the fire by owning and running a country weekly. He bought the Florence *Blade-Tribune.* The paper was housed in an adobe building. It was hand-set and printed on a flat-bed press, first on one side and then on the other. The *Blade-Tribune* also did job printing. The staff consisted of my Uncle Andy, two Mexican compositor-printers, and during that particular time, me. I delivered job printing, answered the telephone, called people on a list of local big shots furnished by my uncle to find out what they had been doing, took notes in pencil. Then I laboriously pecked out the items on an old Remington typewriter with separate keys for capital and lower-case letters. When my first batch of locals appeared in print I was enormously proud. I even got the names of some of the drummers who came to town to call on the merchants. I took pains to spell their names and those of their firms right. I quoted them on various matters. My Uncle Andy often laughed when he read my copy but he seldom changed it much and he always turned it over to a compositor to set.

I made some friends of my own age in Florence. Two were sisters, a vivacious redhead and a lovely blonde, about my own age. Later I was to date them both when I was a student at the Tempe Normal. Another was the nervous, frail son of the prison doctor. Two other friends were brothers who lived in a romantic old house which is still standing in Florence. The house itself fronted on the street and was built of thick adobe with high, barred windows. The patio was surrounded by an eight-foot wall of adobe and topped with broken beer bottles embedded in cement. It was a fort that could not be taken easily.

The father of the boys held some clerical job at the courthouse and the mother was Mexican. She was a superb cook in either Mexican or American style, and often my Uncle Jim and I were invited there to dinner. Both boys have since become distinguished citizens of Arizona.

I MUST HAVE BEEN twelve years old when my Uncle Jim was called to Phoenix to preside at a murder trial. For some reason the judge of the Maricopa court had disqualified himself and the rather sordid business was dropped into Jim's lap.

The story that lay behind the murder was both old and familiar. A beautiful young woman who lived in a Southern city had been having an affair with one of her husband's friends. The husband had somehow found out what was going on and was properly indignant. His wife's lover, who was a tubercular, fled from the husband's wrath.

Like many tuberculars of that time he wound up in Arizona. He got a wall tent, had a wooden floor installed, and lived in it on the bank of a canal not far from my home town of Tempe. At the time of the trial I saw a picture of him in the *Arizona Republic* and remembered that he was the thin young man with sandy hair and flushed tanned cheeks whom I had seen driving into town in a red Reo.

Precisely how the outraged husband found out where his wife's lover had come to roost I do not know, but he did find out. The tubercular was living under another name, but the husband came to Tempe, inquired as to where the man he described was to be found. He rented a livery-stable buggy, drove out to his former friend's tent, and shot him. He then drove back to Tempe, delivered his buggy to the livery stable, paid for it, and told the startled constable that he had just killed a man.

His story was that he had simply wanted to talk to the man. He had arrived in the middle of the night when his former friend was sleeping. He entered the tent, threw the beam of a flashlight into the sleeping man's face, and called out his name. His defense was that when his former friend awakened and realized who was behind the light he had reached under his pillow for a revolver. The outraged husband had then, according to his story, shot in self-defense. It was true that the officers who investigated the killing did find a revolver under the pillow of the murdered man.

How long the trial went on I cannot say. My Uncle Jim and I stayed at a hotel with an open porch around each floor and slept outside on cots. It was August and fearfully hot. My Uncle Jim used to parade around the big hotel room wearing BVD's, a strange one-piece undergarment customary in those days. Jim was six feet two and a half inches tall and weighed at least 250 pounds. In his BVD's he looked like a frigate under full sail.

We had three or four electric fans in the room and the only way we could get relief from the heat was to strip down to our underwear and let the hot wind from the fans cool us by evaporating our profuse sweat. I can still remember Jim sitting in a rocking chair in the voluminous white underwear, smoking a cigar, drinking beer, and going over legal-looking papers. With his white hair and mustache he was, even in that get-up, a dignified and commanding figure.

When we turned in on our cots it was still very hot and we lay there sweating in our pajamas. Along about midnight it became cooler and I can remember awakening often to pull a sheet over me. I can still remember the *clump-clump-clump* of horses' hoofs against the pavement, an occasional half-drunken voice from the dark streets below.

We ate lunch every day in a German restaurant not far from the Maricopa County courthouse. I was introduced to rye bread, limburger cheese, sauerkraut and sausage, Wiener schnitzel. Every day I had my little glass of beer. Possibly it was because my taste buds were young, sensitive, and unspoiled by tobacco, or maybe it was because in those days beer had more hops in it and was more carefully brewed than it is today, but at any rate I have never since tasted beer so delicious. After court was adjourned for the day, Jim always had his two ritualistic Old-Fashioneds and I my grape juice and seltzer water.

In those pre-prohibition days there must have been some fairly sophisticated restaurants in Phoenix. At least I remember them as being very elegant. In the evenings when it had cooled off a bit, Jim liked to make something of a ceremony of dinner. We generally went out with friends of his. I can remember dining out in a patio where evaporation from grass and trees made it cool and pleasant. I can remember rich sauces and icy wine in silver buckets. On these occasions Jim always saw that I had a glass of wine.

Once Robert Maintland Pillson, the Tempe banker, came in with his beautiful wife. Mrs. Pillson called my uncle "dear Jim" and Jim gallantly kissed her on both cheeks. I was shocked. The Woolfs didn't kiss other men's wives, even on the cheek and when the women's husbands were present. Mrs. Pillson patted me on the cheek and told me that Buddy missed me and I ought to come back to Tempe to play tennis with him. She also noticed that I had a wine glass by my plate. "My God, Jim, are you mad?" she said. "Letting Jack drink champagne! If his mother and old J. W. Woolf found this out they'd have cat fits!"

"Tush, my dear," Uncle Jim said. "When I was growing up in California we had wine with every meal and I am a model of industry and decorum!"

While the trial was going on I sat on the platform on which my uncle's bench rested. I listened to all the testimony. The defense attorney was a small man with a large head and a great shock of gray hair. I liked him very much, as my sympathies were with the handsome defendant and the beautiful, wronged wife. I disliked the prosecuting attorney, who called the crime "coldblooded, premeditated murder" and who in his closing speech to the jury demanded that the clean-cut young defendant be hanged in the dreadful execution chambers I had seen at the Florence prison.

The defendant, a slender man who could not have been over thirty, answered simply and apparently honestly the questions the attorneys asked him. The man he had killed, he said, had been a friend. He had not wanted to kill him, he said, but he had carried a revolver because he was afraid this other man might be armed and desperate. He had simply wanted to talk over the dilemma the three of them were in. When he had found out about the affair he and his wife had separated, but after the killing she had rallied to his support and they had now decided to try to rebuild their lives. He said that when the other man had reached under his pillow he felt he had no choice but to kill him. The prosecuting attorney could not shake his story.

Even as a child I was conscious of feminine beauty, and I was aware then as I remember now that the defendant's wife was a lovely creature indeed. She was slender, had a delicate oval face, large brown eyes, glowing red-brown hair. I can still remember her testimony. It was the day of the split skirt, and when she climbed up and into the witness chair a lovely silken leg flashed out of the tight skirt like a scimitar from its sheath. That day she wore a rust-colored dress and a saucy matching hat on one side of her head.

The attorney for the defense questioned her gently and delicately about her illicit relationship with the dead man. He established that the man was a trusted friend of both this lovely young woman and her husband. This man, she said in her Southern drawl, had asked her up to his apartment and had offered her some champagne. Unacquainted with the properties of the stuff she had drunk two or three glasses. Finding herself both faint and dizzy, she had seen a bed through an open door and had gone to it to lie down.

Then, she said, Mistah Jones (or whatever his name was) had got on the bed beside her. She was so dizzy she hardly knew what he was doing, but he had hugged and kissed her, and then (she sobbed and dabbed her eyes with a tiny white handkerchief) he had *fo'ced* her. I hung on her every word.

Gently the kind defense attorney asked her to go on.

She just felt terrible, she testified. Just *awful.* She could hardly face her husband, whom she dearly loved. She didn't know what she was going to do. She decided to talk this awful thing over with her seducer, so once more she went to his apartment and the rascal *fo'ced* her again.

I was not used to the Southern accent. I was not certain what "fo'ced" meant, but I suspected the worst. As she sat weeping in her remorse and humiliation there was not a sound in the courtroom. Everyone heard me as I piped shrilly, "Uncle Jim, what's 'fo'ced'?" There was a roar of laughter. The witness blushed. The courtly attorney for the defense scowled. Suddenly my uncle was pounding on the bench and demanding order and decorum in the courtroom.

When the prosecuting attorney cross-questioned the beautiful young woman, she wept, and as I watched I became aware that she had the complete sympathy of the all-male jury. When her testimony was concluded I was likewise aware that I was not the only one who enjoyed the flash of that slender, silken leg.

The next day the attorneys wound up and the case went to the jury. I doubt if the jury had been out for fifteen minutes when the foreman returned with his verdict "not guilty."

The beautiful adultress threw her arms around her husband and kissed him. Both of them shook hands with the members of the jury. Then they came up and shook hands with Uncle Jim, thanked him for the way he had conducted the trial. The beautiful young woman patted me on the head and told me she had been watching me and she thought I was cute.

There was much talking in the courtroom and in the judge's chambers after Uncle Jim had retired. Finally, the two of us were in a horse-drawn cab and on our way back to the hotel.

"Wasn't Mrs. Smith beautiful!" I said. "I think she is the prettiest woman I have ever seen!"

"Quite a luscious little wench, I must say!" Uncle Jim said. "I have seen the time when I could have used a little of that myself, but, alas, for various reasons such high jinks are now out of the question."

"Wasn't it awful what that man did to her!"

Uncle Jim laughed. "I doubt if he had to 'fo'ce' her very much," he said, "and I imagine she rather liked getting 'fo'ced' and that she was 'fo'ced' a good deal more often than she let on. 'Fo'cing' generally requires some cooperation."

I was shocked.

"Uncle Jim, don't you believe all she said? Do you blame her?"

"Jack, son," Uncle Jim said. "I don't want to make a cynic out of you. That will come soon enough anyway and in the natural course of events. I am glad the case came out as it did. One man's dead. It wouldn't right any wrong to hang another one. If anyone deserves punishment it is that beautiful, vain, and selfish girl. By rights someone ought to beat her tail until it bleeds.

"The only one I feel sorry for is her husband. He loves that flighty little bitch and he has a hell of a load to carry the rest of his life. I hope the two of them have enough sense to get the hell out of the place where everyone knows what has happened and go someplace where they can start over again.

"I don't blame anyone particularly. The guy that got in bed with her probably had plenty of encouragement, and a beauty like that would tempt a saint. I don't blame her husband for being wild with jealousy. If I had been in his shoes I'd certainly have done my best to beat that fellow within an inch of his life and I might even have killed him. I have seen too much of life to try to predict what I would have done or what someone else might do.

"The man who got killed deserved what he got. The son of a bitch knew he was taking a big chance. He knew that if the girl's husband found out he might very well get killed. That's why the cowardly bastard ran like hell and wound up in Arizona. He wasn't married. He could have faced up to the situation and could have offered to marry the girl when she got a divorce. If he had done the manly thing, I doubt if the girl's husband would have killed him.

"But he ran away. He left that vain and beautiful girl to stand her husband's anger and jealousy, the disapproval of others, her own guilt—and he left her to bear the whole load alone. It's all a hell of a mess, but things like that happen."

# 10 · Mother's New House

IT was my mother's evil fate to be born to a mother who for most of her life rode on her back like an old woman of the sea. My mother was the oldest girl in the Woolf family, the second-oldest child. My grandmother very early taught her to perform all the housewifely chores ranch and farm women turn their hands to. Before my mother was in her teens she could cook; bake bread; kill, dress, and disjoint chickens; sew; mend; wash; iron; clean house.

Because of her accomplishments, my mother was a very useful person to have around a farm house and she worked long hours for nothing. My grandmother was both possessive and thrifty. She opposed my mother's marriage to my father from the start and eventually managed to break it up. Before my father had come along and had married my mother when she was twenty-seven, my grandmother had chased off a couple of other suitors. After her divorce, my mother lapsed into the familiar role of mother's helper.

When Grandfather moved his tribe into the big monstrosity of concrete blocks in 1910, my mother, as I have previously related, went along with my sister and me in tow. My mother was teaching and had two children to care for, but it fell to her lot to do most of the housework. Years before, my grandmother had fallen and hurt her spine so that for a time she was partly paralyzed. For the rest of her life she walked with the aid of one crutch. I have often wondered if the crutch was simply not a prop that helped her rule her family and get her own way.

Even after some financial reverses my grandfather could have well afforded a maid and a housekeeper, but most of the time he was lost in his own interesting thoughts and I do not suppose the idea occurred to him. My grandmother, on the other hand, must have been aware that teaching and taking care of a big house was a back-breaker for my mother. But not only did she never express either sympathy or appreciation but she insisted that my mother pay half the expenses of running the establishment. My grandmother was about as stingy a person as I have ever known. As far as I can remember she never in her life gave me a present. At the time my mother's two young sisters were teaching near by and were home every weekend. Both were in the throes of choosing mates. Every weekend there were at least two ardent swains for house guests and two big meals had to be cooked and served every day.

Fried chicken was the standard mainstay for Sunday dinner, along with salad, biscuits, milk gravy, mashed potatoes, string beans or peas, pie or cake. Like all thrifty people of that day my grandparents kept a flock of chickens that furnished both meat and eggs. Tempting nests filled with straw and supplied with decoy china eggs were provided for the hens, but some of the Plymouth Rocks and white Leghorns had reverted to their jungle-fowl instincts and preferred to lay their eggs in odd and interesting places. One of my duties while I lived at Grandfather's place was to gather the eggs morning and night. I made a game out of searching out those hidden nests.

When a Sunday dinner was in the offing, it was generally my duty to catch the fryers that were to be sacrificed to our voracious appetites. My grandfather had made an implement about eight or ten feet long with a hook on the end, something like that of a shepherd's crook but smaller, so that if it went around the chicken's lower leg the foot would not go through.

Along in the morning my grandmother would say: "Boy, it's time to catch the chickens. Mind you get tender young cockerels." I'd pick up the chicken-catcher, toss out a handful of wheat, and cry seductively, "Here, chickie, chickie, chickie." The greedy birds would drop whatever they were doing and come running. While they were eating, making pleasant clucking sounds of feeding, and pecking and spurring each other, I'd sneakily slip the crook on the far side of a juicy young cock's leg. When I gave a yank he would vainly try to escape, squawking bitterly. His companions would squawk and scatter. Then I'd stuff my captive into a gunny sack and he'd shut up.

For a minute or two the rest of the flock would stay away from the delectable wheat, wondering what the hell had happened to good old Joe. Then their greed would overcome their caution and they'd come flocking back to feed and quarrel once more. Another yank, another young cock to keep old Joe company in the gunny sack. I kept this up until I had enough cocks to feed the family and the guests. Then I took them around to the woodpile, picked up a sharp hatchet kept for the purpose. One by one I held them by the hind legs, laid their necks on the chopping block. They always looked at me with a combination of trepidation and reproach, as resigned to their fate as Mary Queen of Scots. One blow of the sharp hatchet and the head with the reproachful eyes was on the ground on one side of the chopping block and the fluttering body on the other. I then took the decapitated chickens in to my mother in the kitchen. She plunged them into boiling water to loosen the feathers, quickly plucked them, dressed them, and cut them up for frying.

My grandparents followed the pioneer American tradition of the bountiful larder for their feasts days of Thanksgiving, Christmas, and New Year's Day. These ritualistic orgies always called for turkey. A big bird would be purchased from a farmer from two weeks to a month before the great day. Then it would be put in a separate coop to be fattened. The day before the feast, my grandmother always hobbled out on her one crutch, instructed me to hang the turkey up by the hind legs. She always cut the poor bird's throat with a razor-sharp butcher knife and stood by as it bled to death, its wings beating a slower and slower tempo as life departed the body. The big birds always shed a great quantity of gouty dark-red blood. These spectacles revolted me, for by the time the date of the turkey's execution arrived he and I were pals. I would have been feeding him for two or three weeks.

But my qualms were always forgotten when I sat down to a holiday feast and they never interfered with my enjoyment of the white breast of turkey and my mother's dressing. In addition to roast turkey the well-ordered household of a good provider like my grandfather always served a home-baked ham studded with cloves. At Thanksgiving there was almost always, in addition, roast prime ribs of beef or the roasted ham of a buck mule deer; and once at Christmastime my Uncle John provided the family with the hindquarter of a desert bighorn ram. My mother's turkey dressing (an old Kentucky recipe from the McConnell family) combines cornbread, stale biscuits, rye bread, sage, onion, egg. My wife learned to make it from my mother and has passed the art on to my two daughters. It makes most turkey dressing seem dull indeed.

Besides the turkey, the ham, and generally venison, there were mountains of mashed potatoes, scalloped oysters, asparagus, carrots, peas, salad, fruit punch for the children, coffee for the elders. For dessert there would be pumpkin pie with whipped cream, apple pie, home-made ice cream, always fruit cake, and generally some sort of a layer cake. I always ate myself into a comatose state and was as quiet and bulging as a python that has devoured an impala. In the years before Grandfather's death my mother always did most of the work of preparing these feasts. Generally my Uncle Charles and Ruby, his wife, would be there with their two red-headed children. Often my Uncle John with his wife and daughter would show up along with my Uncles Bill and Arthur, possibly with girl friends, and my two aunts with suitors.

In the fall of 1912 my mother decided that living with her parents and being a maid of all work as well as a teacher and the mother of two children was too much for her. She decided to build a house on a lot she bought from Grandfather a block to the east of Grandfather's house. In the meantime she had got a position as critic-teacher in the training school at the Tempe Normal. The job paid somewhat better than did a teaching job in the public schools, was more secure, and had more prestige. But she had to embark on an endless round of attending summer schools in order to reach the goal of a degree.

We moved to a rented house about a half mile from my grandfather's place in the fall of 1912 and lived there until Mother's own house was finished in 1913. To help her with her housework, my mother took in a pretty blond ranch girl from southern Arizona, who worked in exchange for her board and room. Arthur, my mother's youngest brother, met her and at the end of the year they got married. Over a half century later at a party in New Delhi I met a gorgeous blonde, the wife of an American diplomat, William Decker. I was struck by something vaguely familiar about her. Before her marriage she had been Gloria Harrison, the daughter of the brother of Mary Harrison, the ranch girl who married Arthur Woolf and who became my beloved Aunt Mary. I decided right then that Gloria and I were kissing cousins.

My mother made two efforts to escape my grandmother's tyranny —one when she got married, the other when she moved away from my grandfather's big house. Both were futile. After the wedding, her mother dragged her back home and broke up her marriage. Mother's house at 922 Forest Avenue was finished in 1913. Since it was just on the other side of a city block from Grandfather's house, Mother always helped out on special occasions. Both her younger sisters got married, and grumbling because of the expense, my grandmother employed a succession of sullen maids of all work. My grandfather died in 1915. After he was buried and the estate settled my grandmother sold the big concrete block house, had a smaller house built next door to my mother's house, and was on my mother's neck until she died full of years and meanness in 1934. Friends of mine on the *Arizona Republic* in Phoenix knew I was a former newspaperman and that at the time I was a professor of journalism at the

University of Arizona. They asked me to do the old girl's obituary. I suppose it still exists in the family archives.

My mother was not a pretty woman. She had neither a lovely face nor a beautiful figure. From some ancestor she had inherited buttocks so flat as to be practically nonexistent, a deformity which, alas, I inherited and which, it grieves me to relate, I passed on to my son Bradford. I have on occasion been called "Elephant Ass" (for obvious reasons) and when I was in boot camp in the navy I was called for a time "Cactus Jack the Assless Wonder" because I came from Arizona and because if I had any buttocks at all it was not visible to the naked eye.

From my Grandfather Woolf my mother had inherited thick golden hair, small blue eyes, and a compact figure. Her skin was very fair and with her great mass of golden hair she was often taken for a Scandinavian. Her nose was homely, pointed and long, with rather wide nostrils. This she inherited from her McConnell ancestors. Apparently the nose was far less persistent than the funny bottom (another trait to be blamed on the McConnell genes) as neither my sister Helen nor I inherited it and it has not skipped a generation to land on our children.

Nevertheless, with her clear, fair skin, her mass of glowing hair, and her good carriage my mother must have been a rather handsome woman. My father, who thought himself a judge of female flesh, thought her beautiful. My Uncle Jim O'Connor, who in his way was a sophisticate and a man of the world, once told me that he considered my mother a striking woman with the most beautiful hair he had ever seen. It was so long that if she sat in a straight chair when she had it down it overlapped on the floor by a foot.

My mother was only thirty-three when she and my father were divorced, but as far as I know she had no further interest in men. Now and then some divorced man or widower of suitable age would start making eyes at her, but she never went out with any of her would-be suitors, never as far as I know gave any of them the slightest encouragement.

When one of her sisters asked her why she had spurned the advances of a widowed professor at the normal, I remember how her eyes flashed.

"I don't want to have anything to do with him!" she said. "What do I need a man around the house for? Where would I put one if I got married? How do I know he'd be nice to my children? I have my own house, my job, my children. Why should I want a man around?"

My mother, I believe, was basically hostile toward men. Whether it was because she was for a long time the only girl in a large family of boys, whether she had seen that in pioneer life the women did the drudgery and men had the fun, or whether she felt that, in teaching, women did the work and men got the administrative jobs and the big salaries I do not know. I am sure, though, that she was hostile to males in general. The only time she and I ever had difficulties was when my glands, working in their mysterious ways, began to fill me full of strange desires, odd and voluptuous fantasies, sent me wandering in the night uttering outlandish cries.

I remember one occasion when I was about twelve and was beginning to feel the definite first stirrings of maleness, some other youngsters and I were swimming in the nude at what was called the Point of Rocks, a great basaltic boulder that was partly on an ancient lava flow and projected into the Salt River on the far side of the Big Butte, where the reservoir for the city of Tempe was located. The Point was a pleasant spot. In those days the Salt River, except for floods after melting snows or heavy rains in the mountains, ran clear and cool. There were willows and cottonwoods and clean white sand, catfish, and a strange fish called the bony tail. When frosts came in the north ducks rested on the Salt, fed out in the grain fields. There were quail in the thickets and mourning and whitewing doves made nests in the cottonwoods. The river sands were always clean and the hole at the Point of Rocks was always deep. Today, alas, every drop of water that can be impounded has been taken from the Salt. The clean sand of its once-snowy bed is littered with old automobile tires, rusty car bodies, tin cans, empty beer bottles.

But in those wonderful days of 1914 the river bottom was a pleasant and useful place. From April to October people swam in it. Some of the churches held baptizings in it. Boys took girls on solitary hikes down in the river bottoms and many a girl became a woman there. I used to go down there to trap coons, to shoot doves, quail, and ducks.

This fine spring day at least a dozen of us were diving off the big basaltic rock. We were throwing nickels and pennies into the clear water, then diving in after them and catching them before they hit the bottom. Some of the more agile were turning flips on the clean white sand. Some of the more indolent were stretched out voluptuously on the sand so their bottoms could absorb the sun.

My mother had forbidden me to go swimming with the boys. Her excuse was that she was afraid I would drown. Actually I had been swimming quite well since I was nine and anyone who drowned at the Point would have had to work at it. In reality, I am sure she resented that I spent less and less time reading and talking over what I had read with her and more and more time with my fellows, playing rough games, telling dirty jokes, speculating what older boys did to the girls they disappeared with into the willows.

I have known many widows and divorcées, and even some women with what appear to be adequate husbands, who have managed to keep their sons under their thumbs all their lives. One brilliant man now dead was a scholar and a university administrator. During the day he was a respected man of parts. When he got home he was mother's little boy. She made him escort her everywhere. She chose his clothes. She never let him have a date with any women except homely old maids. Once, when he was under forty, he attempted to defy her and made a date with a pretty young woman of twenty-four or so. Mama made him call up and break it.

Emotionally, my mother was Mama's little girl most of her life, and it wasn't until her last years that she began to see her own mother in her true light as a selfish and hostile old crone, something of which I was aware by the time I was ten. If I had been less stubborn, if I had not been blessed with a stiff neck and a good deal of iron in my soul, or perhaps if my mother had been less busy with her teaching and her housekeeping, she might have succeeded in making me Mama's little boy.

It was that day at the Point of Rocks that I dimly realized that she simply did not want me to grow up and to become male. With her blue eyes glittering like those of Grandfather Woolf she marched right in among that mob of naked little boys, grabbed me by the ear, made me dress before my friends, and herded me home. I loathed her for it. Within the next week I must have had a dozen fights and I constantly went about with puffy eyes, cut lips, and skinned knuckles. Every time anyone tried to tease me about that disgraceful and degrading episode, I belted him. Generally a fight resulted. To prove my masculinity I got into the river near Mesa when the swift, chocolate-colored flood water from melting snow in the mountains came down two or three weeks later and swam and floated, generally clinging to driftwood, the seven miles to Tempe. The next day I heard one of the big boys in eighth grade say to another: "Did you hear what that crazy Jack O'Connor done yesterday afternoon? He swum clear down the river from Mesa to between the buttes. It's a wonder the little bastard didn't get drownded!" That was my knighthood.

My mother was a very admirable person. If some of her conduct seemed unreasonable at the time it was because she was driven by unconscious motives. Her two children were increasingly her world and it is only natural that she wanted to cling to them—or wanted them to cling to her. Every normal parent has a fleeting feeling of loneliness and sorrow when he realizes that a beloved child has spread his wings and flown far away and that henceforth when they met it would be as two adults and not as parent and child.

My Grandfather Woolf built his big house hoping that if he did so his sons and daughters would never leave him to loneliness and old age. But within five years after he had moved in he was dead and the children he had hoped to gather around him were scattered from St. Louis to California. My mother wanted me to remain forever her precocious little boy, a lad who did well in school, read many books, discussed them with her intelligently. The only result was that for some years I was bitter and rebellious and our relationship was strained. For my part I have watched my own beloved children grow up, spread their wings, and fly away with as much sadness as joy.

THE HOUSE INTO WHICH we moved in 1913 cost my mother $1,500. Most of the money was borrowed at 8 per cent interest. At the time my mother's salary was, I believe, about one hundred dollars a month. In those days some men raised families on sixty and seventy-five dollars a month. The house was stoutly built of pine lumber by an honest carpenter. On one side were two bedrooms with a bath between them, on the other the living room and kitchen. A large screened porch ran across the rear of the house.

Mother cooked on a gas stove, but such heat as there was in the house in winter was furnished by a wood stove in the living room. In it we burned mesquite, a very hard, dense desert wood that burns about like coal. From time to time my mother bought a wagon load of stove-length mesquite from a Pima or Maricopa Indian peddler. At one time mesquite trees grew all over the desert surrounding the Salt River valley, and for fifty years or so the trees furnished the firewood for those who lived in southern Arizona. Indians would cut down a tree, chop it into stove lengths, split it, then haul it to town cunningly stacked in farm wagons so that the load would appear larger than it actually was. It was part of the haggling for the householder to investigate the load and to protest at the deceit. Then when the terms were amicably settled my mother always gave the Indian a plate of food, which he ate sitting on the back steps. He, in turn, as his gesture, always stacked the mesquite in the woodshed. The pleasant smell of burning mesquite is one of my cherished memories of the mild southern Arizona winters. It never occurred to any of us that one day all of the trees in this great mesquite forest would be cut down.

In those early years in my mother's house, my sister Helen and I slept on the sleeping porch. Helen was then seven years old, a charming little blue-eyed girl with curly brown hair, and every night I told her a long-winded tale to put her to sleep. Mostly they were about my adventures with lions and rhinos on the African veld. I had read Stanley and Livingstone's books about their journeys in Africa. I also read every month my grandfather's copies of *Outdoor Life, Field & Stream,* and *Outdoor Recreation.* I had also seen and been entranced by the motion pictures of game taken in British East Africa (now Kenya) by an American named Paul J. Rainey. At eleven I was a hardened gun enthusiast. I owned a 20-gauge single-barreled shotgun my grandfather had given me, an old .30/40 Krag military rifle I had bought from a bindle stiff for a dollar and a half, and a .22 rimfire Marlin. I knew the ballistics of most of the sporting cartridges of that day, British as well as American. The spring I was eleven I had suffered from a broken heart when Anna Levitsky, my beautiful Jewish blonde, my one true love, the first girl who ever kissed me, had run off with a rich boy from back East. The fact that she was eight years older than I did not make the pain less keen. I knew that I would never love again, and I planned to spend my life collecting ivory and capturing animals for zoos in British East Africa. Possibly I'd also take some movies of charging lions and elephants and sell them for fantastic sums. Then when I was rich, famous, brown from the tropic sun and lean and romantically haggard from malaria, blackwater fever, and cobra bites, handsome in my pith helmet and my khaki shorts I'd look up the beautiful Anna. She would be sorry then that she had spurned me for the guy with the red Stutz.

Before I was twelve I had planned my African battery—a .465 or .470 Nitro Express double rifle for buffalo, rhino, and elephants, a .350 Rigby for the largest antelope, and a .30/06 Springfield for the rest. I saw myself striding across the veld followed by Kamau, my faithful Kikuyu gunbearer, and a string of thirty porters. I was a lonely and romantic figure. Sometimes tears came into my eyes when I thought of myself.

Now and then I gave Helen a change from the dangers of Africa by spinning her a tale of shooting tigers in the Indian Terai or hunting Stone sheep and grizzlies in the Cassiars of northern British Columbia. I though of these bedtime stories many years later, the first night of my first safari when I sat with a sundowner in my hand by a fire in the chill dusk of the high Masai plain and listened to the lions begin to roar as they came out for their night's hunting.

Yet another favorite locale for my adventures was the subarctic. There I would build myself a snug cabin, cook delicious meals, read interesting books, watch the northern lights. I would trap silver fox, mink, marten, and fisher, shoot caribou and moose for meat for myself and my sled dogs. The snow I imagined was fluffy, not very cold. The only snow I had ever seen was on the top of distant mountains.

From November through March the nights were pleasantly nippy out there on the sleeping porch. Perhaps my years on the porch are responsible for the fact that I always sleep best in a cold room. But it is seldom really cold in the Salt River valley. My grandfather's big house was the first one in Tempe to have central heat. Most houses had stoves or fireplaces in the living rooms. Some had heat only from a wood stove in the kitchen. My mother permitted Helen to undress by the living-room stove. She undressed in the front room, and I in the back. On the roof of the new house was a solar heater, coils of pipe under glass. This, along with the fireless cooker, was one of the latest wonders of science in 1913, but in the winter when hot baths were most appreciated the water our solar heater produced was only lukewarm. Mother bought a gas heater and had it installed in the bathroom. All of us were afraid of the damned thing and it blew up regularly twice a year. Only Mother was supposed to light it.

In the winter when we bathed (which was by no means every day) we first got out fresh towels. Then we lit the portable kerosene heater so we wouldn't freeze to death when we undressed in the cold bathroom. Then we gritted our teeth, muttered a prayer, lit a kitchen match, turned on the gas in the heater, and thrust the burning match in the hole. If the timing was wrong and there was too much gas loose in the heater the thing blew up. The top went sailing off and the pipe came crashing down. When I was about fifteen a young man and his pretty blond wife visited us for about a week for reasons so obscure that I have long since forgotten them. The young man was away looking for a job, playing pool or something late one afternoon while my mother was still at school, when his pretty wife decided to undertake the serious business of bathing. I started the kerosene heater in the bathroom for her, got out fresh towels. She asked me how the heater worked and I told her as well as I could. Presently, she disappeared into the bathroom. She had left the door open between the living room, where there was a fire in the stove, and the bedroom she shared with her husband. It was a cold January day and she wanted a little heat. I was reading a book when I heard a tremendous roar. The heater had blown up. I looked up to see our pretty house guest shoot out of the bathroom into the bedroom, a look of astonishment and terror on her face. She was wearing a towel after a fashion but it had missed practically all of the strategic places. After that I felt more kindly toward the heater.

My mother always had to get over to the training school by eight thirty and some of the time she had to be on duty by eight. She fed us quickly, dressed, and was off. It was only about two blocks from the training school to our house, and at noon we all hurried home for soup and sandwiches. Mother was usually home by five thirty to cook dinner.

During the week there was little time to do more than make the beds, wash the dishes, and sweep. I brought in wood for the woodbox by the living-room stove, and when I got home in the afternoons I built the fire, put away groceries that had been delivered.

Mother had two children to feed and clothe, payments to make on the mortgage, and in addition she had to lay aside some money so she could go somewhere for summer school to work for her degree. She had little money to throw around. In those early years I always raised a winter garden—lettuce, radishes, onions, carrots. Once I spaded up the whole vacant lot next door and planted it to potatoes.

Mother celebrated our moving into the new house by purchasing a new icebox. One often sees the term "icebox" in recipes (icebox cookies and so on) but most people have never seen a real icebox. This one was really a box. It had a golden-oak exterior and opened at the top like an old-fashioned trunk. Twice a week the iceman came, stopped his two-horse team, walked around to the open rear of the wagon, chipped fifty pounds off of a three hundred-pound cake, carried it in with tongs, and put it in the icebox. The children around aways grabbed pieces of ice that had been chipped off in the back of the wagon and sucked them. Girls and sissies held the pieces in cloth and sucked through the cloth.

Mother had to watch her pennies, and to keep the cake of ice from melting too soon she used to wrap it with newspapers. I used to try to tell her that the way ice made things cool was by melting. She would never believe me, but it irked her that milk she tried to save went "blinky" so quickly.

The city water in Tempe tasted salty from some chemical and was so hard that soap curdled in it. Mother used to save the distilled water from the drip pan under the icebox to wash her hair in and to do fine laundry in. Another source of soft water was the rainwater that ran off the roof. Mother always kept a washtub under the rain spout and a tubful of rain water was a source of satisfaction to her thrifty soul.

All of the fodder raised in the garden came in handy, but Mother's most important move to pare expenses was to purchase Blackie, the nymphomaniac cow. By 1913 my Grandfather Woolf had sold his rubber-tired buggy and Pet, his fine trotting mare, and had replaced them with a four-cylinder Overland touring car. With only one cow in his Bermuda grass pasture he had plenty of grazing. He suggested that Mother buy a cow to use the grass.

So she bought a heifer named Blackie. She was half Holstein and half Jersey. She produced vast quantities of rich, creamy milk, but she was probably the meanest damned cow that ever lived. I milked her morning and night. Mother always saved the water that she had boiled potatoes in and all the potato peelings. This stuff I mixed with bran and hot water and gave to the thankless Blackie as an hors d'oeuvre. She was passionately fond of the nauseating mess and when I crossed the fence with my bucket she always greeted me joyfully, and to show her love and appreciation she butted me with her nose all the way to the shed where I fed and milked her.

There was nothing Blackie loved more than to kick over the milk bucket just about the time I had it full. I finally had to abandon two-handed milking for that reason. I milked with my right hand, held the bucket in my left. When Blackie couldn't kick the bucket she kicked me. I still have scars on my legs from her hoofs, and on my arms where I was cut when she dragged me through barbed-wire fences.

Blackie gave far more milk than we could use, even though we lavished pure cream on oatmeal and corn flakes and drank several glasses of icy milk for lunch and dinner. So presently we had a couple of customers, as at that time there was no commercial dairy in Tempe. One was a dour professor of pedagogy and his dour wife. The other was a young entomologist, a recent college graduate, who worked for the United States Department of Agriculture. Every morning I delivered a two-quart lard bucket of milk at the back door of each of my customers. I always knocked to let them know that the milk was there so they could put it in their iceboxes.

I used to carry a bucket of milk on each handlebar of my bicycle, leave the bicycle in front of the house, and then walk around the house with the milk. One Sunday morning in early summer I heard a noise as I walked around the sleeping porch of the young entomologist's house. I looked in and down, and there within a few feet of me were the young man and his pretty wife making love. I knew that such things went on. In fact, I often speculated about them. But this was too much. I put down the bucket of milk and fled. I would never go back. My mother told the young man that for some reason I had refused to deliver any more milk at his house. He told her he understood. From that time until he was transferred to another post I would cross the street to avoid meeting either him or his wife face to face. I felt a deep and terrible shame and I imagined they did.

Under average conditions Blackie was a problem. She was as agile as a deer and she often slipped through the fence until I tied a V-shaped branch to her neck to prevent her doing so. When she was in heat she was a holy terror. She went through fences as if they weren't there and found herself the nearest bull. There was nothing maidenly or modest about Blackie. Then I was off on my bicycle to look for her and carrying a rope to lead her back with.

When her wild sex cravings had been satisfied, she always came willingly and in fact seemed rather glad to see me, as I no doubt reminded her of the delicious bran mash laced with potato peelings which I fed her twice a day. Often she would trot to the fence of the field she had invaded to meet me. Then I would put the rope around her neck and ride the bicycle home with her trotting happily behind me. But if Blackie felt her love life incomplete she was about as easy to handle as a rhinoceros.

Once, after I had hunted hard for her four hours, I finally located her about five miles from home engaged in an amour with a particularly truculent Jersey bull. I finally bluffed the bull away from her, got her through a gate, and was starting to lead her off behind the bicycle. All seemed to be going well when Blackie decided that of all the gentlemen cows she had known intimately (a not inconsiderable number, by the way, for when Blackie had hot pants practically anything on four legs looked good to her) this mean old Jersey was the very nicest of all. She tossed her head (and incidentally tossed me one way and the bicycle another), turned around and dragged me through two barbed-wire fences she had taken in her stride.

Blackie's crowning adventure came years later, not long before I joined the army at the age of fifteen. I awkened one morning to find that the urge was on Blackie and she had broken out. I picked up my rope, a .32-caliber revolver firing blank cartridges I had got to discourage amorous bulls, got on my bicycle and started out. I went to all of the pastures where Blackie's favorite paramours were to be found. All the bulls were grazing peacefully and I could see that the ugly and disturbing thoughts of sex were far from their minds. I went farther and farther afield. No Blackie. It was growing late and I was miles from home. I had eaten no breakfast. I was thirsty and faint with hunger.

Then far in the distance I heard a strange roaring noise. Following a vague hunch, I pedaled in that direction. Presently I could tell that the noise was made by dozens of bellowing bulls. I rode on. The source of all the noise was a big alfalfa field where about one hundred old Hereford ranch bulls were being fattened before they were shipped off to be made into bologna.

All were wildly excited. About half of them were fighting furiously. Some bore formidable wounds. All were bawling. Most of those who were not fighting were pawing the ground, shaking their heads and bellowing. In the center of the field a knot of about thirty bulls was milling around. Now and then I'd see the head and forequarters of a bull rise above the pack as he covered a cow. No one needed to tell me that I had found Blackie.

In my life I have gone into the brush after wounded lions and tigers. I have stood up to the charge of two African Cape buffalo and one grizzly bear. But the bravest thing I have ever done was to walk into that field full of sex-crazed bulls and remove the object of their lust. Blackie was glad to see me; for once in her life she had had enough. Scared to death, I got the rope on her and began leading her through that mob of bulls. On the way to the gate, three of the bulls covered her. Twice I had to fire my revolver in the face of a truculent monster.

When I got her back to her pasture she wasn't her usual lively and agile self. She ate little and lay down most of the day.

"Poor little thing," my mother said when I told her what had happened. "What a shocking experience!"

"Well, dammit!" I said. "She brought it on herself!"

I do not think that it is necessary for me to say that because of Blackie's moral laxity her calves were of doubtful parentage. I did not follow their careers, as mother always sold them when they were young. I remember one that looked pure Jersey, one that showed he was part Hereford, and one that was probably fathered by some old brush-popping long-horned range bull.

Blackie reminded me of a Mexican washerwoman with a rather catholic taste in boy friends whom the wits about Tempe called Mama All Nations. One of her children was black, had kinky hair, and was assumed to be the offspring of a Mississippian who had for some months shined shoes at one of the pool halls. Another certainly looked as if he had a considerable number of Chinese genes in his inheritance. A couple of them looked to be pretty much Mexican or Indian, but one little fellow had blue eyes and fair hair. The sports around town used to kid each other about being his father.

# 11 · The Desert and the Mountains

FROM October through January we generally ate a great many ducks at my mother's house. In the days before World War I there was always adequate water in the Salt River and many of the valley farmers were still raising wheat. Mallards used to rest on the river and then fly out into the fields to feed. Mallards were the most common duck to use the minor Salt River flyway when they were headed for their wintering grounds, the marshes of the Colorado River delta. There were also many teal, both green-wing and cinnamon, spoonbills, pintails, blue bills, a few Rocky Mountain goldeneyes, a few redheads. Years later I shot four or five canvasbacks in northern Arizona but I never saw one as long as I did my hunting on the Salt.

My mother, who had to count the cost of everything, preferred that I hunt ducks instead of smaller birds like quail and doves because even the little teal was a chunky bird you could sink your teeth into and it gave a pretty fair return for the investment in shotgun shells. She liked the big fat mallards even better because they produced an even better return of meat to powder and shot.

I used to keep a burlap bag cut so that I could carry it over my shoulder, my 20-gauge single-barreled shotgun, and a box of shells hidden under a hedge on the normal campus. Along with my hunting equipment I kept an old pair of shoes, a sweater, and a worn-out pair of bib overalls. Often instead of going to school I would make a quick change behind the hedge, hide my school clothes, and take off in my ragged, dirty hunting costume with my shotgun and my gunny sack. A clear little stream of water ran between banks lined with watercress just east of the little butte. For some reason it was known as the slew. When I reached that I always carefully removed my shoes and stockings, rolled up my pants legs before crossing. Shortly after that, however, I usually got excited and plunged into the waist-deep water without taking off my overalls to retrieve a duck and from then on I was wet all day.

Sometimes I would bring home only three or four ducks. Once I brought in a bulging gunny sack containing twenty-three mallards and teal. That was quite a load. It was customary among the country people who were my mother's forebears for the women to clean

and dress the game birds. When I hunted with Grandfather either my grandmother or my mother always cleaned the game, even when we brought in around one hundred whitewing doves. Tired as my mother must have been she always cleaned and plucked the ducks, the quail, the whitewings, and the mourning doves I brought in. It never occurred to me until I got married that a man might clean game birds if there was a woman around. My wife was a city girl unused to country ways. She was born in Springfield, Missouri, of parents who had met at the University of Illinois. She grew up in St. Louis. When I brought in my first bag of quail after our marriage and told her to get cracking, she told me that if I wanted to eat those awful things I could clean them myself.

Sometimes, after I enrolled in the high-school department in the normal, I would be out on the river before the sun was up. I would hide in the willows and try to catch the mallards as they lifted off to fly out to the grain fields. Often I would have a good bag before school time. Sometimes I'd shoot only in the mornings. Sometimes I'd stay all day. During the midday hours I would wade across the river and hunt Gambel's quail on the north side in what is now part of Scottsdale but which was then desert and river bottom bordered by alfalfa fields. When my mother asked me where I had eaten lunch I would tell her that I had gone home with Gordon Goodwin, Leldon Windes, or Cedric or Harold Austin.

A little bragging on my mother's part resulted in my getting my wings clipped. One of the faculty members who fancied himself a hunter told my mother proudly that the evening before he had knocked off five nice mallards. My mother said that was fine but her boy Jack could go out and bring in from ten to twenty-five after school almost any time he felt like it. The teacher did a little investigating and reported me. I was called up before Dr. Matthews, who gave me a lecture, reminded me of my distinguished relatives, pleaded with me to get down to work and to stop driving my wonderful mother mad with worry.

In the days before the First World War few people in Arizona hunted. In all the years that I shot ducks on the Salt River upstream from Tempe I don't suppose I saw a dozen other hunters. I can remember running across only one other quail hunter between the river and Scottsdale, which was then the sleepiest of sleepy little country towns. This chap was a middle-aged Easterner, who was visiting friends in Phoenix. They had told him that there were many quail around Phoenix and he had shipped an English pointer out in an express car. Both he and the pointer were having a tough time because they were hunting where there was no ground cover and the smart little Gambel's quail simply would not stay put. The hunter swore and the fine pointer got so frustrated that he forgot his manners and barked. I joined forces with them and found a field of wheat stubble where the quail were feeding morning and evenings. There the pointer worked very well.

Those who hunted in the pre-World War I days in Arizona were mostly meat hunters. They enjoyed getting out into the desert and the mountains but meat came before recreation or exercise or shooting skill. Although my Grandfather Woolf had been a part-time market hunter during his days along the New Mexico–Colorado line and had sold dozens if not hundreds of deer to butcher shops in Trinidad, Colorado, he had a rigid code of ethics as far as winged game was concerned. Game that took to the air, he told me, was to be shot for sport, and anyone who shot anything on the ground or water before it flew was a pretty low fellow.

I wish I could say that I always followed my grandfather's precepts, but I did not. I wanted to show a good ratio of meat to shells expended so Mother would continue to let me charge shotgun shells at Curry's Tempe Hardware, so if I had a chance to blast a flock of ducks on the water or rake a covey of quail on the ground I never failed to do so. One time on a cold December morning, so cold that when I took off my shoes and rolled up my pants to cross the slew there was ice at the edges and heavy frost all around, I really had a chance to make a killing. I had gone perhaps a mile upstream and had picked off a couple of mallards out of flocks that had flushed ahead of me and had taken off over the willows within range, when I saw what looked like a boulder-covered sandbar about four hundred or five hundred yards ahead.

That puzzled me because the boulders had no business being

there. I knew every foot of the river, and what I was looking at was supposed to be a sandbar. As I watched I saw wings flap and I realized that the sandbar was solid with resting ducks. My greedy mind began to formulate a plan. I would make a long circle through the willows in order to stay out of sight and then I would crawl straight toward that enormous flock of ducks. I planned to approach behind a low fringe of young willows that grew along the bank.

I finally made it. As I peered through the willows there were ducks everywhere on that bar. It had been unseasonably cold in Tempe and bitterly cold in Arizona's high mountains and in Utah. This was why there were so many resting ducks on the Salt.

By this time I had bought with money I had saved by working in the summer a secondhand Winchester Model 97 pump gun. It had a 30-inch, full choke barrel and held six shells. As I contemplated the havoc I was going to wreak my greed began to make me shake. I tried to decide just where I would lay my first shot in order to bag the maximum number of ducks. I was still trying to make up my mind when I suddenly became aware that an old hen mallard was peering through a hole in the willows and looking me right in the eye. I froze, hoping she had not recognized me. But she had. She let out a squawk and bounced straight into the air. In an instant the air was full of ducks and the thunder of wings as at least three thousand mallards took off. I jumped to my feet, firing wildly into that mass of duck. It seems incredible, but I got not one!

My usual method of hunting was to locate a flock of ducks resting in the water. Then I'd stalk them, wiggling along on my belly, pushing my shotgun ahead of me if necessary. When I got within sure range (twenty-five to forty yards) I would try to shoot so that the pattern would cover at least two or three ducks. Then as the rest of the flock took off I would try to bring down another duck or two on the wing. Strange things happen. Just as my emptying my gun into that mass of mallards and not getting a feather sounds incredible, so this story will sound equally incredible. One day I sneaked up on a flock of teal and rolled a couple over in the water. The flock took off to my right. I led one of the teal about two feet and shot. Seven plump teal came tumbling down!

The most popular game bird in Arizona in those pre-World War I days was the whitewing dove. If I remember correctly the season started on July 1. The birds flew in from Mexico in June to nest, and when the season opened nesting time was in full swing. But no one seemed to be bothered by the fact that when the old birds were killed the squabs perished in the nests. Whitewing shooting was both easy work and a sociable event. In one of the chapters on my Grandfather Woolf I have told how gunners would come from California and from the Eastern states and set up camps. The local gunners would go out with stools to sit on between shots, with food and cold drinks.

In the summers I visited my Uncle Jim O'Connor in Florence; he and I used to shoot whitewings right from the yard as a flight went over there both mornings and evenings. But once a week or so Jim liked to foregather with some cronies by a "tank"* where the whitewings came in for water. Jim liked to make a real production out of these shoots. He always had a washtub filled with ice and bottles of beer, makings for martinis and bourbon Old-Fashioneds, mayonnaise, butter (kept cold in the ice tub with the beer), delicious potato salad (which was always made by the wife of Heinie Schultz, one of the gunners), various kinds of sausage, cheese, pickles, and olives. The gunners always sat on camp stools with bottles of beer beside them. Often they held their guns in their left hands, their cigars in their right. Handling a cigar and a bottle of beer at the same time with the same hand must have been difficult but they managed.

My Uncle Jim was a fine shot but physically rather lazy. While we were shooting he hardly moved five feet from his stool. I always

* In Arizona lingo a "tank" is a pond created by a dam built across an arroyo to catch and hold rainwater for cattle or for irrigation. It probably derives from the Spanish word *tanque.*

hunted up and brought back the birds that both of us killed. Jim had a stunt he was pretty good at. When a whitewing came in rather low and directly toward him, he would shoot it, kill it, and reach out and catch it as it fell. I have tried to pull that stunt myself but have never been able to bring it off gracefully.

Then along about sundown, when the nighthawks came out to dart and swerve after insects on long, narrow wings, and the air began to cool after the fierce heat of the day, Jim would get out a folding table, set it up, and cover it with goodies. His cronies would gather around, brag about their shooting, make sandwiches, dish up potato salad on paper plates, eat hugely, and drink lots of beer. Among the whitewing hunters I remember Jim McGee, the sheriff; Heinie Schultz, the Jewish Ford dealer, whose wife made the wonderful potato salad; Ramon Nicholas, a Mexican cattle rancher who had lost his left arm but who shot one-handed with a tremendously strong right.

Getting ahead of this story, the numbers of whitewings began to fall off noticeably around 1916–17 when the raising of long-staple cotton replaced that of wheat and when a vast quantity of mesquite where the birds nested had been cut down. I have been told that the birds are now present in much greater numbers than when I moved away from southern Arizona in 1948. Biologists showed that the shooting of the birds at nesting time was probably the principal factor in their decrease. As soon as the opening of the season was set on September 1 the birds began to increase once more.

Quail were also more plentiful over most of Arizona prior to 1917 than they are today, as overgrazing on desert lands had not caused the cover to deteriorate as much as now. Very few people hunted quail, as most of the birds were out in the desert. Roads were poor, tires uncertain, and quail hunting hard work. Except close to towns like Tucson, few people bothered to hunt quail.

I suppose I had a hunting license in those pre-World War I days, but I cannot remember buying one until the fall of 1921. It cost either a dollar or a dollar and a half. Arizona had a game department, but the chief game warden, as the head of the department was then called, was a political appointee who often had only very vague interest in game. The wardens were likewise political appointees, who spent more time mending political fences than finding out how the game was doing. I never actually saw a game warden in the field in Arizona until 1934.

THE MOST EXCITING HUNTING event in Arizona in the old days was the opening of the deer and turkey season. This, as I remember, was always on October 1. The number of deer was then probably at an all-time low. There was almost no law enforcement, and the feeling of miners and ranchers was that it was their right to shoot anything at any time. Many ranchers shot deer whenever they had the opportunity, as by doing so they could eat venison and sell the calves. There was still a fair herd of mule deer in the high, wooded mountain and plateau country of central Arizona and there were a good many Arizona whitetails in the rough mountain ranges that jut up from the southern Arizona lowlands. But the desert mule deer had been pretty well shot out, particularly in the desert country within easy reach of the populous Salt River valley. The native Arizona elk had been exterminated by meat hunters before 1900, and in those days before 1914 the few remaining grizzlies were also being rapidly killed off. As late as the middle 1920's there were still a few grizzlies in Sycamore Canyon south of Williams, in the White Mountains, and in the Santa Catalina Mountains just north of Tucson.

Most deer hunters from around Phoenix hunted to the north, as the nearest reasonably good deer country was in the arid mountain and canyon country seventy-five to a hundred miles from Phoenix. Every year Pinney & Robinson, a Phoenix sporting-goods store on the corner of Central Avenue and Monroe, gave a rifle to the first hunter bringing in a deer. The event was always a major local sports story. A crowd gathered around the store on the morning of the opening of deer season waiting for the winning hunter to show up. Photos of hunter and deer along with a blow-by-blow account of the hunt always appeared in the papers. However, human nature being what it is, some of those bucks got into Phoenix so early that they must have been shot long before daylight. Likewise, some of them smelled bad and showed evidence of having been shot at least twenty-four hours before.

Few people from the Salt River valley hunted deer, and even fewer had ever shot one. It was not uncommon for deer hunters to drive into deer country, camp, and hunt for a week without seeing so much as a doe. Anyone who had actually killed a deer was something of a celebrity.

I shot my first deer out of season, sadly enough, when I was twelve years old with a .30/40 Krag, a military rifle used in the Spanish-American War. I had found an area of desert all tracked up by a little bunch of mule deer, so I went back there early one morning, sneaked around trying to find one. As luck would have it, I saw a young buck before it saw me. I got a fearful case of buck fever. The buck was not far away but the front sight wobbled all around, on the buck and off. I finally yanked the trigger and the buck bounded off. I knew I had missed him. I stood there for a moment hating myself, feeling guilty and deeply depressed.

I walked over to the spot where the buck had been standing. I saw his plunging tracks where he had taken off. I followed them a little way—and I saw a splash of blood. I started so violently that the shock and excitement gave me a headache. I went a little farther and saw another big splash of crimson blood. In a few more yards I saw a gray form lying beside a palo verde.

ARIZONA WAS A MARVELOUSLY free country to grow up in. Most of the land not under irrigation belonged to the federal government or the state. Almost all the desert was open range, where anyone could run cattle and where cattlemen went together to sort the animals out in annual roundups. Those who controlled the water used the land around it for nothing. It was not until the middle 1920's that the state began giving leases and obtaining revenue (very little revenue at that!) from the lands it had acquired from the public domain through various public acts—to the university, to the school districts, and so on. It was not until the 1930's that what remained of the public domain began to be controlled and supervised to some extent through the Taylor Grazing Act. The national forests were established in the early part of the century. My Grandfather Woolf saw the destruction to watersheds that unrestricted lumbering and grazing had brought on. He was one of the farsighted Arizonans who wanted the forest reserves established. Those who had been cutting free timber and grazing livestock for nothing were very bitter.

We who were growing up in Arizona then wandered free on the desert and in the mountains. During all my boyhood in the state I never saw a "Posted" or "No Trespassing" sign. Today the big cattle outfits have largely bought the small ones out, but before World War I there were many little outfits—a windmill, a corral made of twisted mesquite limbs, an adobe house, a ramada with a couple of chairs, a cooler with burlap sides, and an olla. A lot of little outfits tried to make a living out of a hundred cows, maybe out of fifty cows.

The ones who were soft or lazy were starved out or sold out. The shrewd and tough little ranchers became big ranchers. On the open range one of the ways a little rancher became a big one was by "sleepering." In riding the open range he would see a fairly large calf that had not been earmarked or branded running with a cow belonging to another rancher. The hustling small rancher would rope the calf, tie it up, and cut the same earmark in its ear that its mother had. He did so hoping that the cowboys riding range for the rancher who owned the cow would see that the calf was earmarked and assume that it had likewise been branded.

The tough and hustling little rancher would keep his eye on the cow and her calf (and the other calves he had "sleepered") and then when the calves were weaned and started running by themselves he would catch them, cut out the old earmark, cut his in, and put his brand on them. At roundup time he claimed them.

The hustling little rancher often built up his herd very rapidly by

this and by other methods. Sometimes ranchers who practiced "sleepering" and other bits of chicanery got shot. Sometimes they just disappeared. But often they got rich. Trying to make a living out of fifty to a hundred and fifty cows was tough. The man who rode the range had to be out in hot weather and in cold. Riding horses at a dead run over rough mountain country is dangerous. Horses can stumble and throw their riders. They can fall on

him and kill him. A good friend of mine lay with a broken pelvis under a horse with a broken back, died slowly and horribly. Ranchers lived lonely and isolated lives, and many ranch houses could be reached only by saddle horse and pack train.

But these little ranchers were always friendly and hospitable, much more so than the big, rich ranchers. Because they saw few people they were always glad to see a new face. They were always glad to tell hunters where they had seen several coveys of quail or where a great many whitewings were coming into a tank to water. After you had a couple of drinks with a rancher or had broken bread with him he would even tell you about the canyon where he'd seen a big desert mule deer buck (which he always called a "blacktail").

Before World War I not many of these small ranchers had automobiles. Roads were bad and tires were worse. They seldom got to town. Often they had to ride ten or fifteen miles to pick up the mail the rural mail carrier who made his route twice a week left there. Most of them ate poorly. They lived on biscuits (made with water, canned milk, salt, shortening, and baking powder, and mixed right in a hole in the flour in the top of the sack and often baked in a Dutch oven), frijoles, jerky (strips of beef or venison dried in the sun), bacon, and coffee. They didn't use many canned goods except canned milk, but they all liked canned tomatoes.

Some of those small ranchers who were bachelors were excellent housekeepers, whose adobe houses or log huts were always clean and neat. Others kept a few hounds to chase mountain lions with and to keep the dishes clean. Sometimes if they thought about it they rinsed out a dish or a skillet the hounds had licked before they used it, but more often they forgot about it.

Most of these cowmen who lived alone had stomach trouble. They ate too many heavy biscuits, too much milk gravy. If they had venison or beef they fried it until it was black clear through. The frijoles they ate were generally hot with chili. They consumed too much starch. As a consequence they generally got potgutted in middle age and wore their pendulous bellies over their belts.

Their costume was a blue chambray shirt, a pair of levis, a blue denim jacket, and a pair of high-heeled cowboy boots. On their heads they wore beaten-up old "ten-gallon" hats. If it looked like a bad rain they tied a "slicker" on behind the saddle. If it was exceptionally cold they might put on a wool shirt or even two wool shirts and wear a pair of leather gloves. When they rode they wore a pair of leather "chaps" to turn brush and thorns. Before World War I those who rode the range almost invariably carried a revolver, generally a single-action .45-caliber Colt. Some took with them Winchester Model 94 carbines in .25/35, .30/30, or .32 Special caliber. If they did they generally carried it in a scabbard (often homemade out of rawhide) butt up and to the rear on the right side. I often wonder what some of these old-time cowmen would think of the fancy cowboy clothes worn today.

But they were a fine and hospitable lot of people. When I used to hunt quail and desert mule deer the small ranchers were always glad to see me, always asked me to come back for "dinner" at noon. Arizona was a thinly populated state then and everybody knew or had heard of everybody else. A few questions about where I was from, what my name was, and who I knew generally established that I was old J. W. Woolf's grandson, nephew of Bill and Jim O'Connor, and Charlie, John, and Billy Woolf. ("Christ, old Johnny Woolf and me we got drunk as hoot owls and got into a fist fight down at a bar at Dos Cabezas one time, but we was so goddam borracho we couldn't hurt each other much! Old Johnny and me, we was compadres then and we slept in the same bed in the same room in the hotel. When I woke up my dad-burned thumb was all swole up and sore as hell, and I says: 'For Christ sake, Johnny, I must of hit somebody last night. Look at this-here thumb!' And old Johnny he said: 'You're damn right you hit someone, you crazy bastard! It was me! Boy, was we drunk!' He showed me his left ear and it was swole up as bad as my thumb. A great guy, Johnny Woolf, a real compadre. Any nephew of Johnny Woolf's a friend of mine!")

If the small cattleman had a wife and family there was usually an attempt to make things a little more homelike. Then there was often a kitchen garden near the house. Often the family kept a milk cow. I'll never forget one of the best meals I ever ate. A friend and I were hunting quail about thirty-five miles out of Tempe when the rancher, a man whom neither of us knew, rode up and told us of a spot about a mile away near a tank where quail were quite plentiful. A while later we saw him as he again rode up. "For Christ's sake," he said, "ain't you two boys ever coming to dinner? The missus is expecting you!"

We had hot biscuits, cold milk (it was in December), fresh butter, and green onions from a winter garden.

Some of the freedom in the back country began to go when the big ranchers started to buy out the little ones, as the rich are always less hospitable than the poor. Loss of freedom to go anywhere took another downward step when grazing leases were granted on state and federal lands and ranchers illegally posted them. Thoughtless hunters sometimes left gates open, camped around waterholes and kept the cattle away from them. Then during and after World War II many rich Easterners moved to Arizona, bought cattle spreads for more than they were worth so they could wear cowboy suits, play cowboy, and also show a loss on their cattle operations for tax purposes. Then as hordes of unacclimated members of the proletariat swarmed into Tucson and Phoenix, bought four-wheel-drive automobiles and motorcycles and went swarming over the countryside, the "No Trespassing" signs bloomed like flowers in the spring. The old open range of my boyhood gave one last gasp and died.

THE DESERT IS SOMETHING you get used to. Any human being or any animal that grows up on the desert quickly learns that just about everything has thorns on it and that bumping into the thorns is a painful experience. I no doubt learned this lesson painfully, but I did so at such an early age that I have no recollection of it. Dogs, horses, everything else have to learn the same way.

I can hunt desert mule deer all day and never get into thorns. I can chase a wounded quail or a big buck with a broken leg through a chollal (a big patch of vicious cholla) without bumping into thorns. I am not conscious of avoiding them: I simply avoid them. This is so nearly subconscious on the part of a desert dweller that it can almost be called instinct. Smart dogs quickly learn to avoid cholla. A bird dog first brought to the desert is full of thorns the first few days he hunts. But from then on he learns to stay out of them.

I came back to Arizona after an absence of several years with wife and young in 1931. For three years we lived at high, cool Flagstaff where the country is just about thornless. Then in 1934 the president and board of regents of the University of Arizona decided they needed a professor of journalism. They put the finger on me, so the O'Connors moved to Tucson, which is in the desert. In a week or so we went on our first desert picnic. We drove into a clean, sandy arroyo and stopped. I was starting to get the picnic things out when my wife and two boys all began howling. All were full of cholla.

Some years later a former student of mine who had grown up

in the East but who loved the desert got married and brought his Eastern bride, a beautiful girl of twenty, back to Arizona on their honeymoon. He liked to shoot, so he came by with his bride and invited me to go with them out to an old rifle range in the desert east of Tucson. We were getting our rifles out when we heard the bride cry out. She had backed into a cholla plant and her poor little fanny was full of cholla balls. We laid her bottom up across the hood of the car, and putting a stick on each side of a ball I removed the balls one by one. Then I got out a pair of pliers and pulled more than seventy thorns out of her bleeding and quivering behind. The cholla needles are curved like fishhooks, but the points are so fine and sharp they are almost invisible. The balls will hang on the hide of a passing animal. The thorns work gradually deeper. Finally the ball is brushed off, leaving some thorns in. It falls on the ground and after a rain it sends out roots and becomes a new cholla plant.

Pack rats drag cholla balls together and build elaborate fortified nests. Birds build nests in cholla and are safe from predators. There are many varieties, but the meanest is the Bigelow cholla. Some varieties of cholla have beautiful flowers in the spring. The thorns of the cholla burn as if they had been dipped in gasoline and they can be used to signal for help by someone lost in the desert. The prickly pear has flat leaves protected by thorns that are less vicious than those of the wicked cholla. The beautiful ocotillo likewise has thorns, as does the catclaw (a small bush) and the mesquite tree.

The great saguaros (giant candelabrum cacti) have become one of the leading symbols of the West. Any time a hack artist has to design a jacket for a Western novel—no matter what the setting is—a book about cattle country, or wallpaper with a Western motif, he falls back on the good old saguaro. Actually, the saguaro grows nowhere in the United States but Arizona, and even in the deserts of the Mexican state of Sonora the saguaro is soon replaced as one goes south by its Mexican relative the sahueso. No saguaro has ever crossed the Colorado River into California or Nevada unless some person helped it, and the giant cacti are cut off from New Mexico by a belt of high, unsuitable country in eastern Arizona. Like most desert vegetation the saguaro is protected by thorns, but the cactus wren nests in it and the desert bighorns have learned to girdle it when they need water in time of desperate drought.

The barrel cactus (bisnaga) is short and fat. It looks like a barrel and it is full of water. Its thorns are as cruel as the claws of a tiger, but the desert sheep break open the cactus for the cool green water. The fruit of the saguaro and the sahueso are sought by the birds, and desert deer and sheep all relish the fruit of the wicked and treacherous cholla. In August when the fruit of the organ cactus is ripe and red in the western desert of Sonora the whitewing doves devour them and the Seri Indians wander through the desert living on the fruit. The droppings of both whitewings and Seris are scarlet then.

Many a greenhorn who did not know the desert has died of thirst when he was surrounded by plump bisnagas filled with cool green water. Likewise many a greenhorn had drawn his last breath lying in the sands of a dry arroyo when, if he had but known it, he could have struck cool plentiful water by digging down a few feet. These places where the water runs close to the surface beneath the sands are known as *arivipas.* Their location is known to desert dwellers, human and animal. I have seen where deer and sheep have pawed to make themselves *pozos,* or wells, and once north of Tucson after a desperately dry summer I was hunting quail along a dry arroyo when suddenly I found myself in the midst of a coyote congregation. I soon found out why. The intelligent animals had dug themselves a pozo six or eight feet deep in the bed of the arroyo and at the bottom was several inches of cool, clear water. They knew the location of the arivipa as well as anyone.

In my youth a confectionery store called Donofrios in Phoenix made a specialty of "cactus candy." It was made from the pulp of one of the large cacti preserved in sugar. What kind of cactus was used I am not sure but it runs in my mind that it was the bisnaga. The fruit of the prickly pear makes delicious jelly, but it must literally be handled with gloves, as the rind is covered with tens of thousands of wicked, almost microscopic thorns.

Spring in the desert is lovely. The paloverde (Spanish for green tree) trees are masses of yellow bloom and they are always filled with clouds of humming, wicked little desert bees. The ironwoods (*palo fierro*) look like distant bluishwhite smoke when they bloom. The ocotillos are all tipped in scarlet, and the bisnagas and saguaros bear handsome flowers. After rainy winters the desert is carpeted with California poppies and other flowers.

The desert dweller is a lover of water. He cherishes lifegiving springs and rivers. He builds his houses with high, thick walls and with few windows so they will be dark and cool. The desert dweller works in the cool of morning and evening, dozes during the heat of the day. He imagines that when he dies he will go to a cool heaven of green trees, cold clear water, and if he goes to hell it will simply be his familiar desert only more so—hotter, more glaring, drier. The sunbathers of the Southwest are not natives of the desert, and neither are those who build houses with picture windows. The desert dweller wants to shut the sun out—not let it in.

To illustrate the feeling of the desert dweller for water and mountains and coolness, I must spin a tale about a humble Mexican restaurant that existed many years ago in Tempe. It was owned by a couple of poor, unsophisticated *paisanos* who had moved to Arizona from Sonora. The man was a bit more enterprising than most, and the wife was a very good cook. When they found that both gringos and Mexicans would pay money for her excellent Sonora-style dishes they opened a little restaurant. The food was authentic, hot, and cheap. I used to eat there often and so did many other gringos.

I loved the food but I also came to admire a mural. It was the creation of a simple Mexican sign painter so unsophisticated as to make Grandma Moses seem as urbane as Picasso. The mural was of the cool, magical north country that desert dwellers dream of.

Both owner and artist were very proud of it. The mural showed a lake with high, snow-capped, and timbered mountains in the background. At one end of the lake was brown-and-white moose. Neither artist nor owner had ever seen a moose, but they had seen pinto horses, so why not a pinto moose? The moose was being stalked by two hunters in a canoe. From the wake the canoe left in the blue, blue water of the lake the hunters must have been paddling it at the rate of at least thirty-five knots. The sun was shining brightly, but in this magic never-never land the shadows cast by the trees didn't go away from the sun: they went toward it. Tempe's Mexicans loved the mural. They used to come and gaze at it, think how cool it must be there, how nice it would be to have all that water available to bathe in and to irrigate with, and how much meat there was on the pinto bull moose. Then they would say: *"Ah, que linda, que agradable!"* sigh, and sit down to their frijoles, enchiladas, and tortillas.

LIKE ANYONE WHO SPENDS his life in the desert, those of us who grew up in southern Arizona thought of the mountains as a sort of a foretaste of heaven. Actually what we referred to as "mountains" was largely the great Mogollon plateau that runs across central Arizona. On it there are piles of cinders, rock, and lava that have formed mountains. Some of the highest points of the San Francisco peaks are well above timberline and so is the top of Mount Baldy in the White Mountains. But for the most part the plateau is between 7,000 and 8,000 feet in elevation.

The air in the mountains is thin. In the shade it is always cool and at night it is chilly. During the last part of July and August there are often thunderstorms in the mountains with floods of cold, driving rain. When the storms die out and the rain ceases and the rumble of thunder moves off like a distant cannonade, the cool damp air is fragrant with the smell of yellow pines.

But to me the autumn was the magic time in the mountains. Then as October came the aspens turned yellow and the leaves danced as the trees swayed in the wind like golden sequins on the dress of a lovely slender girl. The oaks turned red and in the mornings frost lay thick on the grass and the edges of the little streams were laced with ice. Then the mule deer bucks were fat. Their antlers were polished and their hides thick. The wild turkeys that had hatched the previous spring were grown and plump after a lush summer of grasshoppers and rose haws and pine seeds. The black bears were starting to put on their winter's fat when the first frosts came. Then lucky desert dwellers headed for the mountains with heavily laden Model T Fords creaking and groaning over steep and rocky roads. Sometimes they came back with deer and turkey, sometimes even with bear. But the game had been pretty well shot down before World War I and more often than not they came back empty-handed, weary, constipated, their faces and clothes smudged with smoke from campfires of pine knots.

Like most desert-raised youngsters I felt very romantic about snow. Sometimes in November, always by December, those of us who lived in the warm Salt River valley would see storms whiten the tops of the distant mountains to the north like the Four Peaks and the Mazatzals. I longed to touch snow, that wonderful stuff, to be in a snowstorm, to roll in snow, to revel in it. I touched my first snow when I was in my early teens. I had gone to Florence on the railroad to spend a few days with my Uncle Jim O'Connor's family. There had been a big general storm and I could see that the tops of the Catalina Mountains about thirty miles away toward Tucson were white. When my train pulled into the little station at Florence my astonished eyes discovered that the tops of a half dozen freight cars that had just pulled in from the copper-mining town of Ray were covered with about six inches of something white. It could only be snow. The instant the train stopped I jumped out, climbed up on a car and touched the fabulous stuff. It was coarse, granular—so much grainy ice. Halfheartedly I made a snowball and threw it at my cousin Wallace.

But all through my childhood I was bitterly envious of the children who lived in that fabulous country known as Back East.

They had beautiful, fluffy snow. They had jolly fights with snowballs. They made snowmen and built snow forts. They wore woolen caps and romantic-looking woolen mufflers. They rode in sleighs, skated on real ice, coasted down hills on sleds. They had white Christmases and there was some excuse for Santa Claus's sleigh. But in the Salt River valley, alas, Christmas Day was usually warm and sunny and there were grapefruit and oranges on the trees in Grandfather Woolf's yard.

It seldom got very cold during a normal winter in the valley. Sometimes during late December and January there would be frost on the grass in the early mornings. Sometimes there would be a thin skim of ice on the tubs in which my mother thriftily caught the nice soft rainwater that ran off the roof. But in all the years during which I was growing up in Tempe I never saw so much as one falling snowflake. As my sister Helen said to a visitor from the East one time, "I have never seen snow but I have seen wild ice!"

# 12 · The Automobile Age

I CANNOT remember seeing an automobile until I was four or five. That would have been in 1906 or 1907. My first automobile must have been a bit old-fashioned even then, as I have a very definite memory that the engine was under the seat and that it steered by a tiller instead of a wheel. I can remember standing by

it and noticing that it lurched and shook with each belch of the motor.

The first time I rode in an automobile has completely escaped my memory, but I can well remember the first long automobile trip I took. This must have been about 1910. My Uncle John Woolf came by my Grandfather Woolf's new house and picked me up to take me to Florence to visit my Uncle Jim O'Connor and his family. His car was a Reo and it was red. It runs in my mind that it had two cylinders, but it may have had four. It also had six spare tires and it turned out that we needed them all. We left

Grandfather's place about eight o'clock in the morning. My mother offered to put up a lunch, but John, who was playing the big shot, refused it. "Pooh, Ida," he said. "It would just be a waste of time. We'll be in Florence eating a good hot meal at the hotel at noon."

We made the seven miles to Mesa without incident but two or three miles beyond, while we were still going through irrigated farm land, the Reo had its first flat tire. While John was changing tires, a crowd of about twenty people collected. Every wagon on the road stopped, and a couple of young men working in a nearby field laid down their tools and came over to gape. I remember one of the farmers saying that he was of a mind to get one of them contraptions.

In 1910 or shortly after there was a graded road from Mesa most of the way to Florence, but experienced motorists avoided it. It was not maintained and it had never been surfaced. In dry weather it was deep in powdery dust and pockmarked with villainous chuckholes. In wet weather it was a sea of bottomless mud. It was called the State Highway and everyone who owned an automobile and had tried it warned all he met to stay away from it. Motorists preferred to make their own roads, and the desert between Mesa and Florence was covered with dozens of tracks. The first daring automobile drivers followed an old wagon road, but when high centers became too high they simply turned off into the virgin desert. Other motorists followed their tracks. Presently the new road was the established one. When it in turn got difficult to negotiate, or when a mud puddle looked too formidable, motorists struck out on their own.

The roads between farm fields in the Salt River valley were always deep in mud during the winter rains. An automobile could not get over them at all and they were difficult and sometimes impassable even for horse-drawn wagons. The farm roads around Tempe were not paved until 1918 or 1919, and as late as 1923 there was still no surfaced road between Florence and Mesa. When it rained you simply put on chains, hit the soft spots as fast as you could go, and prayed.

Tires must have been incredibly bad back in 1910. Uncle John's Reo had one flat after another and John spent far more time patching tubes and changing tires than he did driving. By two o'clock in the afternoon I was famished.

"Uncle John, haven't you got *anything* to eat?" I asked.

"Not a thing," John said.

"Mother wanted to fix a lunch and you wouldn't let her."

"Goddammit, don't whine at me! I'm as hungry as you are!"

To repair a tube John would pump it up to find where the air was leaking out, spitting on all suspected leaks to see if the spit bubbled. If we ran over some cactus there might be four or five leaks in one tube. Then he marked the leaks with chalk. He next sandpapered the area around each hole, then clamped on a vulcanizing attachment, and a little fire burned as the "hot patch" went on.

Doggedly John drove on, halting every few miles to repair another tire. The sun went down. It began to grow dark and Uncle John turned on the acetylene gas from the Prestolite tank on the runningboard of the Reo, opened up the glass of the headlights, and lit the hissing jets with a kitchen match. They popped sharply as they ignited and instantly the desert track in front of us was bathed in clear white light.

We went on, plunging from rut to chuckhole. Faint with hunger I got carsick and started vomiting. John stopped the car to see if I could get rid of whatever I had left. "Oh Christ, what next!" he said.

We had water and gas cans along. Now and then he'd stop to fill the radiator or put in more gasoline. About nine o'clock he delivered me to my Uncle Jim O'Connor's house.

"Jim," he said, "you'd better give this poor little bastard something to eat. We've had a hell of a time and the kid hasn't had a bite since early morning. He's been puking his toenails up for the past ten or fifteen miles."

Supper was long since over, but there was a freezer full of chocolate ice cream. I ate a big dish of it and promptly lost it. I have hated chocolate ice cream ever since.

I LEARNED TO DRIVE an automobile after a fashion on my Uncle Jim O'Connor's Cadillac in 1913 when I was eleven. The car was rather old then, as people who bought good automobiles did not relinquish them lightly in those days. The Cadillac was a touring car with a right-hand drive and the gear shift on the runningboard. There were no front doors, and as I remember this noble vehicle the rear seat must have been seven feet off the ground. The car was always driven with the top up; if it rained, curtains had to be put on. These were kept under the back seat.

Since the Cadillac had no self-starter, it had to be cranked by hand. Hand-cranking was fraught with risks, and automobile owners were always getting their arms broken if the motor coughed suddenly and spun the crank. The old Cad had a massive motor that turned over very slowly, and when it was weaving through the desert tracks at fifteen and twenty miles an hour it went *glubeldy, glubeldy, glubeldy.* When not in use the Cadillac lived under a ramada of its own. Jim's Mexican hired man kept it reverently cleaned and polished, the motor free from oil and dirt. He even had an olla filled with cool water hanging in the Cadillac's ramada, apparently under the impression that the car might want a drink sometime.

In 1913 Jim's Cadillac was beginning to look a bit old-fashioned. The rear end looked like that of a carriage, and most automobile bodies were built the same way. But the Ford touring cars had smooth curved rears that could be easily and cheaply stamped out. In a few years all car bodies were so made. The Fords and most new cars of other makes had front doors—except that the left-hand door on the Ford was false and did not open. The new Fords in 1913 had electric lights that ran off the magneto, but when the going got tough and the car slowed down the lights grew dim. Because of this many automobile owners were skeptical as to whether electric lights would ever be practical.

But when the automobile age really got going it came on with a rush. For many years Tempe's street-cleaning department had consisted of a single gnomelike Mexican, stooped, rickety, bent, and ancient. He went up and down Mill Avenue with a handcart, a shovel, and a willow broom which he made new each day from willow branches cut down in the river bottom. He swept up the voluminous droppings left by the horses hitched in front of the stores, shoveled them into the cart, and disposed of them—where, I do not know. As the automobile displaced the horse there was less and less manure left on Mill Avenue. Finally the city council dispensed with the services of this poor old man. His cart, his shovel, his willow broom disappeared forever. I paid no attention to the event at the time, and indeed had not thought of it until the writing of this book began to stir dusty and moth-eaten memories. There was, of course, no such nonsense in those days as a pension for long and faithful service. Let us hope that this poor old man had a loving son somewhere who could provide him with shelter, tortillas, frijoles, and maybe even an occasional nip of tequila in the sunset of his useful life. The other part of Tempe's street department consisted of a sprinkling cart drawn by two large horses, one of which had a monstrously deformed front hoof at least three times bigger than his other hoofs. During the dry summers, and at other times if the dust got bad, the sprinkling cart went over town laying the dust. Small children followed it, shrieking and howling as they jumped in and out of the cool water.

The automobile industry was the growth industry of those pre-World War I days, but many an investor, including my Grandfather Woolf, got burned. I have read that a few hundred dollars invested in Ford made men millionaires, but those who guessed wrong and invested in many of the other automobile-manufacturing companies lost their shirts. There were many makes—the E.M.F. (which wits called the Every Morning Fixum), the Mitchell (which as I remember had an off-breed shift on the order of that on the Dodge), the majestic Winton, the Hupmobile, the Case, the Stevens-Duryea, the Pope-Hartford, the Packard (which lasted into the modern era), the Maxwell (which, I believe, was bought by Walter Chrysler and formed the basis for the Chrysler Motor Company), the American, the Hudson (the first car I remember that did not use a magneto), the aristocratic Pierce-Arrow, the Stearns-Knight and the Willys-Knight (both had sleeve-valve Knight motors), the Franklin (a great favorite with doctors over the United States because it had an air-cooled motor and no radiator to freeze up), the speedy Mercer, and many others.

But it was the Model T Ford that really ushered in the automobile age in Arizona. The Ford was cheap, reasonably rugged, easy to repair, and easy on gasoline. Time payments came into being, and people who had ridden bicycles all their lives drove Fords to work. No longer did one hear jokes about footprints upside down on the dashboard of the buggy. Instead there were jokes about what happened in the rear seats of Fords. Whether the Ford Motor Company was shrewd enough to start or encourage the craze for Ford jokes I do not know, but the jokes were wonderful promotion for the Model T. As I think back I cannot remember a single Ford joke, and even at the time I didn't think many of them funny; but they were so popular that books of Ford jokes were published and sold for fifty cents and a dollar on newsstands. People paid their money for them.

At first there were no filling stations and no garages. If an automobile owner wanted some air in a tire he got out a hand pump and inflated it himself. There was a gas pump for a good many years in front of the Birchett Brothers' grocery store on Mill Avenue and one in front of the Case tractor agency (which also sold Case automobiles). Carl Spain (who married Lena Woolf, my second cousin) worked in his father's blacksmith shop. He was a mechanical genius who could fix anything, so presently he found himself doing more work on automobiles than on general blacksmithing.

The first filling station in Tempe were started by a couple of local boys at the corner of Mill Avenue and Eighth Street. They had an air compressor and anyone who wanted to could fill his tires for nothing. They advertised the fact with a big sign that said FREE AIR. This was *progress* and everyone in Tempe was very proud of the innovation. When the boys filled up someone's gas tank they also wiped off his windshield if they thought of it. There were no amenities. If the dusty traveler wanted to wash he was welcome to use the radiator water in the can by the gas pump, and if he wanted to relieve himself he could go behind the building.

Road races were very popular in those early years of the automobile age. To promote the Arizona state fair, which was held each fall, two road races were held—Los Angeles to Phoenix and El Paso to Phoenix. Racing cars that took part in the El Paso–Phoenix race came hell-bent right through downtown Tempe, and when the people heard the roar of a racing motor in the distance they ran out of stores and offices and stood along the sidewalks of Mill Avenue to watch the dusty, muddy, desperately weary drivers, each accompanied by a mechanic, go roaring by. Real highways were almost nonexistent in those days, and since the fair was held in November when it might be wet if the winter rains were early, the road racers sometimes had to ford streams and plow through mud. They tore up their tires on stones, punctured them with cactus thorns. They took wrong roads and got lost. They wrecked their cars by hitting cows. Those that won prize money really earned it. I remember meeting one of the road-race drivers once, a man who had been a big-league pitcher before he became a race driver. His name was "Cannon Ball" Baker, and as I remember him he must have been six and a half feet tall.

Uncle Jim O'Connor generally drove over from Florence with his family to take in the Arizona state fair, and he always took me along. There were automobile and motorcycle races, horse races with little jockeys perched on beautiful long-legged thoroughbreds, and harness races with trotters pulling funny little carts. There were pens filled with prize cattle and sheep and displaying blue and red ribbons, exhibits of gargantuan vegetables, of preserved fruit, pies, cakes, and all manner of domestic arts. Uncle Jim O'Connor stuffed all of us kids at noon on lemonade, ice-cream cones, hamburgers, hot dogs, and cotton candy. At night we had a proper dinner, and he saw that we were all bedded down snugly in a three-bedroom suite he always reserved at his favorite hotel.

The world changes a little every day, and then we wake up to find familiar things have gone forever. None of us realized then how profoundly the automobile was to change our world. But it did. Fewer and fewer horses and buggies were hitched in front of the stores on Mill Avenue. In 1908 almost all the vehicles were horse-drawn and people stared at automobiles. By 1914 buggies were rare and distinctly old-fashioned. The hansom cabs drawn by beautiful horses no longer met the trains at the railway station in Phoenix and the hotels replaced their horse-drawn buses with automobiles. The grocery stores bought light trucks for deliveries. The Fike brothers started a bus line between Phoenix, Tempe, and Mesa. They used hard-working little Model T Ford motors and large custom bodies that carried twenty or twenty-five passengers. But in keeping with the Western tradition the buses were called "stages," as the horse-drawn stagecoach survived in Arizona well into this century.

When I was a boy in Arizona the verb "to pack" was synonymous with "to carry" or "to transport." Even today "to pack" is still used in that manner in parts of Arizona and other sections of the West. I can't remember just when I saw it but I ran into a serve-yourself grocery store called "Pick and Pack." In my youth pack-train, mules, and horses were widely used means of transporting goods. There were dozens of ranches so isolated that everything from the outside had to be packed on a horse or a mule. Those old packers could do wonders. They packed stoves, furniture, machinery into remote mines and ranches. By putting them between two stout horses in the manner of a palanquin they even packed in pianos and organs.

But the automobile brought a demand for better roads. Presently an automobile or a truck could go where only a sturdy wagon drawn by six stout mules had formerly gone. Then roads were driven back into the hills so that automobiles could be used instead of saddle and pack horses. Since World War II the natives of Arizona have been pretty well swamped by hordes of newcomers that have made Arizona one of the fastest-growing states in the Union, but pockets of old-timers with their quaint ways and odd vocabularies still remain. On my last visit to Arizona I stopped for lunch at a little restaurant next door to a saloon. I asked the waitress if she could go next door and bring me a bottle of beer. "No, Ah cain't because Ah'm a lady," she said, "but it's all right if you pack it in yourself!"

UNTIL WELL ALONG in the 1920's Arizona roads were pretty terrible. Most were unpaved, dusty, full of chuckholes. In the mountains where road work was expensive they were narrow, steep, and rocky. Often the motorist went up and down hill by jumping his car from ledge to ledge. Cooling systems on pre-World War I automobiles were not too good, and motorists going up long grades had to stop two or three times to let their motors cool and to fill the boiling radiators. The city of Flagstaff is about 220 miles from Phoenix, and I can remember when a motorist who made the trip in one day got his name and his picture in the papers. Daring motorists began driving from Phoenix to Los Angeles in numbers about the time of World War I. For the conservative, making the four hundred miles in three days was considered good time. A two-day trip was something to be remarked upon.

Motorists did not undertake trips of several hundred miles lightly. They carried from two to four spare tires, various spare parts for the motor, a shovel, tire patches, an extra jack, tire tools, perhaps a winch so the car could be pulled out of mud holes, and a revolver for protection against robbers and wild animals. Only the most feckless motorist would begin a journey without extra oil, gasoline, and water. The supply of these necessities was carried on the runningboard in a set of red, white, and blue cans. The red can contained the gasoline, and I believe the blue can contained the oil. It was also wise to take along a supply of iron rations to keep body and soul together in case the car got stuck, a bridge washed out, or an arroyo came up from a sudden rain. In the desert the sandy dry washes called arroyos that would not have a drop of water in them eleven and a half months a year could become raging torrents three and four feet deep in a few minutes after a heavy rain somewhere. Unwary motorists were always having their cars washed downstream and ruined, and in some cases these sudden floods drowned the motorists themselves.

I remember the first time I ever went by automobile from Tempe to Los Angeles. My Uncle Bill Woolf was driving over to see his wife, Crickett, and his young son, Bill, Jr., who were spending the summer on the beach to escape the southern Arizona heat. A Tempe family was going to drive over at the same time and they asked if they could go along with us in convoy to lessen the hazards of the drive. Bill's car was new and in perfect repair but the other car was a bit doubtful.

Bill, Mother, my sister Helen, and I were in one car, the other family consisting of the driver, his wife, and a little boy and a charming little blond girl in the other. We got a good early start and set out at a good sturdy twenty miles an hour. By the time we reached the outskirts of the village of Buckeye around noon to eat lunch on a canal bank, we had stopped to change tires at least three times and to tinker with the motor in the other car about twice.

Exactly what was wrong with the other car I do not know, but the motor got more and more dyspeptic. Finally my Uncle Bill decided to tow it. We arrived at Yuma just across the Colorado River from California about dusk. Bill bribed a mechanic to work overtime on the other car. We ate dinner in a steaming restaurant and all turned in on the open porch of the hotel. It was bad enough outside. Inside the rooms it would have been unbearable. It had been 126 in Yuma that day and I am sure the thermometer never went below 100 all night.

The next morning the other car was running and we set out for Los Angeles. We soon encountered the plank road through the sand dunes. This consisted of planks laid side by side and just wide enough for one car. At intervals the planks were in double widths so that one car could turn off to allow another to pass. In some places the sand had blown over the planks so that passage was difficult. In others the sand had blown from a section of plank, so that the road was slanted and hazardous. As I remember it the road extended for fifteen or twenty miles.

Once over the road we drove through dismal and fearfully hot little towns in the Imperial Valley, past the Salton Sea. Then we toiled up a narrow road to a pass in the Coast Range. Once on top the country changed. We could see hills covered with yellow grass and spotted with oaks and in the distance the mists of the Pacific Ocean. It was instantly cooler. That night in Los Angeles when we went to bed it was deliciously cool and we slept under blankets. No wonder many of those who grew up in the Arizona desert wound up living in southern California. All through their youth they looked upon it as the promised land!

# 13 · First Love

WHEN I was growing up in Tempe there were very few people of the Jewish faith in town. Phoenix was only nine miles away. It was much larger. It was growing faster, and as the use of the automobile spread, more and more people went there to shop. Since Jews tend to be smart business people most of them set up shop in growing Phoenix rather than in a backwater like Tempe.

When I was a boy Goldwater's dry-goods store in Phoenix was already prosperous and well known, and Korrick's, which was then called the New York Store, was the largest of the Phoenix department stores. Both were Jewish enterprises.

But this chapter has very little connection with Phoenix and none at all with well-known and prosperous department stores. It is about a Jewish family and the beautiful Jewish girl who was my first love. This is a tale of a great love that had a lot going against it from the start. In a way it could be said that it had a happy ending. In another way it couldn't. One of the reasons why my first love, the beautiful Anna Levistky, and I did not marry and live happily ever after was that at the time our romance began she was nineteen years old and I, alas, had just turned eleven. In spite of the difference in our ages, I must add, however, that I loved her dearly and I think she was rather fond of me.

The two Levitsky brothers in Tempe owned stores. Moe had a grocery store on Eighth Street across from one corner of the normal-school campus. Actually the store was on the Mexican Town side of the street, but in addition to a large Mexican trade he got many customers from the east end of town, since his was the most conveniently located store for the people who lived on that side of the normal-school campus.

Moe was a sad-looking old bachelor with stringly blond hair and large melancholy blue eyes. He had no happy banter for his customers and he almost never smiled. He was hollow-chested, thin, and he looked ill. It was generally believed that he was a lunger, as people with tuberculosis were called.

It was also agreed that Moe Levitsky was the biggest sucker for a hard-luck story in town. It was said that if it hadn't been for Moe half the people in Mexican Town would have had to go hungry between jobs and paydays. Dr. B. B. Moeur, our family physician, told me after Moe's death that the little Jewish storekeeper fed one poor lunger who lived in a tent by the canal near the Little Butte for over a year, never was paid a nickel, never asked for one.

All the little boys in town knew that Moe was a soft touch. They would go up to his candy case, put down a nickel, and say: "Mr. Levitsky, I want five cents' worth of candy." Moe would say: "O.K., son, what kind?" He would pick up a scoop and a big sack. The little boy would point. "Some of this and some of this and some of this and some of this." Moe would shovel the candy in as long as the boy had enough nerve to keep on pointing out what he liked. A nickel bag of Moe's candy was as big as a fifty-cent bag anywhere else.

If Moe was especially fond of one of the boys he might tousle his hair sadly and say, "Now run on, son. Don't get a bellyache."

When we were living in the tents Mother ran an account with Moe and she used to send me up to his store for twenty cents' worth of ground round, a dozen eggs, or fifteen cents' worth of potatoes. I always asked for the privilege of going up to pay the bill because Moe always came through with a generous *pelon*—a Spanish word for a gift thrown in free with a purchase or with the payment of a bill. On the rare occasions when I had a nickel of my own Moe always loaded me up with candy.

Isadore Levitsky, Moe's brother, owned a dry-goods store off Mill Avenue downtown. It was a cluttered, dusty place and Isadore's customers were the poor—mostly Indians and Mexicans. His merchandise consisted largely of cheap work clothes, blue chambray shirts, overalls, cheap work shoes, calico dresses, cotton socks, cheap and showy trinkets, straw hats.

I got mixed up with the Levitskys because I had invented a game known simply as "Knights." This was the early fall of 1912 and I was ten years old. My mother had got a job as a critic-teacher at the normal and we had moved out of my grandfather's house into a rented house while Mother was waiting for her own house to be finished. I had read *Ivanhoe* and had become fascinated by knights, armor, and the Middle Ages. I drew pictures on stout cardboard of knights wearing various kinds of armor, colored them with crayons, and then cut them out. I also drew pictures of horses, all saddled and ready to go. My knights were drawn so that with their two legs and the scabbards for the swords they could be placed firmly on the saddles. Then I affixed spears betwen horse and knight. The knights were then ready to joust. Each contestant pushed his knight violently along the floor toward the knight of the other contestant. Then they backed off and went at it again. The first knight that fell off his horse lost the joust.

I used to prowl around the stores in Tempe looking for suitable cardboard with which to construct my knights. Much of the cardboard was so thin as to be worthless. Some was so heavy it could not be cut with my mother's scissors. For some reason the yard behind Isadore Levitsky's Bon Ton store was piled high with empty cartons made of exactly the right kind of cardboard. Isadore was older than Moe. He was stooped and below average height and had a rickety walk. As far as I can remember I never heard him laugh. He had graying blond hair, blue eyes, and a "Jewish" nose.

I knew a little about old Isadore Levitsky and his tribe just as everyone in a small town knows about everyone else. His life had been a tragic one. He and Moe had been forced to flee from Russia. They had landed in New York with Isadore's family. There they had known great poverty and more tragedy. Isadore's beautiful wife had died and had left him with three children, one the baby Anna, who was born in New York.

Somehow the two brothers and Isadore's three children managed to get to Arizona. They had picked the territory because both had weak chests and the doctors in New York had advised going where there was warmth and sunshine.

They had little money but they both managed to open their humble stores. Moe lived behind his. Isadore, who had three children to look for, bought a small frame house not far from his store. Somewhere he acquired an old Jewish woman the Levitskys called Aunt Minna to cook and care for his children.

The oldest child was Ike. Everybody loved him and everybody said he was a real wild man who wasn't afraid of anything and could whip his weight in wildcats. I have no recollection of him, but as people described him he was of middle height with blue eyes, wavy blond hair, a lithe, muscular body, and a handsome face. He could run faster than anyone in town. He was a crack football player, a lightning-fast shortstop. He belonged to the volunteer fire department and he took more crazy chances than any of the other firemen. He was good-natured and had a sunny disposition, but when he got into a fight he was a tough hombre.

Much to old Isadore's disappointment Ike wouldn't have anything to do with the store. When he was quite young Ike got a summer job on a cattle ranch because the owner took a fancy to him. He became an expert rider and roper and used to compete in the primitive rodeos that were held throughout Arizona on various holidays.

He married a frail, pretty Jewish girl from Phoenix and she bore two boys—Hal and Ike, Jr. Next he got interested in automobile racing. He competed in road races all over the Southwest and on dirt tracks at county fairs. He was killed in a crackup somewhere in California, and within a year his young wife was dead of what was then called "galloping consumption." Isadore took the two little boys to raise. Both were goodlooking and blond. Hal, the elder, had a nose like his grandfather, but Ike, Jr., two years younger, was reputed to look just like his father. He was a handsome kid with a perfect Grecian profile.

I was pawing one day through the cartons behind old Isadore's store when the two Levitsky boys came out and asked me what I was doing. I knew both the boys, though not very well. Hal was in a grade above mine, Ike in a grade below. I explained my game of knights. The two went home with me and we played the game with my collection. They borrowed some of my knights and horses so they could make their own. They traced around them, colored them, and cut them out. From then on for several months the Levitsky house became the scene of many a joust and tourney.

Until I started thinking of the various Levitskys and their place in my life as this book began to shape up, I took their house and their way of life for granted, as children do. Now I marvel at how that small house contained all the Levitskys.

When all the members of the tribe were home there were eight of them—Isadore; Aunt Minna; Hal; Ike; Abe Goldstein, Isadore's son-in-law; Rachael, his wife; Joe Goldstein, the son; and the beautiful Anna. The house was small. I can remember only two bedrooms. There was a screened porch in the rear of the house, a living room, one bathroom, and a kitchen. Where all those people slept I have no idea.

I adored the Levitsky house. It was cluttered, noisy, and it was always filled with the delicious smells of Aunt Minna's cooking. Aunt Minna was always cooking and eating. She was a merry woman, short and dark, and she had a tremendous bottom that filled me with awe.

Isadore's dead wife must have been dark, because his eldest daughter, Rachael Goldstein, had large brown eyes and wavy dark hair. Even at the age of ten I was conscious that she was a great beauty. She had the exotic look of the Near East—full red lips, large languid eyes. As became her type of beauty she was a bit on the voluptuous side with full breasts and lovely round, white arms. I was not the only one who was aware of her beauty, as Rachael herself undoubtedly appreciated it deeply. She spent a great deal of time in front of a mirror. She wore dainty shoes and silk stockings and was always prettily dressed. She read. She embroidered. She seldom helped Aunt Minna with the chores and she paid little attention to Joe, her one child.

Her husband, Abe, was as homely as Rachael was beautiful. He was short, had kinky hair, large, yellow protruding teeth, bulging dark eyes. He had short legs but astonishingly large feet and he walked with them turned well out with a sort of a waddle as if he were afraid that if he did not he would get them tangled up. Abe was a salesman. Apparently he was not a very successful salesman, as it was necessary for his wife and child to stay with his father-in-law. What he sold I haven't the faintest idea, but whatever it was he had to travel to sell it. He returned late on Fridays, left early in the afternoons on Sundays.

Joe, his son, was Ike's age, nine. This unfortunate child, this son of a beautiful mother, looked and walked exactly like his homely father. He was the same age as Ike within a few weeks, but Ike was gay, witty, lively, imaginative. Joe was without imagination, had no sense of humor, seldom laughed. But he was very intelligent, worked hard, and in school his grades were never lower than 95. While Hal, Ike, and I were having jousts with our cardboard knights, laughing and shouting, Joe sometimes watched us as if he thought us insane. To us our knights were King Arthur, Lancelot, Galahad, Ivanhoe, Richard the Lion-Hearted. To Joe they were simply ridiculous-shaped pieces of colored cardboard.

Hal, Ike, and I gave little thought to the future except that we were all certain that we would be rich and famous, would marry beautiful women, and travel in faraway places. Joe had his life planned in detail. He would be a dentist, he said. Dentistry was a good, honest, well-paying occupation. It was pleasant indoor work. One could study dentistry more cheaply than medicine, and the practicing dentist did not have to make disagreeable house and night calls. Hal, Ike, and I thought of prospecting for gold in Alaska and the Yukon and of going to British East Africa to shoot elephants for their ivory. Hal sometimes thought he'd like to get rich by inventing something. Ike one moment thought he'd like to be an actor and the next he considered a career as a rancher and bronco buster. Sometimes I thought I'd like to be a cartoonist, sometimes a writer. Joe told us we were all talking through our hats—that we ought to select something safe and sure, something that paid well. Medicine, dentistry, and undertaking were all good solid occupations, he said. Everyone was born, got sick, developed bad teeth, died and got buried. In any of these you couldn't lose!

Anna Levitsky, Isadore's youngest child, had been born in this country. When I first started playing with the Levitsky boys she was eighteen, soon to be nineteen. She was then a junior at the normal, which means that she was a college freshman, as the teaching course at normal was for two years. I had seen Anna around town and at the normal campus and I had always admired her greatly.

When she came home from school the day I fell in love with her, she had on a white middy blouse and dark skirt. She wore her wavy blond hair in a thick braid and that day it was tied up with a blue ribbon. She had long dark lashes and rather dark eyebrows for one so fair. Her pretty nose was short, slightly aquiline, and her lips were full. When she smiled, which was practically all of the time, she had a dimple in one cheek. Years later when I saw her after I was grown I was surprised to find that she was a small woman—five feet two or three.

When she came in that day the two Levitsky boys and I were sitting on the floor of the Levitsky parlor having a tourney. Our knights were spread around us.

She sat down on the floor with us.

"What are these? Knights? How do you play the game?"

Hal showed her. She picked up a knight, examined it.

"Say, this is cute," she said. "Whose idea was this?" She turned to me. "You're clever," she said. "You have imagination. Are you going to let me play?"

After we had played with the cardboard knights for a while she took the three of us down to Laird & Dines' drug store and bought four ice-cream cones. We licked them joyfully as we went back to the Levitsky house. "Aunt Minna will be sore about these cones," she said happily, "but I don't give a darn. She says eating before a meal destroys your appetite. Look at her! She eats all the time and she has an appetite like an alligator."

I was going to the training school at the normal where my mother was a critic-teacher. That was the fall of 1912. I often saw Anna on the campus. She always waved to me. Sometimes she'd catch up with me and we'd walk together.

Anna was much like her brother, the dead Ike. She always walked fast. She was quick, and had great muscular coordination. The normal-school girls had to take exercises in classes held in the basement of the gymnasium. The uniform was a white middy blouse, baggy black bloomers, and black stockings. I used to sit in the window after school with other sixth-graders and watch the girls march to the music of a phonograph, twirling their dumb-bells. When Anna caught sight of me she always smiled and waved. She wore silk stockings and I could tell she had the most beautiful legs and the nicest figure in the gym class.

She was good at basketball. The games were played outdoors, and I used to go over to watch and cheer. Baseball was the favorite game of sixth-, seventh-, and eighth-graders, and every day after school most of the vacant lots in town would be filled with baseball players. Now and then Anna would come by and join in the game. She could field the ball better, hit it harder, run bases faster than the biggest boys—even those who were fourteen and fifteen years old.

Any girl as pretty and as lively as my beautiful Anna was bound to have boy friends. Presently I began to see her walking slowly home from the normal with various gangly boys. I loathed every one of them.

One Saturday along in December I was playing at the Levitsky house when I went charging through the unlocked door into the bathroom. The little room was warm and steamy and my beautiful Anna was standing in the tub drying her rosy body with a white towel. Her wavy blond hair was piled on top of her head. She looked very young and very beautiful.

She gave me a startled look.

"Damn you," she said. "Knock before you come in here!"

She must have seen the tears in my eyes as I retreated. A moment later she came into the living room barefoot and wearing a kimono.

She held me briefly in her arms and kissed me on the forehead. "Honey," she said, "I'm sorry I yelled at you. I know you didn't mean anything." She smelled warm and soapy and sweet. I loved her more than ever.

Sometime after Christmas a young man in a red automobile started bringing Anna back to the Levitsky house. Often they sat in front of the house and talked long and in low tones.

Hal and Ike told me he was a rich boy from the East who had been going to college back there. The year before he had been very ill with pneumonia and his parents had sent him out to stay with relatives in the dry mild climate of Phoenix so he wouldn't get "lung trouble." He had decided to take a few courses at the normal, just to have something to do, and every day he drove over. I imagine his car was a Stutz Bear Cat, but I would not swear to it. It had two bucket seats and no side doors. It had a round gasoline tank behind the seats and three or four spare tires. When the boy who owned it opened the muffler the car made a fearful racket and Hal told me that Anna had said that the car had hit seventy on a straight stretch on the way to Mesa. Hal also reported that she had said that the wind was so strong she could hardly get her breath.

I loathed that young man who owned the red car. I imagined myself rescuing Anna from him. He'd be trying to do something dreadful to her and I would come riding swiftly up on my bicycle.

"Let that pure young lady alone, you beast!" When I had rescued her, that beast, in my fantasy, always slunk off and Anna embraced me, smelling warm and sweet and soapy the way she had that day after I had blundered into the bathroom.

But in reality it looked as if Anna didn't want to be rescued. I noticed that the red car did not stop in front of the Levitsky house and the boys told me that Anna had had a terrible quarrel with her father. He had forbidden her to go out with the red-car boy any more. But I would see her out riding with him anyway. Once I saw them in the car on an isolated spot on the campus *kissing.* I sneaked away and tried to pretend I hadn't really witnessed the disgusting sight.

Anna seemed distracted. Two or three times she passed me up at the normal and didn't see me. I discovered that the boy with the red car would take her within a couple of blocks of her house and then drop her off. It seemed pretty sneaky to me.

I was still pretty mad at Anna the night of Hal's birthday party. It was along in the spring sometime because I remember that the orange trees in my grandfather's yard were in bloom then and I still remember the cloying, heavy smell, sweet and sensual.

There were probably twenty-five children at Hal's party. Hal was twelve, not quite a year older than I was. I had been eleven the previous January. It was a fine party. The guests were about evenly divided between boys and girls. Since a few of them were thirteen and fourteen some of the girls had begun to swell in interesting places and some of the boys were sort of getting ideas. We played Run Sheep Run, Hide and Go Seek, and Farmer in the Dell.

For a while old Isadore sat around and beamed at us, but presently he went to bed. Aunt Minna fed us after Hal had blown out the candles on his birthday cake—huge mounds of rich homemade ice cream and big hunks of cake. Mrs. Goldstein just sat around looking beautiful and mysterious.

Then, as usually happened at parties about that time, someone suggested we play Post Office. There was a closet off the little front hall which served as the post office. A stamp was exactly what it said—a stamp on the foot, and this is what the virtuous and modest girls always sent word out that they had for the boys. A letter was a kiss, and a package was a hug. The bolder boys would say they had a package and a couple of letters for a certain girl. Then giggling and blushing the girl would go in. Then the boy would come out, smugly wiping his lips and the girl would ask for some other boy.

I had been in a couple of times. Both times the girls said they had stamps for me—and that is just what they had. One hefty lass delivered such a stamp that she almost broke my instep. I tried to give a letter to one shy girl. She ducked and all I got was a taste of her hair.

The time went on. Some of the guests were getting bolder. Then the front door opened and the beautiful Anna, glowing and lovely, came in from a date.

"Anna's gotta play Post Office. Anna's gotta play Post Office!" a couple of the older boys yelled.

In a moment one of the boys said he had a package and a letter for Anna Levitsky. Anna disappeared into the closet, and the boy came out looking important. I hated him!

Then my heart almost stopped beating. The postmistress passed the word that Anna had a package and a letter for Jack O'Connor.

With my heart pounding I went in. Anna was wearing perfume and she smelled very sweet there in the darkness. She put her arms around me and kissed me on the lips. We weren't lip kissers around the Woolf menage; as far as I can remember this was the first time anyone had ever kissed me on the mouth. I haven't forgotten yet how warm and sweet and soft her lips were.

"You're a sweet, funny kid!" she said.

"I love you, Anna," I whispered.

I didn't know it then but she was telling me goodbye. She left the closet and the postmistress had to ask me twice who I had mail for. I asked for the girl who had darn near broken my instep. I thought I'd really give her a stamp she'd never forget, but I chickened out and gave her a little hug instead. I thought she was kind of cute anyway but I didn't love her like I loved Anna.

The next afternoon I didn't have anything to do. It was Saturday and there was no school. I went over to the Levitsky house to see if I could work up a baseball game. As I walked up on the porch, I heard a terrible wailing. It puzzled and frightened me.

I was about to sneak off when the door opened and Hal came out. "I saw you from the window," he said.

"What's the matter? Who's that crying?" I asked.

"Grandfather," he said. Then he started to weep. "It's about Anna. She got up early and left the house. A little while ago Grandfather got a telegram. She had married that goy with the red car and had already left on the train."

Old Isadore Levitsky had been through enough trouble to unhinge a dozen people, but Anna's running away and getting married just about finished him. He got a coffin, had the rabbi in Phoenix go through with funeral services for Anna. Then he had the empty coffin buried. Hal and Ike told me he never mentioned Anna again.

I didn't see the two Levitsky boys so often after that. I spent the summer of 1913 with my Uncle Jim O'Connor's in Florence, and the next fall when I was in seventh grade all of us thought the game of Knights was sort of childish and silly.

Over the course of the years I heard that Anna was living in New York and that she had two children. Old Isadore Levitsky died eventually. He left a few thousand dollars to his children and grandchildren—how he managed it I do not know, as his store certainly never looked like a very profitable operation. Aunt Minna had a stroke and died within a couple of weeks of old Isadore's death. The Goldsteins moved to Phoenix, where Abe got a job selling automobiles. Joe Goldstein went to dental college and eventually became an orthodontist.

Tempe got poorer and poorer as a business town, and after Isadore died his store stood vacant for years. Moe lived much longer, but on one occasion when I hadn't been to Tempe for some time I drove down Eighth Street and saw that his store was vacant and boarded up.

I ONLY SAW ANNA once after that night when we played Post Office at the birthday party. This was in June 1923, just after I had graduated from the two-year course at the normal. Another guy and I had stagged it to an alfresco dance place on the north edge of Phoenix called the Arbor. It was way out at the end of Central Avenue beside a canal and on the edge of the desert.

When this guy I went with and I got there I saw Hal Levitsky sitting in a booth beside the dance floor. His date had her back to me. I could see she was a blonde with long hair. Hal waved and motioned for me to come over. My heart skipped a couple of beats when I realized his date was Anna. I would have known her anywhere. She hadn't changed much. Her hair had a little less gold in it than I had remembered. Her face seemed a little thinner and her blue eyes seemed larger and darker. Perhaps that was because she was using mascara and eye shadow. It was as if she had spent the ten years since I had seen her last slowly growing more beautiful. Because I was a kid when I had seen her last I was surprised that she was so small—a couple of inches over five feet, maybe.

She wore her blond hair over her ears and in a big bun at the nape of her neck. A beautiful woman with classic features and a good figure always looks best in simple clothes without a lot of frills to get in the way and spoil the effect. I can't remember much about how Anna was dressed that night except that she was wearing a simple summer dress of some soft, light-blue material. The skirt was short, just below her knees, and her legs were lovely.

I guess Hal didn't see much percentage in dancing with his aunt even if she was a great beauty. As soon as Anna and I started talking he excused himself and spent the rest of the evening dancing and drinking Coke and bootleg Mexican whiskey with a pal of his named Joe Grunion and his date.

That was all right with me, because Anna was a gorgeous woman and a wonderful dancer. Hal had a bottle of Mexican tequila called José Cuervo, which means Joe Crow in Spanish, under his seat. Anna and I made lemonades with charged water, quartered lemons, and sugar. Then we put our glasses down out of sight and dumped some tequila in. As I remember, it was a pretty good drink.

Anna told me that she had been in Santa Barbara, where her parents-in-law now spent most of their time. She said she had left her two children with them to spend most of the summer. Now she was on her way back to New York, she said, but she thought she would stop off in Phoenix to see her relatives.

We danced just about every dance. Along about midnight Hal came over and told us that he was going to have to take Joe Grunion and his date home because old Joe was really boiled and his date was afraid to ride with him. He gave me the keys to his car and asked me if I minded taking Anna back to the hotel where she was staying.

I told Anna that I was still in love with her. She laughed, reached across the table and squeezed my hand.

"Better stop!" she said. "You make me feel about nineteen again!" Then she went on: "You were a funny little kid. I always thought you had a gleam in your eye that didn't belong in the eye of a ten-year-old."

"Eleven!" I said.

"Was that time you burst into the bathroom and caught me without a stitch on deliberate or accidental?"

"Accidental, but only because I didn't have the guts to do it deliberately. I used to dream of peeking in your window to watch you undress!"

Anna giggled. "You probably would have missed me and seen Aunt Minna," she said. "Boy, would you have got your money's worth!"

NOT LONG BEFORE I had collected fifty dollars from an engraving company for laying out a brochure and writing the copy and captions for a dude ranch. I had some money with me, so I took Anna to the American Kitchen, a Chinese all-night restaurant on Central Avenue in Phoenix. I could only remember Anna and a waiter, but in the next week about a dozen people I knew asked me where I found that beautiful broad I had in there that morning and who in the hell was she.

I never saw Anna again and heard from her directly only once. In 1930, when my first book came out, she wrote me a little note in care of my publisher. Once when I ran into Hal in a clothing store in Phoenix he told me that she'd had another child a couple of years after I had seen her last. Now and then I used to see her picture in the society section of *The New York Times.* I noted that she was an Episcopalian. Even in newspaper halftones she was a knockout.

# 14 · Me and the Movies

I CANNOT remember what year it was when I saw my first motion picture, but I do know that it was at the Goodwin Opera House in Tempe. I must have been around seven or eight. This, I admit, is an advanced age for one to start a career as a movie fan, but in those days my mother was having a hard time and she felt she could budget very little for recreation. On Sunday afternoons about that time she used to take my sister and me down to Laird & Dines' drug store, where she bought us each an ice-cream soda (ten cents). She never had one herself, as she felt she could not afford it. Helen always ordered strawberry and I pineapple. This was recreation. Movies were out of the question.

How I managed to get to my first movie I cannot say. I had heard of such things and was intensely curious. The Opera House had, I believe, originally been a store building. The rear was not raised and everyone sat on collapsible chairs. I remember that when the operator of the motion-picture machine was tuning up his projector and was focusing a clear white light on the screen, some latecomers walked in. I could see their silhouettes sharp and black against the screen and thought that was the motion-picture show. I was prepared to enjoy it. When my first movie came on it was a western full of gunplay, handsome horses, chases, and cowboys and Indians.

The Goodwin Opera House was owned by Billy Goodwin, the father of my friend Gordon. Billy also owned an open-air theater called the Airdome across the street. This was used in the hot summer months. The Opera House and the Airdome were operated as family enterprises. Just before curtain time Gordon and his father used to drive their Model T Ford through the streets of Tempe shouting through a megaphone: "Show tonight at the Goodwin Opera House. Pearl White in *The Perils of Pauline.* See what happens next!" Mr. Goodwin generally operated the projector. Mrs. Goodwin sat at the piano looking up at the screen and playing suitable music—soft, tender stuff during romantic scenes, thunderous stuff with a lot of bass chords when there were fights and chases. Gordon often sold or took tickets. Because Gordon and I were pals, I could usually get in free.

Like most pre-World War I children I became an ardent fan of Pearl White, the heroine of *The Perils of Pauline,* the first smash-hit serial. I suspect la belle White was a natural brunette because the movies showed blond hair but large dark eyes. Poor Pearl had a hell of a time. Every episode ended with the villains about to do away with her at last. She would be gagged and bound to a railroad track and a train would be rushing toward her or she could be hanging by her fingernails to a ledge and about to drop ten or fifteen stories to the street. For some time I was really hooked. I would worry for a week about the poor girl's predicament and then when Saturday night came I would rush down to the theater to see how she escaped.

But no matter how desperate her situation looked at the end of one episode, Pearl always got out of it quickly at the beginning of the next and then immediately got herself into another pickle. Finally I decided that I was worrying unduly from week to week and that the producers of *The Perils of Pauline* were not about to end a good thing by bumping old Pearl off.

I laughed at the Charlie Chaplin one-reelers, mooned over the love life of Francis X. Bushman and Beverly Baine, longed to have the horse-faced, slit-eyed look of William S. Hart, the first great western star. Perhaps the world is too sophisticated today for comedies like the Mack Sennett two-reelers with the custard pies, the chases by low-comedy cops, the pratfalls, and the beautiful and well-stacked bathing beauties like Marie Prevost and Phyllis Haver, but I remember them as a riot.

I suppose, in these days of air-conditioned homes, stores, and automobiles, that southern Arizona summers are more bearable than they used to be, but when I was a boy in the Salt River valley I always hated the summer heat—a thick, heavy, all-enveloping heat that smothered me like a blanket. There were two schools of thought about the heat. One was that it was bad for white men and if they didn't get out for a time each summer they would wither up and die. The other was that the copious sweating the heat brought about was good for people and flushed the poisons out of their systems.

The Woolfs and the O'Connors all felt that in spite of its advantages southern Arizona was not really a white man's country in the summer and that some respite was necessary, particularly for the aged, the young, and the tender. My Uncle Jim O'Connor owned a summer cottage at Venice, California, and my Grandfather Woolf owned one at a resort called Iron Springs near Prescott, Arizona, at an altitude of about 6,000 feet. At either place it was delightfully cool, and at Iron Springs during summer thunder showers it was almost cold.

My mother, my sister Helen, and I spent parts of several summers with the Woolfs at Iron Springs and the Jim O'Connors at Venice, and it was near Venice that I had my first contact with movie-making. Venice had been developed as a summer resort, and as a gimmick the promoters had built some concrete-lined canals filled with seawater so the place would live up to its name. I once saw some of the original promotional brochures for the place and the canals were supposed to be filled with gondolas complete with handsome gondoliers who yodeled happily, or did whatever gondoliers are supposed to do. But as I remember pre-World War I Venice the canals were unused, grown with aquatic weeds, and interesting-looking little crabs scurried around the edges.

There was an amusement pier at Venice and one a mile or so

beyond at Ocean Park. Both piers had roller coasters, various slides, games, shooting galleries, and establishments where one could purchase cotton candy, Coney Island red hots (five cents), and delicious hamburgers (ten cents). At the end of the Venice pier was a building constructed as a replica of a ship (a Spanish galleon, as I remember it). The place was known as the Ship Café and it was supposed to have been a very good restaurant before prohibition. Since the food was good and the restaurant was expensive many movie actors were supposed to patronize the place. I once gaped through a window there and saw Mary Pickford—or at least someone the other children said was Mary Pickford—eating lunch.

Down the beach the houses began to thin out until one came to a cluster of cottages, a pier, and a few stores called Redondo. Beyond that was El Segundo, where at that time the sewage from Los Angeles was dumped into the Pacific Ocean. This was a region of bare sand dunes with a little sparse vegetation growing on them. How far this was from my Uncle Jim O'Connor's cottage at Venice I do not know, but it could not have been more than three or four miles. As you shall see, I used to walk there and back every day.

At any rate, the word got around somehow that a movie was being made in the sand dunes near El Segundo. My cousin Wallace O'Connor, who became one of the world's great swimmers and water-polo players but who is now dead, and a couple of other youngsters went along with me. The business fascinated me. The people were manufacturing various episodes in a serial. The star was Ruth Roland, who had succeeded Pearl White as the No. 1 serial queen. The man who was evidently cast as the heavy was a tough-looking character of about thirty-five named Eddie Polo. The young lady who if not the villainess was at least not all that she should be was a pretty but hard-faced blonde.

Apparently the serial was supposed to take place in cattle country, as the actors dressed like cowboys, rode horses, and carried six-shooters. There were two corrals, one for the horses, and one for the prop cattle that the actors chased around from time to time. Near them was a pile of baled alfalfa hay. This was a necessity, as in these barren dunes a kangaroo rat would have starved to death.

The making of most movies in those days must have been quite inexpensive compared to the staggering budgets today. As I remember it there were never more than thirty people, counting cameramen, actors, extras, prop men, and watchmen on the set. Such sets as they had were cheap and flimsy, false fronts of houses and stores propped up in the sand by two-by-fours. A villain being shot off the top of a sand dune was simply a dummy filled with straw and pushed over by a prop man.

Several tents (rather large as I remember them) had been erected to serve as dressing rooms. As the star, Ruth Roland had one to herself. The tough blonde and another girl had a second. Eddie Polo had one by himself and the other male actors all crowded into another.

That first day the four of us stared at everything with the unabashed curiosity of children. When noon came a batch of cardboard lunch boxes were distributed and everybody ate. The sight of all those moving jaws activated our own salivary glands. We thought of delicious hot dogs and hamburgers and left to see if we could find some provider at Redondo.

The next day only Wallace and I showed up. When noon came I was sitting in the sand watching Ruth Roland daintily eating a sandwich.

Presently she became aware of my presence.

"Hey, towhead," she said. "Are you hungry?"

"Yes ma'am," I said.

"Want a sandwich?" she asked.

"If you don't want it," I answered politely.

She handed me a banana and a ham sandwich wrapped in wax paper. Then she turned to Eddie Polo. "Eddie, give the other kid some of your lunch. You're too damned fat anyway." Eddie handed Wallace a sandwich.

"Towhead," Miss Roland said to me, "what's your name?"

"Jack," I said.

"Jack, do you think I am beautiful?"

"Yes ma'am."

"Do you love me?"

"Yes ma'am." (Rather doubtfully.)

"You're cute," she said. "Come here and give me a kiss!"

She gave me a hug and planted a kiss on my cheek. When I got back to the summer cottage in Venice my mother saw the famous Roland mouth reproduced in lipstick on my cheek.

From then on until we went back to Arizona I was a fairly useful member of the company. I carried Miss Roland's makeup kit so she could repair her face between takes. I held horses for the cowboys. I caught cows and led them back to the corral. I ran errands, relayed messages, worshipped Miss Roland. She saw that a catered lunch was brought from Los Angeles for me every day and the two of us always ate lunch together. When I told Ruth Roland that I was leaving the next day for Arizona, she kissed me and told me she wanted me to come back and marry her when I grew up.

Many years later I was in the office of a Hollywood agent talking about a possible job in the movies when the agent's secretary told him that Miss Roland was on the phone. I sat there while he talked: "Yes, Miss Roland, no, Miss Roland, of course, Miss Roland."

I interrupted him. "Are you talking to Ruth Roland?" He nodded. "Let me talk to her when you get through," I said. "Tell her it's an old friend."

"Guy here in my office wants to talk to you. Says he's an old friend. Looks harmless. Shall I put him on?"

He handed me the phone.

"Miss Roland," I began. "I used to be in love with you."

"Who are you?" she asked. "A lot of people have been in love with me!"

"Do you remember a towheaded kid that hung around you and ran errands for you years ago when you and Eddie Polo were making a serial down in the sand dunes near El Segundo?"

"For Christ's sake," Miss Roland said. "Sure I remember. Wait a minute . . . you're Jack. I haven't thought of you for years—a real nosy towheaded kid with green eyes and a hell of a tan. What ever happened to you?"

"Oh, the usual thing," I said. "I went to college, got married. I've done some writing."

"If you're not doing anything right now, why don't you run out and see me?" she said. "I'd sort of like to see what you look like!" She gave me her address.

Unlike a great many of the early movie stars Ruth Roland had hung onto her money and she lived in considerable elegance. She had invested widely in southern California real estate and was a very rich woman. At that time she was still a good-looking woman, I guessed not far from sixty. She was worth many millions when she died.

We had a couple of drinks. She expressed great amazement at how I had grown, asked me what sort of life I'd had and what I planned to do with the rest of it. I told her I was damned if I knew. She said that was the spirit. About all you could do in this world was to watch and see what they threw at you and then duck.

Actually we didn't have much to talk about, as we soon exhausted the subject of making serials on the sand dunes near El Segundo with Eddie Polo, and what a nosy little guy I had been—nosy but sweet. We talked a little about the cheap little broads you see in pictures these days, had another drink. Then I left.

BACK IN THE DAYS BEFORE World War I the making of motion pictures appeared to be very casual. A great many scenes were shot outdoors using the public streets and parks for sets. By 1915 most of the citizens of Los Angeles and Hollywood were pretty blasé about movies and movie actors.

Famous actors had not retreated behind the walls of big houses then. I have seen well-known movie actors lined up in rocking chairs on the porch of the old Hollywood Hotel and such stars as Norma and Constance Talmadge dancing at the Alexandria.

I must have been about thirteen and a student in the academic department (high school) of the Tempe Normal when I was an extra in a movie called *The Yaqui.* It starred Hobart Bosworth, a painter turned actor, who had spent a couple of years painting in the Salt River valley, and who had broken bread at my grandfather's house.

The director hired as extras the entire cadet company at the normal because they had uniforms identical to those worn by the United States Army. In my big dramatic scene, I (along with the

other members of the cadet company) was supposed to be guarding the border against an invastion of Mexican bandits or something. I assumed a very dramatic stance and a determined, jut-jawed look, knowing that millions would see my handsome face and manly figure. Outside camera range a couple of stooges ran up and down waving smoke sticks. This was supposed to be the smoke of battle drifting over from Mexico. The Mexicans and all other armies were using smokeless powder in small-arms ammunition then and it gave off very little smoke, but such technicalities didn't bother Hollywood in those days. I waited for months (and so did practically everyone in Tempe) for *The Yaqui* to show up at the Goodwin Opera House. I was bitterly disappointed. Those damned stooges with the smoke sticks had laid the smoke so well that I had been completely smoked out of a movie career. However, I got a catered box lunch and three dollars.

As a youth I used to be in Los Angeles now and then and I always had my ears open for news of mob scenes being shot. My recollections may be wrong but as I remember it ordinary extras who appeared in their own clothes and simply milled about got five dollars a day. If they put on any sort of costume from a dinner jacket to a suit of armor they got seven-fifty, and if they got into a scene as an individual (approached one of the stars, let us say, and appeared to say something) they got twenty-five dollars. I was an extra in several movies in Hollywood and in Culver City. I was part of a fight audience in a picture starring Jack Dempsey, and I wore a suit of armor when I was supposed to be a Roman legionary. Another time I wore a sarape, a straw hat, and some dark makeup and was a Mexican. It was fun and during my acting career I got a lot of excellent telephone numbers.

I also had the opportunity to look over some of the reigning movie queens. Most of them appeared to be prettier on the screen than they were in the flesh. Most of them were smaller than they appeared to be in pictures, and I always felt that it would not be difficult to find any number of girls prettier than most Hollywood stars on any college campus. I also thought that many of the girls who never made it in Hollywood, girls who were extras or who played bit parts, were far prettier than most of the stars. But the stars had something these girls didn't have—that mysterious quality of being able to light up before a camera.

The two-reel comedies of Charlie Chaplin were a tremendous

hit in those innocent days before World War I, when a Chaplin rage swept the United States. It was comparable to the Beatles rage of the mid-1960's. Movie theaters, dance halls, schools all held Charlie Chaplin contests and awarded prizes. There were Chaplin imitators four years old and Chaplin imitators fifty years old, all complete with derby, baggy pants, tight coat, oversize shoes, and cane. I thought Chaplin funny but not that funny and being up to my fundament in Charlie Chaplin imitators bored the hell out of me.

We had to go to Phoenix to see *The Birth of a Nation,* but *Intolerance,* also made by D. W. Griffith, came to the Goodwin Opera House in Tempe. I was quite taken by Constance Talmadge, who had a role in it, and sent in twenty-five cents (coin, not stamps) for an autographed picture. I also got a Personal Letter from Miss Talmadge. It began "Dear Fan."

I had a tender spot in my heart for a pretty movie actress about my age. She was often called Hollywood's Youngest Star. She played sweet roles, wore her blond hair in curls *à la* Mary Pickford, and to look at her you'd think butter wouldn't melt in her mouth. I'll never forget how shocked I was when she got her demure little self involved in a juicy Hollywood scandal. It seems that along with several other well-known actresses she was playing footsie with a Hollywood director who was old enough to be her father and who was a famed roué. Anyway, someone bumped the guy off (a fate he richly deserved, I must say). It turned out that the director had the gals coming and going in and out of his snuggery in shifts and that he maintained what can only be described as a seraglio. Reading about all this hanky-panky and knowing that my dream girl was mixed up in it was an exceedingly traumatic experience for me. I don't think I have ever quite recovered. If I am a cynic in my sunset years it is largely the fault of that beautiful young lady with golden curls and round blue eyes!

# 15 · The Happy Summertime

WHEN I was growing up in Tempe before World War I it was generally believed that any boy with the right stuff in him would go out and get a job. This was supposed to lighten the burden on his parents, to enable him to earn enough money for clothes to start school in the next fall and lay aside some spending money, to stiffen his backbone, and also to show him that the best things of life weren't free.

What with paying for a house, supporting herself and two children, and in addition trying to put away enough to go to summer school and work toward her degree, and to pay premiums on a life insurance policy, my mother had no easy time. She felt that I ought to get summer jobs and even jobs after school. Furthermore, some of her relatives were always asking her (in my presence) why that big lummox Jack didn't go out and get a job and help support himself. My Grandmother Woolf was always insisting that great big slob ought to find something to do instead of mooning around all the time with a book or running around wasting his time and getting into mischief with Billy Goodwin's boy.

My Aunt Ruby, Charles Woolf's wife, told my mother (also in my presence) that the big worthless boy that eats like two men should be made to go out and get a job. Later she told my mother that in her circumstances she was foolish to think of attempting to send me to college, that the thing to do was to kick me out and make me go to work and earn my own keep. She also added that hard work was a great builder of character. I felt she was undoubtedly right, but if her son Harold (who was and is a nice guy) ever had a summer job I never heard of it. Instead she and Charles thought the best was none too good for their own children. Both went to Tempe High School, but Harold went on to Stanford and Harvard Business School, and Dorothy, his sister, went to exclusive (and expensive) Mills College at Oakland, California. When I came back to Tempe in 1921 my mind was made up to go to the normal for a couple of years and then go on to some university. I was in the bedroom one day when Aunt Ruby was calling on Mother.

"I hope you're not planning to keep that big worthless lout up while he goes to the normal!" Ruby said. "A poor grass widow like you shouldn't think of letting him go on to school. If I were you I'd simply turn him out and let him shift for himself!"

I did not see my mother, of course, but I can well imagine that her blue eyes blazed. "Ruby," she said. "I'm sick of this. You're talking about my life, my money, and my son. What I do with any of these things is my business, not yours. I notice you and Charles are planning to send Harold to college. I think Jack's a smart boy and worthy of an education. I'll do what I can for him!"

As far as I know my Aunt Ruby never mentioned the subject again, but the result of her sniping at me and my grandmother's constant nagging left me with a sneaking notion that I was probably a lazy and worthless oaf. I still think they were at least half right.

Jobs of any kind were not easy to get in Tempe, particularly for young boys with no skills. There were only two large employers of labor in or around Tempe. One was the normal and the other was the creamery, which was about a mile from town. Occasionally a job opened up with one of the merchants, and farmers hired help to harvest various crops, but for the most part there was very little I could find to turn my hand to.

The first job I ever had was cleaning bricks. I must have been about nine or ten. A portion of the training school at the normal was to be torn down and the bricks were to be cleaned and used in another structure. Several small boys were hired to clean the bricks as they were loosened from the walls and sent sliding down V-shaped chutes. There was a chute for each small boy. The boss of the brick-cleaning operation gave us each a trowel, picked up a brick, and showed us how to knock the mortar off. When he had demonstrated with several bricks he told us we were on our own. We were to be paid so much for each one hundred bricks we cleaned. The bricks came tumbling down the chutes. We all fell to whacking away at the bricks with our trowels.

As I whacked I began to notice what happened when the bricks shot down the chute. If they came all the way to the bottom and struck a brick that remained at the bottom of the chute, they were pretty certain to break corners off. That would not do. I let several bricks stay in the chute thinking that if they were stopped sooner and before they had got up full velocity the bricks might not break as they came down. They didn't. I noticed also that when they came just the right distance they not only did not break but the impact of one brick's striking another often knocked all the mortar off, always knocked most of it off and loosened the rest.

I was very proud of my discovery. As the bricks came down I would pick them up, knock off loose mortar, and put them on my neat stack of cleaned bricks. My pile was growing about three times as fast as that of any other boy. The others either let the bricks tumble out the end of the chute onto the ground or stopped them by letting them hit one brick. In one case the mortar all remained and it took considerable work to knock it off. In the other the brick was generally broken. As the workmen who were loosening the bricks saw my stock of cleaned bricks grow they sent more down my chute.

Whoever was in charge of the brick-cleaning operation went away to supervise something else. Noon came. I ate the two sandwiches my mother had put up for me, had a drink of water at a fountain, and rested in the shade until the workmen who were dismantling the building finished their nooning and went to work again. They complimented me on my big stack of bricks.

As the hours went on my stack grew and grew and I happily contemplated the money I had coming to me. But along about four o'clock the foreman came back. He went around the other stacks, picked up some of the bricks, looked at them. Then he came and stood beside me to watch me work.

Presently he punched me on the shoulder and yelled: "Hey, you, what in the hell do you think you're doing?"

"Cleaning bricks," I said, startled.

"Goddammit," he said, "I hired you to clean bricks with a trowel and not pull any of that fancy stuff. For Christ's sake, them bricks is three-fourths clean when you pick them up."

"I don't think it makes any difference how I clean bricks just so I clean them!" I said.

"For Christ's sake," he said, "you let them bricks roll out on the ground like the others are doing. I hired you to *clean* bricks and not to pull that crap!"

Furious, I let the bricks bounce out on the ground. At five o'clock, when quitting time came, I was fired.

"Twelve bucks!" the boss said. "This sneaky little devil's cleaned twelve bucks' worth of bricks. What do you think of that? Hell, that's twice what I make!"

Outraged and weeping, I went home. The next Saturday I collected my twelve dollars from Linsey Austin, the superintendent of grounds. I had learned something about human nature, but exactly what it was I did not know at the time.

AT VARIOUS TIMES I ALSO WORKED at the creamery. The firm manufactured ice, which it sold at a dock at the plant and which it also sold through town by means of an ice wagon drawn by two horses. The creamery bought milk from farmers and then boiled it down, put it in cans, pasted various labels on them, and shipped them out. The creamery's own brand name was Lily, and the label showed a graceful and virginally white lily. But cans filled with milk from the same batch were also pasted with a half dozen other labels. Since being an employee of Lily I have always been a bit skeptical about brand names on canned food generally and on canned milk especially.

On various occasions I worked at the creamery, usually when the firm was hard put for labor and was scraping the bottom of the barrel. I think I got ten cents an hour for a ten-hour day the first time I worked there, fifteen cents an hour the last time. In those days the gang bosses got twenty and twenty-two cents an hour. The moron I had known in fourth grade and who had chased me home a couple of times before I worked him over with a baseball bat was the boss of a gang there. He told me he was getting twenty-two cents an hour—$2.20 for a ten-hour day, $13.20 for a six-day week. This was less than sixty dollars a month, and at that time he was supporting a wife and five children. He was half-soling his shoes with old automobile casings. In his dim anthropoid way he was worried about his future—or lack of it, and he had long since forgiven me for trying to fracture his skull with the bat.

I remember wheeling cartons of tinned milk to freight cars. Possibly that's the only sort of job I ever held at the creamery. I remember the cloying, nauseating smell of boiling milk over everything. I can still almost feel the moist, clinging, stinking air. I loathed the creamery, the people I worked with, the bosses, the exhausting, tiresome, degrading work I did. We went to work at seven thirty, got off at five thirty, were allowed to stop work for a few minutes to gobble lunch. Since I had to punch the time clock at seven thirty I had to get up at six in order to dress, eat my breakfast, and walk the mile to the creamery. When the shift was over I was always exhausted—from the heat, from the degradation, from the stench, from boredom. In hot southern Arizona it did not really cool off until about two o'clock in the morning. When the alarm awakened me at six I was deep in a sleep of exhaustion. I'll never forget those endless days of trundling a hand truck loaded with cartons of milk. I had an Ingersoll watch held by a string and tucked in a little pocket on the bib of my overalls. I used to look at it every few minutes. The hands moved so slowly that I used to wonder if the damned thing was working.

The creamery continued to operate week after week, year after year. For all I know it is still there, still stinking, still hiring teen-age boys to push hand trucks loaded with milk cartons. I never worked at the creamery unless I was broke and unless I couldn't possibly get another job.

Who owned the creamery I have no idea. Nor do I know whether it was profitable or not. Undoubtedly whoever ran it had a board of directors on his neck and if he exploited morons and teen-agers he was probably himself exploited. He probably didn't make much money. The father of a friend of mine was a chemist there and the combination of his small salary and the laziness of his slattern wife made the family live very poorly indeed. I was asked to stay for dinner one night. All they had was eggs fried in lard and watermelon.

But my labors at the creamery did give me some understanding of the poor helpless people who spend their lives in jobs like that. It also taught me that hard physical labor was not for me.

I could generally get a summer job when I needed it at the normal. Linsey Austin, the superintendent of grounds, was the father of two friends of mine, Harold and Cedric, and an uncle on his mother's side of Gordon Goodwin. At the normal I would chop weeds at twenty-five cents an hour—two dollars for an eight-hour day. Weed chopping bored the very hell out of me, but it was far easier work than pushing hand trucks at the creamery, and I could walk to work in five minutes or so and go home for lunch. Later in the summer, just before the normal opened in September, I could usually get a job washing windows.

I have mentioned in an earlier chapter that one summer I hauled sand from the river bed to a construction job for about a month. Every morning at seven thirty I got to the stable, where I hitched up my team. Then I drove down to the river and laboriously shoveled a load of sand into the wagon. Then beating the horses mightily, I got them to pull the heavy wagon out of the soft sand onto harder ground. It was at least a mile from the river bed to the construction site. When I got there I unloaded the sand by working loose one board in the wagon bed. The sand then started to run out. Then I'd get another board loose and turn it on its side. When all the sand had run out, I would get in the wagon, bat the horses, and head for the river again.

I didn't mind the job. Shoveling heavy sand was hard work, but I did it down by the river, where the water and the willows smelled fresh and cool. Driving to the construction site and back, I had plenty of time to think and to dream. It was hot, but out in the open air there was almost always some movement of the dry air to evaporate the sweat and keep things bearable.

It generally took me about a half hour to harness my team to the wagon, another half hour to drive down to the river, and probably another thirty minutes to fill the wagon bed with sand. I would guess it took me around thirty minutes to drive the horses each way. At noon I unhitched the horses, took them down to the river for water. I then ate a couple of sandwiches, took a drink from my canteen. After I had lain in the shade for a few minutes I filled up the wagon with sand, hitched up the horses, and drove again to the construction site. Once there, I always paused to have a drink of ice water which the contractor furnished for his workmen. I tried to be back at the stables at five o'clock so I could unhitch my team, put them in their stalls, fork down a feed of alfalfa hay for them, examine their backs to see if they had any harness sores, and give them a fast going-over with the curry comb.

My working hours were from seven thirty to five thirty. I seldom got home before six fifteen. I would fill the tub with cold water, then lie in it and read the Phoenix *Gazette.* If Mother was away going to summer school in pursuit of a degree, I "batched." This meant that when the alarm went off at six o'clock in the morning, I got up, fried myself a couple of pieces of bacon and one egg, ate this with a couple of pieces of toast (one with jam), drank a glass of milk, and headed for the stable. My lunch was always two cheese sandwiches and an apple. For dinner I sometimes cooked myself a hamburger and opened a can of green beans, but that was a lot of trouble and to avoid it I usually walked downtown and ate at Joe Holland's restaurant. Joe was half Chinese and looked all Chinese. He was a fine cook but he had little business, as the citizens of Tempe had neither the time, the money, nor the inclination to eat out. My usual dinner was a rib steak, a boiled potato, a salad of sliced tomatoes, cucumbers, and onions, a piece of apple pie, and a glass of milk. That cost twenty-five cents. For those who had to count their pennies, Joe had what he called his "Working Man's Special"—a big plate of beef stew (slumgullion), all the bread and butter anyone could eat, a piece of apple pie, and all the coffee the diner could drink. The price? Fifteen cents.

Many Chinese seem to have rather high-pitched voices, but Joe had a marvelously deep, rich bass voice. He was an opera nut and had in his living quarters behind the restaurant an Edison phonograph with a wooden horn, which he claimed gave much better reproduction than a metal horn or a phonograph of the new hornless variety. He had a large supply of records and he knew by heart the bass parts of most of them. He was particularly fond of Caruso, who was then a great star. He was a lonely man and sometimes when I was the only customer in the restaurant I would go back to his living quarters with him and listen to him sing along with Caruso.

Joe's father had been English, his mother Chinese. He was born in Hong Kong and grew up in Singapore. Joe spoke excellent English with a decided British accent, something which used to astonish people who knew nothing of his history. If he felt that a customer looked down on him because he was Chinese or if someone addressed him in the Arizona version of pidgin English, old Joe really turned on the Queen's English. You would think he was right out of Oxford.

At the time of which I write Joe Holland must have been in his sixties. He was almost completely bald and his shiny pate was criss-crossed with large blue veins. He had led an adventurous life.

He had cooked on transpacific steamships and in hotels and restaurants along the Pacific Coast. Although he was certainly in his middle forties at the time, he had taken part in the Klondike gold rush in 1898. He had gone to Skagway, Alaska, on a steamship from Seattle and had climbed Chilkoot Pass with a 125-pound pack on his back. He found that panning for gold bored him, so he got a job cooking in a Dawson City restaurant.

Joe found me a good listener.

"You know," he told me once, "I'm aware that I look like a bloody Chink, but at heart I am really British. My father was in the British Colonial service. He died when I was twelve and it wasn't until then that I learned I was a bastard. Seems the old boy had a wife and a family in England. I was very fond of him and his death cut me up. Then my mother took up with another man, a goddam Chinaman. This I couldn't stand. It must seem odd to you, I know, but my father was English and I inherited his attitudes and prejudices. I had been going to a school for gentlemen's sons. Some were all English but some were Eurasians like me.

"So I ran away from home. I have never seen my mother from that day to this. As I remember her she was quite pretty, but she was actually a rather common sort."

What ever happened to old Joe Holland I do not know. All I remember is that when I came back to Tempe in 1921 to start going to school at the normal, he was gone and someone else was running a restaurant in his old location. I can't remember that I ever asked anyone what happened to him.

Remembering as I do how I worked hauling sand over a half century ago, I can see how power and machinery have made things enormously cheaper in terms of human and animal sweat and energy. Even in ten hours I do not think I hauled more than four loads of sand a day to the construction site. I got $2.25 a day. The team I drove must have been worth four or five hundred dollars, as they were big, fine workhorses—Percherons, I believe. They needed a great deal of hay to keep them in condition, and hay in those days sold for about what it does now. The horses continued to eat and to demand care whether they were working or not. The wagon and the harness were expensive. I believe my employer was paid for the sand by the cubic yard, and the sand was probably pretty costly. Today, a big dump truck filled by a steam shovel can probably haul more sand in one trip than the horses and I could in a week.

I likewise worked part of one summer on a farm harvesting hay. I slept on a cot in a barn along with a middle-aged hired man, a bindle stiff who rode freight trains from one area where labor was needed to another. He had worked as a farmhand from southern Arizona and southern California to the prairies of Canada. He had milked cows, picked and packed fruit, harvested hay, alfalfa, beets. Because he could do anything around a farm he got three dollars a day. I got half that. Both of us got our board and room—if you could call our cots in the barn room. The hired man rolled and smoked Bull Durham cigarettes, but this was not an expensive habit as Bull Durham cost five cents a bag and cigarette papers were attached. Every two weeks he got off early on Saturday afternoon and went to Phoenix, where he played a few games of pool, did a little drinking, and went to a bordello to get his "ashes hauled." Before we went to sleep each night he used to reminisce for a few minutes. Getting his ashes hauled sounded to me like a mechanical and depressing experience. I did not envy him.

We arose before dawn, fed and watered the horses, milked the cows. There were six or eight of them. The milk was left by the road where a truck from the creamery picked it up. We then had breakfast—coffee, hot cakes, bacon and ham, two or three eggs. The farmer had no icebox and no ice. Food was kept cool (but not very) in an evaporative cooler that hung outside under a ramada. Its sides were burlap which was kept wet and cooled by the breeze. The butter was always liquid, and milk soured quickly.

I ran a two-horse sulky rake. I sat on an iron seat and guided the horses. The machine was so called because it had two wheels like a sulky—a cart made for one person, like the carts used in harness races—and it had a rake behind. The alfalfa had been cut and had dried into hay in the hot sun. With my machine I raked it into long rows. Every fifteen or twenty yards I bore down with my left foot on a lever so that the rake would lift and drop the hay. Doing that for twelve or thirteen hours gets a bit tiresome, but it is good for the muscle tone.

At noon we unhitched our teams, drove them into the farmyard for water. We then washed up and ate "dinner"—what our hostess called "bottled" meat (meat preserved in jars at the farm—pork and beef), potatoes, vegetables, pie.

We then hitched our horses up again and worked until dark. The hired man drove a buck rake. This had either three or four horses and they "bucked" or pushed a much larger and heavier rake in front of them to put into stacks the rows of hay I had raked up.

As the sun was about to set we unhitched our teams, drove them into the farmyard, watered them, forked hay down for them. Then we milked those damned cows again, washed up, ate "supper," which was exactly like dinner. Then we went to bed. I describe this method of cutting, curing, and stacking hay because in the United States it is as dead as the spinning wheel. Now and then I see a rusty sulky rake sitting around in some isolated mountain meadow in Idaho, and when I do I never fail to shed a reminiscent tear.

As far as I know there were no bathing facilities whatsoever on the farm. The hired man and I washed the dust off with towels and buckets of cold water. On Sundays, I walked the three or four miles to my home in Tempe, cutting through the river bottom. I'd take a good bath, put on clean clothes, and make a real orgy out of going down to Laird & Dines' drug store and devouring a pineapple ice-cream soda and a cherry sundae with chopped nuts and whipped cream.

I generally had some sort of job either all or part of the summer and I usually put enough money aside to buy some clothes and yet squirrel away a little for movies, hamburgers at Joe Holland's restaurant, or Cokes and ice-cream sodas at Laird & Dines' drug store. I harvested milo, picked dates, delivered telegrams at ten cents each, drove a truck for a lumber yard.

I HATED SUMMERS in southern Arizona because of the constant unremitting heat, but I liked them because I did not have to go to school. If I was staying at home, I could always run out and swim in the Salt River with Gordon Goodwin, the Austin boys, or other friends. The Baptist church was always having watermelon or ice-cream socials. It still astonishes me to think of how much ice cream and how many slices of watermelon I could put away.

I also liked having my own money to spend and I enjoyed the feeling of freedom of being able to buy my own clothes, even if Mother went along to see that the material was good and that I got them large enough so that I would have room enough to grow into them.

The best summer job I ever had was the summer of 1916, I believe. I was then fourteen and Gordon Goodwin and I got jobs as carpenter's helpers. A new dormitory was being built at the normal. It was a cost-plus job and the carpenters managed to make their jobs (and ours) last all summer. Also, because it was a cost-plus the contractor was very generous. Gordon and I got fifty cents an hour for an eight-hour day and a six-day week. That was twenty-four dollars a week, not far from what my mother made. The union carpenters, if I remember correctly, made seventy-five cents an hour, thirty-six dollars a week. There was not much for us to do. We brought materials to the carpenters, assisted them slightly, went downtown to buy them Coca-Cola, packages of cigarettes, and plugs of chewing tobacco.

It was also part of our duty to listen to their windy stories. One elderly carpenter was an Irishman, a red-hot union man and something of a radical. He told me that I was a disgrace to my good old Irish name because I went to a Protestant church and took military drill at the normal, as the cadet company was part of the Arizona National Guard. The National Guard all over the United States, he said, were damn strikebreakers, and of all the things he hated, one was a scab, one was a strikebreaker, and the other was an Orangeman. The old boy would get so worked up that he'd glare and yell at me. To hear him talk you'd think I'd been butchering the babies of the Catholic Irish and machine-gunning strikers.

Yet another carpenter, an exceedingly unattractive old goat who chewed tobacco, was an indefatigable and (to hear him tell it) highly successful woman chaser. His specialty seemed to be landladies and the middle-aged wives of men who worked at night. He told me his sordid tales with many a wink and leer, many a bite on his plug of tobacco, and many a squirt of tobacco juice into the shavings.

The carpenter I liked best had graduated from some small college in the Middle West and had tried teaching English and French in a high school for a while. "It drove me crazy," he told me. "Trying to get those morons to write a paragraph you could make heads or tails out of—or even a sentence. And trying to get the little snots to like Shakespeare or even Longfellow . . . If it wasn't the kids it was their goddam mothers. If I didn't give their little darling as good a grade as some other old bitch's little darling they'd come and whine to me or they'd go bellyache to the goddam principal. Then he'd call me in and ask me why little Susie Jones hadn't got as good a grade as little Minnie Smith. Karl Jones, you know, was a very influential man, the son of a bitch would say, and Mildred Jones, the guy's wife, was a very cultured and charming woman. He'd tell me he'd appreciate it if I'd just go over my grade book and see if I hadn't made a mistake or something. For Christ's sake!

"Why in the hell the American people want to throw away all that dough to educate those peasants I'll never know. They educate them so they can read Harold Bell Wright, Zane Grey, Jean Stratton Porter—did you ever read *Pollyanna,* kid? I read about half the first chapter and puked!—Sunday newspapers, and the titles of these damned movies. Now everybody's supposed to go to high school. Someday, for Christ's sake, they'll all be supposed to go to college!"

I liked the misanthropic carpenter immensely and spent much time in rooms he was finishing listening to him denounce schoolteachers (particularly principals and superintendents), the educational system, contemporary novels, women's styles, the Kaiser, and anything else he could think of. He brought me books to read—*McTeague* by Frank Norris, Zola's *Nana, The Arabian Nights,* and Boccaccio's *Decameron.* I could read anything in those days, from *Tarzan of the Apes* to *The Origin of Species.* I enjoyed them all.

It was that summer when I worked as a carpenter's helper that I added to my local reputation as a public nuisance who would come to no good end by getting fined for discharging a firearm within the city limits. It came about this way:

I didn't have to get over to my job until eight o'clock, and the dormitory where I was helping the carpenters was only a half block from my house. Mother was away attending summer school. My sister Helen was with her. I enjoyed my slumber during the cool morning hours and I was always sound asleep when the alarm went off at seven. I then cooked my breakfast, took a cold tub, dressed, and went over to my job.

One morning about six thirty I was awakened by a lanky, pallid Italian boy about my own age. He saw me asleep on the sleeping porch and scratched on the screen until I awakened.

Then he began his spiel: "You wanna some nice muskmelon, green beans, watermelon, new potatoes, squash, rutabaga . . ."

"Look," I said politely enough, "I am the only one here. I just cook breakfast. I don't need any vegetables." He went away, but I was angry and didn't go back to sleep. I felt rather sorry for the boy, as I had seen the poor little vegetable store his parents had opened on Mill Avenue.

The next day he woke me up at the same time with exactly the same spiel. "Listen here," I said, "I told you yesterday that I didn't need any vegetables. If you wake me up again, you'll regret it!"

I had a hunch that the boy would show up again the next day, so before I went to bed I got out the cheap revolver I had got for shooting blank cartridges to intimidate amorous bulls who had been playing footsie with Blackie, our nymphomaniac cow. I went to sleep with the revolver loaded and on the floor beside my bed.

The next morning I was again awakened.

I leaped from my bed wearing pajamas and brandishing the revolver. I shouted that I was going to kill the vegetable peddler. He had left his bicycle in our front yard but he didn't stop to get on it. Instead he tore up the sidewalk toward town howling for mercy. I followed right behind him shooting off blanks and yelling: "This will teach you to wake me up! (*bang!*) I missed you that time but I'll get you right in the ass with this one. (*bang!*) I warned you, didn't I? Now take your medicine. (*bang!*)"

I chased the kid two blocks up to Eighth Street. By that time I had used up my six blank cartridges.

About ten o'clock the town marshal came, hauled me off the job, and took me down to justice court. I got my Uncle Charles Woolf to defend me. I was fined five dollars for discharging a firearm within the city limits. The complaining witness was a sour old maid who ran a boardinghouse at the corner of Forest Avenue and Eighth Street, but everyone on our block was upset. Three old maids lived next door to us and one of them almost had a seizure.

Fred Joyce, who lived a block away, was up early watering his lawn. He heard the shooting and saw the kid come tearing by his place with me after him. He thought the whole thing was very funny but what really fractured him was that the boy left a wavering stream of dampness behind on the sidewalk for the whole two blocks. Fred and I always got along fine. He was the only one in our neighborhood who didn't think I would eventually hang.

The bicycle remained in the front yard all day, but during the night someone removed it.

# 16 · The Age of the Practical Joke

LIKE most old men I am convinced that the world is going to hell and to me there is no greater and more convincing proof of the general degeneracy of mankind than what has happened to the once robust celebration of Halloween. In the places with which I am familiar the observance of this ancient folk rite is now largely in the hands of doting mothers and cute little moppets wearing masks. They ring doorbells, demand a treat by threatening a trick. About the most daring and destructive caper I have known modern children to perform is the soaping of store and car windows.

It wasn't like that in Tempe before World War I, let me tell you! Halloween was really celebrated then! On the morning after, the town looked as if it had been worked over by a puckish Attila the Hun. Many of the tricks were feats that required elaborate planning, imagination, foresight, and engineering skill. It was no small feat, for example, to pick the lock on the front door of the administration building at the normal school, and put a cow and a half ton of hay in President A. J. Matthews's office.

It was routine for the older boys and young men to take buggies and farm wagons apart, carry them to the top of buildings, and reassemble them. Small buildings were moved. Automobiles were repainted and their licenses were switched so that it took a wise man to know his own car.

Somewhere around 1913 or 1914 a sewage system was put in, but before the coming of the sewers, householders had the choice of inside plumbing that drained into a cesspool or the outside plumbing of the privy. Because the privies were cheaper most people chose them. At least three fourths of the houses in and

around Tempe had privies in the back yard. Most were two-holers and each contained a supply of newspapers (the Tempe *News,* the *Arizona Republic,* and the Phoenix *Gazette*) and an outdated Montgomery Ward or Sears, Roebuck catalogue. Some had two large holes and one small one so the whole family could practice togetherness. The few privies in Mexican Town were generally supplied with corncobs, as most Mexicans in those days couldn't read and couldn't order from a catalogue if they did because they seldom had any cash. On the other hand, they used a great deal of corn to make the masa which was basis of both tortillas and tamales. It was the privies that were the principal targets of the younger set of vandals to which I belonged. On the morning after Halloween not a privy in or around Tempe remained standing.

For most of my years in Tempe my best friend was Gordon Goodwin, whose father owned the Goodwin Opera House. The Goodwins were an old Tempe family, and Gordon's mother was an Austin, another old Tempe family. Gordon and I have been friends since we were five. We fought, swam, got in trouble, played tennis, dated, and hunted together. Gordon went to the University of Arizona and Harvard Law School and has now lived in southern California for many years. He was one of the fastest sprinters in the United States when he was in college, and a crack baseball and basketball player; he made varsity letters at Arizona in several sports.

We considered it a poor Halloween indeed if between us we didn't turn over at least ten privies. Two incidents remain in my memory. One dark Halloween night we were joyfully turning over privies along the right-of-way of the Southern Pacific branch line that ran from Phoenix through Tempe to Maricopa, where it hooked up with the main line of the Southern Pacific from New Orleans to Los Angeles. Each crash of a privy was always followed by the barking of dogs, the screams of women and children, and the bitter cursing of householders. As a consequence of all this uproar we were turning over only about every third or fourth privy along the right-of-way.

All went well until we encountered a privy that had been stapled to a page-wire fence. Tipping it over required considerable effort and the creaking and groaning of the fence alerted the householder. He rushed to his back door and shouted, "Stop that, you little sons of bitches!" But the last staple was then pulling out. We gave a final push and over the privy went. An instant later we heard the crash of a shotgun, saw the flash at the muzzle, and a charge of birdshot spattered in the cottonwood just above our heads. Gordon was off like a rocket. I crouched low and got across the tracks so the raised roadbed would be between me and the shotgun. Then I sneaked along until I was about seventy-five yards away from the privy and out of shotgun range.

The householder was examining the overturned amenity and apparently talking to his wife. "Well, by God," he said, "the little bastards done it again. I didn't think they could. I'll swear to Christ I had forty staples a-holdin' it to that-there fence! I sure hope I dusted their butts with some of them Number Sixes!"

I got back on the tracks and started walking in the direction Gordon had taken. About a quarter of a mile from the scene of the privy-tipping I heard a desperate groaning. Then I made out someone sitting on the ground. It was Gordon. In the darkness he had not seen where the tracks crossed an irrigation ditch and one of his legs had gone between two ties. He had been running full tilt and it was a wonder his leg was not broken like a matchstick. As it was, all the hide and considerable flesh had been taken off one of his shins. He probably still wears the scars.

The Catholic church was not supplied with inside plumbing in those days and the priest was an ancient, scholarly, and absent-minded Spaniard. Gordon and I thought it would be a pleasant prank to turn over the priest's privy. It would cost him no great inconvenience since the church was right beside Mexican Town and he could gather a task force of parishioners to right it within minutes. So we crept up, got behind it, and pushed. The edifice had passed the point of no return when we heard a startled cry from within. It was too late. All we could do was to run. Apparently Father Espinosa was in deep meditation and did not notice that his seat was rising and tipping until too late.

Chico Molino, a Mexican friend with whom I played bullring and whose mother made superb enchiladas and tamales, told me later that Father Espinosa's cries for help were soon heard across the way in Mexican Town, and that the good priest, who was a slight man with narrow shoulders, was pulled out through the hole even before the edifice was righted.

GORDON AND I BOTH HAD READ alluring ads by fur dealers in *Hunter-Trader & Trapper.* They invited readers to send in for a price list of furs, and as I remember these firms also sold traps, scent bait, and hide stretchers. Trapping looked like an easy dollar, so we got hold of some traps and set to work. We caught a few coyotes and raccoons but our principal victims were stupid and unwary skunks.

On one occasion we rode our bicycles out to the Double Buttes, a pair of round hills of volcanic origin about two miles southwest of Tempe. We had four traps there and to our delight we found that each contained a skunk. Gordon had his father's .32 Colt automatic pistol and with it he shot the skunks—one from at least fifty yards, a shot both amazing and lucky.

For some reason which escapes me we decided not to skin the four skunks there. Instead we put them into a burlap bag and decided to take them to town before we skinned them. The new Tenth Street grammar school was not far from my home and we decided that the benches and tables where the children ate their lunch would be an ideal location for the skunk-skinning operation.

When we skinned the animals we discovered that the scent bag of one of the skunks (probably the one that Gordon had shot through the brain at fifty yards) was still full of scent. We felt it would be a great pity to waste such a valuable substance so we obtained a bottle somewhere and decanted the precious essence into it.

Then one of us got a brilliant idea. Here was the skunk scent. There was the school. The prank seemed ordained by a higher being. We opened a window, sneaked in, and put a drop or two of skunk essence on every eraser in the building.

That was Sunday. The next day we were both hauled out of school, taken over to the Tenth Street grammar school, and told by the indignant principal to start cleaning up the mess we had left on the benches and tables. Someone had seen us skinning the skunks. School had been dismissed for the day.

In his innocence the principal had thought that the scent from the lunch tables had somehow got wafted into the school building. But the second day, even after Gordon and I had scrubbed the lunch area with disinfectant soap, water, and brushes, the classrooms still stank. School was dismissed for a week while the building was ventilated, fumigated, and perfumed with scents of pine needles, roses, and lilies of the valley. The building still stank.

Finally the school board met with the principal to decide what to do. They couldn't burn down the building very well, and they found it would do no good to sue our parents, since a lawyer had advised them that parents were not responsible for torts committed by their minor children. They could only keep the windows open and try to survive. Gordon and I were heroes to the younger children who attended the school because we were responsible for a week's unexpected vacation. They didn't mind the smell. They said it was sort of wild and woodsy.

For years the Tenth Street school smelled of skunk, particularly on damp days. Gordon and I never told the harried principal that he could solve his problems by getting rid of the erasers.

Not too long after this episode my mother put her foot down. She told me I was to trap no more skunks. Every time I skinned a batch of skunks and forgot to put on my special skunk-skinning costume, it meant that I had another skunk-skinning costume which either had to be kept in the woodshed or burned. Furthermore Gordon and I didn't find skunk trapping very profitable. We would read the price list, decide a certain hide was "Large, black, prime —$7." We would send it in along with others and wait expectantly for a juicy check from Funston. When it came it would be for a hide that was small and unprime and for eighty-five cents.

But I had some traps. If I couldn't catch skunks I felt that I ought to do something useful with them. At that time I was a high-school freshman in the academic department of the normal.

A husband-and-wife team ran the dining hall, where all the students who lived in the dormitories got three squares a day. Board and room were then, if I remember correctly, about twenty dollars a month.

The husband, an Austrian named Krause, was the chef. He ran the kitchen, bought the food, did most of the cooking. His wife supervised the dining room and the student waiters who worked for their board and room. She also taught youngsters from the mines and ranches not to eat with their knives and not to pick their noses or their teeth at the table. According to the story, Mrs. Krause had been "salivated." At one time, the tale ran, she had taken a massive dose of calomel and had then inadvertently taken aboard some acid. The result was that she was "salivated" and all her hair had fallen out. Those who claimed to be in the know said she was completely bald, wore a wig, and painted her eyebrows on.

The Krauses had no children, but they did have a particularly ill-natured and repulsive Mexican hairless dog on which Mrs. Krause lavished her thwarted maternal instincts. I loathed the monster and for some reason it loathed me. Each day my path crossed that of the Krauses. I was going from one classroom building to another and they were headed home for a brief rest between lunch and dinner. The dog was always with them and he never failed to snarl and yap at me. Several times he threatened to bite me. I told Mrs. Krause that if that goddam dog of hers ever succeeded in biting me I was going to kick it no less than 125 feet. She told me that if I touched her darling she'd have me expelled from school.

So every day this miserable mutt, this grotesque caricature of a dog, cruised ahead of the Krauses, grunting, growling, wheezing, breaking wind, sniffing at posts and bushes, peeing on something about every twenty-five feet, and always barking and snapping at me. He was so fat he looked stuffed, and his back was covered with warts, blackheads, and pimples. His eyes bulged out and his face was frozen into an ill-natured and petulant snarl.

I had noticed that he always went to a particular tree in a garden about twenty feet from the sidewalk the Krauses followed. He sniffed at it to see what other dogs had been by. Then he hoisted his leg to leave his own calling card. That done he looked about with his bulging myopic eyes to see if he could locate me to yap and snap at.

So one spring morning, the day after that damned dog had finally nipped my ankle, I got up at first light, dressed hastily, took one of my skunk traps and a small spade. When I got to the garden containing the dog's favorite tree, I looked around to see if anyone was in sight. The coast seemed clear. I quickly dug a shallow hole for my trap at the foot of the tree, set it, covered it with leaves and twigs, and quietly went back home. I devoutly hoped that no other dog would beat the hairless monster to the tree.

But to my great disappointment my plan did not work out perfectly. I had hoped to witness the mutt's falling into a trap, but for some reason Mrs. Krause was off schedule. She and the dog left the dining hall about fifteen minutes early, leaving Krause behind. I was in class when I heard the shrill and desperate yelping and realized what had happened. Those who were present said that when Mrs. Krause rushed in to rescue her pet her red wig fell off and her head shone like a billiard ball.

WHEN I WAS A FRESHMAN in the academic department at the normal I spent a good deal of time reading in the library, and one day as I read, a complicated Halloween prank began to form in my mind. The general tone of the library was greatly uplifted and the decor improved by the presence of about a dozen plaster copies of famous Greek and Roman statues that stood at intervals arounds the walls. Some of the statues were of males and some were of females but none of them had very many clothes on, and some, it saddens me to say, wore nothing but fig leaves.

As Halloween approached I enlisted the aid of two more juvenile delinquents. Along about midnight we climbed up a ladder to one of the windows of the library, jimmied the window, and entered. We were supplied with a pot of glue, the contents of an old horsehair sofa, and all the cast-off clothing we could lay our hands on. We dressed all the statues, gave all the male statues tremendous black beards by putting glue on the faces and then sticking on the horsehair. A more disreputable and degenerate-looking group of statues you never saw.

I surprised my mother the next morning by telling her that I must be at the library when it opened at eight o'clock, as I had to do some outside reading. She was greatly pleased, as she was not used to such zeal. I had always read a great deal, but assigned reading I had generally been able to take or to leave alone.

Two dear little old maids, of whom I was very fond but whose names I have long since forgotten, ran the library. At five minutes to eight the two other young vandals and I were in the hall waiting for the librarians to open up. By seven fifty-nine five or six earnest and studious girls had joined us, looking a bit surprised to find us so avid for knowledge. At exactly eight o'clock one of the librarians came briskly into the building, registered pleasure at seeing an unusually large number of eager young people hungering for learning waiting by the door. She wished us good morning, put a key in the lock, and opened the door.

We all filed in. The librarian didn't even look up. Nor did the girls. My companions in crime and I sat at different tables pretending to be engrossed in magazines taken from the periodical rack. I looked at our handiwork. My heart swelled with creative pride. In the full light of day the effect was even more sensational than it had appeared by flashlight the night before. I particularly liked the appearance of Diana in her corset and baggy drawers. Mercury's best friend would not have recognized him in a ragged shirt, a dirty pair of levis, and a tattered straw hat. During the night he had grown a prodigious set of curly black whiskers.

Then one of the studious girls actually looked at one of the statues, did a double-take, and tittered. The librarian looked up from her desk.

"Miss Brimhall," she said sternly, "please tell me what is it that you find so funny."

Miss Brimhall pointed. The librarian's jaw dropped. Her eyes widened with horror. She screamed. A girl began to laugh. Two or three others came into the library, then more. Somehow the word had got around. Presently Dr. (honorary) A. J. Matthews, the president of the normal, came in. Apparently the librarian had put in a distress call. He rapped on a table to command attention.

"Students," he began. "You have no doubt noticed that some vandals with a misplaced sense of humor have desecrated the beautiful statuary here. I only hope those who did this are not students of the normal, but whoever was involved can rest assured that no stone will be left unturned to find the miscreants, and once found they will be suitably punished. Now, it will be necessary to close the library this morning while this mess is cleaned up. I am very sorry this had to happen. You all may go now."

By ten o'clock a task force of janitors had undressed the statues, removed the whiskers, and washed their faces. The library was reopened.

A couple of days later, I was summoned to the office of the president.

Dr. Matthews was seated behind his big desk, dignified, full-bodied, impeccably tailored.

"I have just talked to Julius," he thundered. "He says he knows nothing about that disgraceful Halloween prank played at the library. He says the two of you weren't together." By Julius he meant Gordon. There had been a Julius Goodwin who was a cousin of Gordon's and who had graduated from the normal some ten years before. Dr. Matthews always called Gordon Julius. To him one young Goodwin was about like another, and none of them could be trusted farther than he could throw a large horse with one hand.

"Yes, sir," I said.

"I noticed you in the library the other morning when Miss Blount called me over. You know the old saying about the criminal returning to the scene of the crime?"

"I have heard it, sir."

"I suppose you were home studying on Halloween night."

"No, sir."

"Where were you then?"

"Out playing tricks on people."

"Such as what?"

"Turning over outdoor toilets."

"You weren't mixed up in the library business, then?"

"No, sir."

"Hn-n-n-n!" said Dr. Matthews, tapping his store teeth with a letter opener. "Hn-n-n-n . . ." Then he turned to me suddenly. "Now I want you to tell me the truth about this. I won't hold it against you! Did you have anything to do with putting that cow in my office?"

"No, sir," I said. "I was about four years old then. That was a long time ago, but I have heard about it."

"Yes, of course," Dr. Matthews said. "That *was* some time ago. I keep forgetting. Now, Jack, I want to warn you that you're getting a bad reputation. You and that Julius Goodwin. Always into something. Mrs. Krause thinks you trapped her dog, for one thing, and no one has forgotten about the matter of the skunks at the Tenth Street school.

"Now, buck up! Be a man! Your mother is a member of the faculty here. Don't embarrass her. Your distinguished grandfather J. W. Woolf obtained the appropriation that allowed this building to be completed. Your uncle Charlies Woolf is on our board. Jack, you are not really a bad boy—you are just mischievous and rattle-brained."

I CAN REMEMBER very well when the Mexican revolution against the Diaz regime broke out in 1910. I read about it in the newspapers, heard the grownups discuss it, and I remember the boys in Tempe's Mexican Town shouting, "Viva Madero! Orosco has taken Juárez!"

The Mexican state of Sonora was immediately below Arizona, and there were battles between Mexican factions at Agua Prieta across the line from Douglas, Arizona, and in Nogales, Sonora, right across from the Arizona town of the same name. Mexican bullets flew across the border, broke American windows, frightened and annoyed Americans. Mexicans stole cattle owned by Americans in Mexico, wrecked mines owned by Americans. When the revolution broke out and for some years afterward my Uncle John Woolf was the manager of the Green Cananea Cattle Company, an enormous ranch in northern Mexico.

I even met Pancho Villa, the famous Mexican bandit general, when he was making his headquarters in Nogales, Sonora. This was around 1914 or 1915. At the time my father was working in Nogales and my Uncle Bill O'Connor was the Santa Cruz County superior judge. I had gone down for a visit. Pancho Villa's headquarters then being across the border in Nogales, and since I had got interested in photography and owned a little film-pack camera, I decided to see if I could take Villa's picture. I crossed the border with my camera, asked where Villa was to be found, and presented myself at his headquarters. A guard told me to go away, that the general was not seeing just any American boy that came along. I was insistent. Presently an officer came out and told me the general was busy and for me to go away.

I told the officer that I was a great admirer of Villa and that I had come many miles, all the way from central Arizona, just to express my admiration and to take his picture. The officer said he was deeply touched but that Villa was busy and for me to go away.

Then the door opened and Villa came out. I recognized him instantly from pictures I had seen in newspapers and magazines. He wanted to know what in the hell all this arguing was about. The officer said this crazy gringo kid claimed to be an admirer of the general and wanted to take his picture, but he (the officer) had told him the general was busy and to go away.

Villa slapped me on the back, told me he liked my looks, and said I could take all the pictures I wanted. He took the guard's 7-mm. Mauser carbine and a cartridge belt away from him, posed for me with them, took another man's big hat off, posed in that. He got on a saddled burro that was nearby, and clowned around as I took his picture. He then told the officer to take a picture of him with me. He put his arm around me and flashed a big grin.

The pictures came out very well. I wish I had them now, but somehow the album I had pasted them in disappeared from my mother's house when it was rented after her death. Since that day I have always had a rather warm spot in my heart for Villa. From what I have read of Khrushchev, he makes me think of Villa. Both were uneducated men of the people. Both could be amiable or deadly. Both were overturned by shrewder, more sophisticated, and equally ruthless men.

It was Pancho Villa who in a way was responsible for one of the most elaborate practical jokes in an era of elaborate practical jokes. In March 1916 his raid on Columbus, New Mexico, had everyone along the Mexican border nervous and excited. If Villa struck in New Mexico he might also strike in Arizona or Texas. General John Pershing was sent to chase Villa around in Chihuahua but he didn't have much luck.

Every spring the cadet company at the Tempe Normal held an annual encampment. Under Captain Fred Irish, who for many years was the company's drill instructor, the company pitched pup tents, cooked their rations, dug trenches, held tactical exercises. Irish was, I am sure, strictly a textbook soldier, but he read his textbooks well and everything was done by the numbers. I doubt if ever in his life he had fired a rifle, yet he gave excellent lectures on all aspects of military rifle shooting.

Irish's wife had run off with another man and had later divorced Irish and had married her lover. Irish was a bitter, lonely man of enormous dignity. I loved rifle shooting and did well at it, but in all other aspects of my military education at the normal I was a failure. I cut the three-times-a-week drill (along with my pal Gordon Goodwin) as often as I dared. I was apt to have buttons off my uniform or my hat on cockeyed. Spit and polish bored me, and I was generally thinking of something else when I was supposed to present arms, do squads right, or something. In my years of military drill at the normal I never rose above buck private.

When I showed up in his cadet company and in his chemistry class Irish took one look at me, disliked me immediately, decided I was a degenerate member of an otherwise respectable family. Once, when he was sitting on a little stool recording the scores as several of us shot at five hundred yards, he put down a "possible" for me and then said: "You are a good shot. Why do you otherwise have to be so worthless?"

I was not the only one who was bored by military training and who didn't exactly love Captain Fred Irish, so Villa's raid on Columbus started the fertile mind of some genius to working. The erosion of the years has erased the name of this brilliant youngster from my memory, so if by some remote chance he should read this book I hereby apologize.

At any rate, he thought it would be a wonderful joke to pretend a raid on the encampment by Mexican bandits. He gathered in some fellow pranksters, including Gordon Goodwin and me. From then on we liberated all the blank cartridges for our Springfield rifles that we could lay hands on. One of the boys somehow got hold of a considerable quantity of the flash powder used before the invention of the electrically triggered flash bulb to take "flash-light" pictures. Someone else got a supply of fuses used in setting off dynamite charges. This was probably easy because many of the male students who lived in the dormitory were sons of miners. Another genius developed a process for making papier-mâché—out of old newspapers, if I remember correctly. Working together happily and secretly, we put a charge of flash powder into waterproof paper, inserted the dynamite fuse, then put about a quarter of an inch of wet papier-mâché around this and let it dry. These were our bombs.

To see how the things worked we went over between the two buttes one evening at dusk, lit a fuse, and tossed a bomb into the air. It exploded with a hell of a bang and lit up the surrounding country. I am sure that half the women in nearby Mexican Town crossed themselves at the spectacle of lightning and thunder on a clear night.

The encampment was to last a week. The big raid by the "Mexican bandits" was set for the fourth night. One by one we slipped through the lines when everyone else in the camp was asleep. In all, there were about eight of us. We had a good supply of the flash-powder bombs, four or five Springfield rifles, and perhaps a hundred blank cartridges.

One of the bombardiers lit a fuse, tossed a bomb into the air. It exploded with a fearful crash and lit up for an instant the low desert hills a mile or two away as bright as midday. Then one of the riflemen fired off four or five cartridges.

"Viva Villa!"

"Viva Mexico!"

"Death to the gringos!"

We heard the sounds of excitement in camp—yells, commands.

We attacked from another direction. More bombs exploded in the air. More blank cartridges popped.

"Viva Villa!"

"Kill the Americans!"

"Remember Columbus, New Mexico!"

We threw more bombs, fired more blank cartridges in the Springfields.

Presently some shooting started in camp. We had all done considerable military rifle shooting by that time and had served in the pits where we had pulled and marked targets. We recognized the sound of bullets coming in our direction. A high-velocity bullet travels faster than sound, and if the bullet is coming toward the listener he hears the crack of the bullet as it breaks the sound barrier through the air and then the report of the rifle. It sounds like this: *Chick-boom.*

"For Christ's sake!" one of the bandits said. "Those guys are *shooting* at us—and they're using *bullets!*"

Until then we had all been having a very good time. We felt we really had shaken up the camp and had annoyed Cap Irish. Now we realized that if our luck turned bad we might stop a bullet. Besides, the sobering thought came to us that we were probably in trouble. Then we heard the sound of a roll call and we *knew* we were in trouble. We decided to split up and sneak back into camp.

I ditched my Springfield in some bushes near a big saguaro where I could find it without trouble, then sneaked close to the latrine tent and listened to hear the guards walking their posts. I found out that the guards met at the latrine tent, then separated. From the length of time it took them to walk their posts I decided that Cap Irish had doubled the guard—and I learned later that I was right.

When I estimated that the guards were a maximum distance from the latrine tent, I crept under the back flap, took down my pants, and sat down on the pole that served as a seat. When the guards neared the tent for their rendezvous I began to groan horribly.

One of them stuck his head in the tent and threw the beam of a flashlight in my face.

"What in the hell's all that shooting and yelling been about?" I asked.

"You been in here all that time? What's the matter?"

"Bellyache," I said. "I heard all that shooting, but I couldn't leave the tent."

"I think that's a lot of b.s.," the guard said. "Some no-good bastards been pretending they was Mexican bandits. It scared the hell out of everybody and old Cap Irish was fit to die. He had ball ammunition issued and we were digging trenches. He figured the greasers were shelling us with high explosives but their shells were short.

"Then some smart guy sort of recognized some of them voices and figured they didn't sound much like Mexicans. He told Cap Irish he ought to have a roll call and see who the hell was absent. Eight of you bastards didn't answer."

I groaned again.

"Yeah," I said, "I heard them calling roll but I couldn't get out of here."

"I'm gonna call the corporal of the guard."

"O.K.," I said. "Call him."

The corporal of the guard and also the first sergeant showed up.

"I was walking my post when all of a sudden I heard somebody groaning like hell in the latrine tent," the guard said. "I looked in and here Jack is sitting on the can. He claims he was here all the time when that shooting broke out and during the roll call. If he was, why in the hell didn't he make noise before?"

"I did, goddammit!" I said. "You were so scared you couldn't hear me! You thought old Pancho Villa really had you by the balls!"

"So you was in there all the time?" the first sergeant said. "You swear it?"

"You're damn right!" I said.

"Well, I'll tell Cap Irish we didn't catch you sneaking in and that you claim you were in the can all the time."

When I was taken to Irish he listened to the first sergeant, looked at me with cold dislike, and did not even address me directly.

"He wasn't caught, so we can't prove he was mixed up in this," he said. "We'll have to turn him loose."

Most of the other bandits were caught as they tried to sneak through the lines. They were all put under arrest, kept under guard in a special compound. For the rest of the encampment they had a fine time. They ate what everyone else ate. They didn't have to dig trenches, take part in tactical exercises in the hot sun, stand guard, do K.P., or perform any of the other dreary tasks. Furthermore everyone looked upon them with deep admiration. They simply lay around playing blackjack, telling dirty stories, and lying about their conquests among the Tempe Normal co-eds. I regretted that I hadn't been caught.

The cadets returned to the normal campus late on a Sunday afternoon. The next day Cap Irish assembled the entire company in the lecture room where he taught chemistry and physics. He harangued us on the viciousness and depravity of this thing that an irresponsible and degenerate minority had done. He said at least one that he was sure had been mixed up in this disgraceful prank had not been apprehended, but he had his eye on him and had nothing but contempt for a liar. As he said this he glared at me. It sounded as if we had desecrated the American flag, had ravished a Red Cross nurse, and had partaken of human flesh. We had made Cap Irish look foolish, and I am sure he never forgave me or anyone else who took part in Villa's raid.

NOT ONLY YOUNGSTERS but grown men played practical jokes. When a young couple got married it was routine for his friends to kidnap both the groom and the bride. It was considered wildly funny to take the groom's shoes away from him and put him down in the desert to make it back to his anxious bride as well as he could. It was also considered riotous to gather around the house where the bride and groom were consummating their union and shout, yell, ring cow bells, pound on tin cans, and bombard the roof with stones.

When I was about eight years old the creamery, which was about a mile from Tempe, imported a chemist from the East. Through his nervous inquiries the other employees realized that he felt that he was in great danger from hostile Indians.

This was simply too good to pass up. Those who worked at the creamery started carrying rifles to work and strapping on revolvers. They told the chemist that an Apache raid was expected at any moment, as Geronimo had broken out and was loose with a war party. They suggested that he purchase a revolver because he might have to fight for his life at any moment.

When they decided they had the poor tenderfoot sufficiently shaken up, about one o'clock in the morning they gathered around the house where he had a room, shot off their revolvers, and gave out Indian yells. The poor chemist, firing wildly, jumped out of his window and took off. He was found the next morning several miles away with his feet full of cactus. Just about everyone in Tempe thought this was the funniest thing that had happened in years.

The badger fight and the snipe hunt were both old Western institutions. In the snipe hunt a tenderfoot is told that when snipe are disturbed at night they will fly toward a light. He is taken to an isolated spot, given a lantern and a burlap bag, and told to hold the bag open with the light in front of it. Soon, they tell him, the snipe will fly into the bag. The others will go chase the snipe off the roost, they tell him. Then everyone else goes home. When he decides he has been taken, the tenderfoot finds his way back as well as he can. It is from the classic snipe hunt that the Western expression "holding the bag" originated.

In the badger fight the tenderfoot is conned into pulling a string which will open a box and bring out a badger to engage in battle with a dog. He is selected, they say, because he is neither pro-badger nor pro-dog and hence will not pull out the badger at a moment that would be disadvantageous to either contestant. The tenderfoot is told that when the two savage animals collide blood literally flies. His well-wishers advise him to roll up the legs of his trousers before he pulls the badger out so that he will not get them covered with blood.

Then the stage is set. A box with a string leading out of it is brought into the arena. This is supposed to contain the badger. A dog is also brought in and is held facing the box and about twenty feet from it. Dog, box, and tenderfoot are surrounded by a group of noisy spectators all making large bets on one animal or the other.

Then the great moment arrives. The signal is given and the tenderfoot yanks on the cord, expecting to see a ferocious badger come squealing out and hurl himself at the dog.

But instead out comes a chamber pot—a full one at that.

All the spectators howl with mirth and the drinks are on the dude.

The humor of pre-World War I Arizona was nothing if not robust!

# 17 · Things of the Spirit

CHURCHES were something that Tempe had plenty of when I was growing up there in the early years of this century. Offhand I can remember churches maintained by the Catholics, the Methodists, the Christians (whom Grandfather Woolf always sniffishly referred to as the Campbellites), the Presbyterians, the Baptists, and the Congregationalists. I may have forgotten a church or two, but six churches complete with congregations, parsons, choir singers, freshly scrubbed youngsters going to Sunday school, bells, parsonages, and hymnals is a pretty fair number for a town of between 1,200 and 1,800. At the time of which I write there was no Mormon church in Tempe, but Mesa, a town only seven miles away, was heavily Mormon, had a temple, and there were Mormon "stake houses" scattered around. Many Mormons farmed near Tempe and many Mormon students attended the normal. No Mormon who felt himself in need of spiritual succor had to go far to get it.

Grandfather Woolf was a Baptist and I inherited the Baptist religion just as I inherited the Democratic party. My grandfather had contributed heavily to the building of the new Baptist church and the parsonage, but just how genuinely religious he actually than he had been as a boy in Kentucky. He was an extremely intelligent man, and for those times he was much better read and much better educated than the average citizen. At the time of which I write he had lived in the West almost forty years. He had known many kinds, classes, and colors of people—men of various faiths and men of no faith at all. Just as he had almost entirely lost his Kentucky accent I believe he had also lost much of the religion of his youth.

I can remember his going to Sunday-morning services very few times. When he did I was so proud of him that I stayed over from Sunday school and sat beside him through the church services. He always looked commanding, handsome, and important in his black suit, hard collar, and derby. The preacher always rushed out to

shake his hand when the services were over and I could tell he was very important the way everyone greeted him and many fawned over him. He always took his attention, as he did just about everything, with great dignity, but now and then I detected a crinkle of amusement around his bright, steely-blue eyes.

A great deal of the time he was out hunting or fishing on Sunday mornings. When he was not he was puttering around in his orchard or garden or reading in his study. Frank Peck, his principal hunting pal, was the cashier of the Tempe National Bank, of which my grandfather was a director, and Sunday was the only morning that Frank coudd get away. Grandfather may have gone to Wednesday-night prayer meeting, for all I know, and I am sure he went occasionally to Sunday-evening services. My grandmother never went at all. She used the fact that a fall had left her slightly crippled and she had to walk with one crutch as an excuse for not going to church; she used the crutch as an excuse for everything she did not want to do.

My mother did not go to church either. She always said she did not have time, as she was busy teaching five days a week and needed the two free days of the weekend to catch up on her housework. Saturdays were for general house cleaning and laundry. I always helped. Often, with the help of my sister Helen, I did the washing. I also took the Navajo rugs out of the living room, shook them, swept them. I mowed the lawn, straightened up my room. Saturday afternoons I was generally off on my bicycle with some friends.

On Sunday mornings my mother finished the ironing. Most of the week she had to do everything with one eye on the clock and I think she simply enjoyed taking her own time and putting things off on Sundays. We generally did not eat our Sunday dinner until midafternoon; I can still remember with horror long hours of waiting for dinner, faint with hunger and with an empty, growling belly.

As I look back on my youth I can see that in a way I was at the Baptist church a sort of a stand-in for my grandfather and my mother when I went to Sunday school. Grandfather would take me hunting on weekdays, sometimes on Sunday afternoons, but he insisted that Sunday mornings were to be reserved for the good of my soul—or maybe his.

I became aware that Grandfather's notions had changed a good deal from what they probably were in his youth when his brother, Frank Woolf, moved out to Arizona in 1913 or 1914. Frank was my grandfather's youngest brother. He had been a successful farmer in Kentucky and he had sold out to move to Arizona with enough to last him to the end of his days. Bob, another of my grandfather's brothers, had followed my grandfather to Arizona previously and had bought a large farm near Phoenix several miles away. In the horse-and-buggy and early automobile days there was not too much communication between the two sections of the Woolf clan. My Great-uncle Bob's wife, Aunt Lottie, had black hair and dark-brown eyes. All her children had brown eyes, were handsome, and looked nothing like the rest of the Woolf family. Not too long before I moved away from Arizona for good, a motorcycle cop in Chandler stopped me for going twenty miles an hour in a fifteen-mile-an-hour school zone. He pulled out a book and started to write up the ticket.

"What's your name?" he asked.

"Jack O'Connor," I said.

"Ida's boy?" he asked.

"Why, yes," I said, puzzled. "My mother's first name is Ida."

He put his book back in his pocket and stuck his right hand into the car.

"Let's forget about that goddam ticket," he said. "You and I are about third cousins. I'm Gene Woolf's son. I read your stuff all the time!" Never let anybody tell you it doesn't pay to have connections. The cop was the grandson of Uncle Bob Woolf, and I noticed that he had inherited Aunt Lottie's brown eyes.

My Great-uncle Frank must have married rather late, as his wife, my Aunt Fanny, seemed to me anyway much younger, and when I was eleven his youngest daughter was thirteen or fourteen and his older daughter about sixteen. The Frank Woolfs were real hard-shell Baptists. Going to church was just about their only recreation, so much so that it was practically an occupation if not actually a vice. The girls both went to Sunday school, stayed over for church, which was usually not over until twelve thirty or sometimes twelve forty-five. They then went home, where Aunt Fanny fried up two to five chickens, depending on whether they had guests or not, made milk gravy, mashed potatoes, served green beans or peas with milk (this is an old-country way of cooking the two vegetables; I think fresh garden peas are delicious cooked that way, but my wife thinks I am a hick for saying so!), creamed cauliflower, milk, coffee, tea, coleslaw, apple or mince or rhubarb pie, cake, maybe homemade ice cream or sherbet. After engorging this gargantuan repast, the Frank Woolfs retired to their bedrooms if there were no guests or only family guests, rested, belched, prayed, gathered strength for the evening services. I have forgotten to record that Uncle Frank always said grace before each meal. Grandfather Woolf generally said grace before the evening meal, but when he did so it was short and snappy: "Our Heavenly Father, we thank Thee for Thy bounty. Amen." Just like that. But Uncle Frank not only thanked the Heavenly Father and asked that the fried chicken, milk gravy, and peas be blessed, but he also prayed that assorted sinners like saloon keepers, gamblers, scarlet women, and scoffers be made to see the light, by the scruff of the neck if necessary. When Uncle Frank was in good form and was communing with the Lord and reminding him of the sinful state of humankind he was a hard man to stop. One of the most painful memories of my childhood is sitting there with head bowed, itching all over, and seeing the delectable fried chicken get colder and colder. I did not encounter the custom of saying grace again until I was a member of the Omega Omega chapter of Sigma Chi at the University of Arkansas.

Uncle Frank's daughters, Ruth and Lena, not only went to all the grown-up services, but also to those for the young. They religiously attended Sunday school every Sunday morning from ten to eleven, but they also went to church from eleven to twelve thirty and to evening services from seven thirty to nine. In addition they went to prayer meeting at seven thirty on Wednesday nights, to choir practice, to Baptists Young People's Union. I think one was held on Tuesday after supper and the other on Thursday. How their tailbones stood it I have no idea. Their lives were a perfect orgy of religious activity. In their house there were no books except the Bible, *Dr. Livingstone's Adventures in Africa* (Dr. Livingstone was a missionary), the *Memoirs of Gen. Ulysses S. Grant,* the *Home Medical Guide,* and a few old textbooks. The only books of fiction in the house were the Little Colonel books and three or four books of the Five Little Peppers series. My second cousin Ruth Woolf was addicted to both. I tried reading a Little Colonel book but I bogged down early. I did get through *The Five Little Peppers and How They Grew.* It was the story of a widow with five children. As far as I can remember they existed largely in cold boiled potatoes with a little salt. I always wondered why they did not eat them hot. My cousin also was hooked on Clarence Budington Kelland's stories about a fat boy named Mark Tidd in the now long-defunct *American Boy.* My Uncle Frank considered most fiction worldly and didn't allow novels in the house, but the stories about Mark Tidd, the Peppers, and the Little Colonel were good clean tales and in them there was no drinking, no carousing, no sex.

I believe that the official name of the church at Tempe was the First Baptist Church, South. It had been founded by people like my grandfather, people who had, unconsciously perhaps, shed many of their Southern folkways and prejudices while they were adventuring, encountering strange people with strange customs, stealing each other's cattle, and shooting Indians. My grandfather, because of his much wider experience and much more adventurous life, was an entirely different sort of person from my Uncle Frank who had stayed in Kentucky with people just like himself.

My grandfather wasn't much of a churchgoer, for various reasons. All the time he had been ranching along the New Mexico-Colorado line he was far from any church and probably got out of the habit. As I have said he hated to give up his Sunday-morning bird shoots with Frank Peck, and he also probably felt that his large donation to the church had pretty well squared him with God. In addition I believe he was aware of a considerable gulf in awareness and sophistication between himself and the newer arrivals from the South. I remember one Sunday when he had come to morning services and I had stayed beside him. I have forgotten what the sermon was about but I was conscious that he was irritated by it. The preacher rushed out so he could be sure to shake Grandfather's hand. Grandfather exchanged a few pleasantries with old friends and we were out on the sidewalk and about to start walking the one block home when one of the newer members of the congregation, an elderly man from some Southern state, came up to him and shouted: "Brother Woolf, are you right with Jesus?" "I really can't say," Grandfather responded coldly. "What about yourself?" He turned then and we headed home together. "Dad-ratted old fool!" he said.

I did not stay after Sunday school to go to church services very often. The sermons were too long and during the warm months the sight of dozens of palm-leaf fans moving as worshippers tried to stir the stagnant air had a soporific effect on me.

One of my few amusements was watching old man Botkin. He was old, tired from scratching in the barren soil among the rocks of the hillsides in the Missouri Ozarks, and also he was a bit balmy. It was as impossible for the old boy to stay awake as it was for me years later to keep my eyes open in some of the windy courses I suffered through in college. But the fact that he knew he was always dozing off and snoring apparently embarrassed the old fellow. When I stayed for church I used to try to sit where I could watch him. As the preacher's voice droned on, his eyes would glaze. Then his lids would begin to droop. I could see him fight to keep them open. Finally they closed and he would begin to nod. Presently he was snoring softly but audibly. Then as his head sank deeper on his chest, his snores became louder. The preacher would glance toward him with a frown of annoyance.

Old man Botkin always woke up with a bang. I believe he liked to pretend that he had not actually been in dreamland but instead had been lost in deep contemplation and prayer. Sometimes he snored so loudly that he woke himself up. Sometimes the preacher started yelling and awakened him, and sometimes his wife, embarrassed by his head flopping around on his limber neck and by his snoring, would give him a sharp punch in the ribs. But he always awoke with a shout, as if he agreed exactly 200 per cent with some point the preacher had made. He'd throw up his head and shout: "Amen," "The Lord be Praised," or "Hallelujah!" Most of the time these comments didn't fit into the context of the sermon at all, but now and then they added considerable spice. The one I particularly cherished came during a sermon which the preacher had advertised weeks in advance as being the one in which he would expose Tempe as a veritable den of iniquity, a hotbed of vice, sin, and riotous living. Actually he didn't have much ammunition—Sunday baseball and bird shooting, boys swimming naked in the river down at the Point of Rocks, scandalous goings-on in the back seats of Model T Fords, betting on quarter-horse races and cockfights in Mexican Town, a nonstop poker game in the back room of the pool hall, the teaching of evolution in the biology department up at the normal. He saved one point until almost the last. There was, he said, a scarlet woman* openly plying her trade and catering to the lusts of wicked and self-indulgent men right here in Tempe. Just then old man Botkin woke up. "Praise the Lord!" he shouted.

Outside of watching old man Botkin at church my only other amusement was playing a game called Between the Sheets. I learned it from Samantha Duncan, a lush lass several years older than I. I sat down by Samantha one day when I was about ten, partly because the seat next to her was vacant and partly because I had a morbid interest in Miss Duncan. She was alleged to "put out." Several of the older boys claimed to have had carnal knowledge of her and it was true that at school and church picnics she was always disappearing for a half hour or so with some boy. Then

* This must have been old Mama All Nations.

when they returned Samantha always appeared somewhat disheveled and the boy she had gone with wore a self-satisfied leer. Or so I thought. Perhaps it all lay in my imagination. Samantha was a voluptuous-looking lass of about fifteen when I was ten. She had hazel eyes, soft, billowing red-brown hair, and plenty of curves in more or less the right places.

At any rate, on the particular Sunday of which I write I sat down by Samantha, stole a speculative sidelong glance at her now and then. She likewise looked at me out of the corners of her eyes.

Presently she dug up a pencil, wrote a note on it, slipped it into a hymnal, and handed it to me. The note said: "Jack, put 'between the sheets' after the title of this and the next three hymns." I did so and the result was startlingly ribald.

MY MEMORIES of Sunday school are somewhat vague. When I was very young I was hustled off to be exposed to it for the good of my soul. As I recall it we children who were being indoctrinated and civilized were separated by both age groups and sex. The younger ones at least were turned over to earnest women for instruction. I remember that we were each given a little colored card illustrating some Biblical scene and we were also given a small four-page paper filled with homilies and other propaganda deemed suitable for children of our limited years and intelligence.

The Sunday-school teachers to whom I was exposed were all earnest women from Southern farms and villages, good, decent, hard-working, kindly women who cooked large fattening meals, washed, ironed, mended, darned, loved and cherished their children, honored their husbands, were fat and matronly at thirty-five, just about sexless at forty. They were women of no education, women whose only travel had been to ride out to Arizona in day coaches, drinking coffee and eating stale box lunches purchased from the news butcher* when they ran out of doughnuts, roast-pork sandwiches, cold biscuits, and fried chicken they had brought from home.

* The man who sold box lunches, pop, candy, newspapers, and magazines on day coaches.

These women had all read and pondered over the Bible but they had read nothing else, and they were all the end products of a series of generations that produced a great deal of religious activity and a good many religious sects, including the Mormons. They were only marginally literate, and they cherished all the folk beliefs of their peasant British ancestors. These good people were against dancing, card-playing, drinking, reading worldly books, the theater; and they all believed in the Bible from cover to cover.

Several decades in the more liberal West had considerably altered the views of my Grandfather Woolf's family. Grandfather frowned on drinking except for medicinal purposes, but he read all manner of worldly books. He was very fond of Sir Walter Scott's novels, of Mark Twain, Dickens. He also hunted and fished on Sunday, and his children had all gone dancing. The more extreme of the Baptists looked upon the piano as a worldly instrument and the violin as a creation of the devil, but there had always been a piano in Grandfather Woolf's house and his daughters had all taken piano lessons. I can remember when my aunts, Irene and Mabel, gave a dance with a hired orchestra of piano, fiddle, and drums. I remember their playing "Shine On, Harvest Moon" and "Everybody's Doing It!"

Grandfather was no intellectual but he read the popular magazines of the day—*The Literary Digest, Everybody's.* I even remember seeing him reading short stories in *Cosmopolitan* and *Metropolitan* and gazing, a bit wistfully perhaps, at the picture of beautiful showgirls which were a regular feature of *Cosmopolitan.* Grandfather had a logical mind and if evidence was reasonable he was convinced. Once in his study he showed me a picture of the Grand Canyon. "Look at that, boy!" he said. "All made by water. I've been there. I've looked down in it. I've ridden into it. I've looked up from the bottom. It's a mile deep from the South Rim. From the other side on top of Buckskin Mountain* it's a mile and a half deep. It was all cut through rock by water and anybody with eyes

* The old-timers called the Kaibab Plateau Buckskin Mountain because of the enormous number of deer hides taken off by early Mormon settlers.

in his head and with any sense can tell it was. Frank thinks it was all made in six days. Ridiculous! Boy, I'm going to have to take you up to see the Canyon someday!"

I am sure that my grandfather shed his belief in the Biblical story of Creation without much pain because the evidence of long and turbulent change of the earth's surface was all around him. Once when I was quite small he rented for the summer a large house near the beach at Santa Monica, California, and invited my mother with her two young children over for a couple of weeks. He took me to Exposition Park to see the skeletons of the various prehistoric animals that had been dug out of the La Brea tar pits. He was keenly interested in them. I was about six at the time but I can still remember getting sick at my stomach from the interminable rides on streetcars.

I am sure it was rather painful for Grandfather to give up his belief in the special creation of man, but when he read the evidence for the long and slow development of the human race he simply could not brush it off, as much as he would have liked to.

It is the nature of children to believe what adults tell them and also to believe what they read unless it sounds too preposterous. When my sister Helen was born I was told that a stork had brought her. As I gazed upon her red and wizened little face, I could see that while the stork had been flying through the sky holding the diaper that contained Helen in his beak she had got badly sunburned. I remember the occasion very well. At the time I was just one month short of being four years old.

I did not start to school until I was eight and until then I had implicit faith in the stork story, as I had been around children of my age very little. My schoolmates quickly set me straight. At first I was incredulous, but by that time I knew that there were certain differences in male and female anatomy. I had also seen some pregnant women. The facts of life as explained to me by my schoolmates suddenly seemed logical. The stories about human birth told me by elders seemed ridiculous. I experienced no trauma. Years later my mother, after a long-winded and hesitant build-up, began blushingly to tell me about the birds and the bees. I told her that I already knew the facts of life and that she could spare us both embarrassment by skipping it. She was greatly relieved.

I first became skeptical about religion as revealed at Tempe's First Baptist Church, South when I discovered that my Sunday-school teacher used very poor English. Everyone in both the Woolf and O'Connor families used impeccable grammar. I didn't know a verb from a predicate adjective but I did know good English from bad English. The fact that she said "I seen," "I taken," "that's what they done," and "it ain't no different" made me skeptical as to her general wisdom. I did not endear myself to her by correcting her grammar.

I began to feel definitely estranged the day my Sunday-school teacher told her class that the Catholic churches all contained stores of rifles, ammunition, and bombs, and that one day the Catholics were going to break out and massacre (she pronounced it mass-a-*kree*) the Protestants. This was undoubtedly some vague tribal memory of seventeenth-century religious conflict, but it seemed downright silly to me. I spoke up and said flatly that I did not believe it, that I knew old Father Espinosa at the Catholic church and that he would not harm a flea, that my Grandmother O'Connor had been a Catholic and that my Uncle Jim O'Connor had gone to a Catholic prep school. I got so furious that I wept. When I told my mother she said that I should not worry, that Mrs. Jenkens was a good woman but not very well educated and "narrow."

Curiously enough it was a sermon on atheism that made an agnostic out of me. The preacher told his congregation about the incredible beliefs of the wicked atheists. They believed, he said, that Jesus was a mortal man, the son of a mortal woman by a mortal man, that he was a teacher, not the son of God. These strange people also believed, he went on, that Jesus had not arisen from the dead, that there was no heaven and no hell. There were gasps of disbelief from the congregation. Some of the women were so shocked that they wept. All of this suddenly seemed reasonable and logical to me and I at once put most of what I had been taught in Sunday school in the pigeonhole where I kept the story of the stork, of Santa Claus, and the garden of Eden.

This must have happened about the time I was eleven. I continued to go to Sunday school with a fair degree of regularity and sometimes I went to church services. I didn't tell my grandfather that I had become a skeptic. I didn't even tell my mother. But the first summer I visited my Uncle Jim O'Connor in Florence I talked things over with Jim one night after dinner. We had eaten one of Jim's complicated and delicious whitewing stews made with potatoes, peas, carrots, onions, pimiento, green chili, a touch of garlic, some wine—in fact just about everything you could think of, including probably some ashes from Jim's cigar.

With the stew we had a salad of tomatoes, onions, cucumbers with real olive oil and wine vinegar dressing, and fresh fruit for dessert. We pulled chairs out into the back yard. As it grew dark the cooling evening breeze sprang up and the windmill began to clank as it turned. Jim sat with a cigar and a big snifter glass of brandy. His favorite dog, a big Airedale named Major, came and lay down at his feet.

"Uncle Jim," I said suddenly, "do you believe in heaven and hell?"

Jim took a long pull on his cigar, then a sniff and a sip of brandy.

"That's a hell of a question to ask a tired old man who's simply trying to enjoy the processes of digestion. Why do you ask?"

"I heard a preacher talk about atheists. What he said they believed sort of sounded true to me."

"Did it bother you?"

"No."

"Well," Jim said. "This heaven and hell business has never sounded particularly plausible to me, but that's neither here nor there. I go ahead and try to be a reasonably decent and honorable guy every day. If I should die and wake up in either place I'd be surprised. But if the belief in either place makes some people happier and more decent and better able to endure the kicks in the tail we all have to take in this world I am all for it. I would not do anything to undermine their belief."

"Yes, sir!"

"And Jack—"

"Yes, Uncle Jim."

"I have always found it a good idea not to worry much about anything you can't do anything about!"

Most of the boys and girls I went to Sunday school with joined the church. After an emotional sermon they would come forward weeping at the enormity of their sins. The preacher would embrace them, also weeping, and then the new converts would sit in front and join in a good cry. Later they would be baptized, sometimes down at the river between the two buttes, but generally in a sort of a small indoor swimming pool under the pulpit. The boys always wore their best dark suits (which were invariably ruined) and the girls white dresses. The preacher dunked them clear under and when they came up they always looked like drowned kittens. The Baptists felt that no one could go to heaven unless he had been totally submerged. The performance always struck me as lacking in dignity. My sister Helen was baptized and it saddened me to see the poor little thing all dressed in white be plunged into the water and come up coughing, spitting, and looking thoroughly miserable.

ALTHOUGH I WAS simply not the religious type or the joining type I continued to go to Sunday school now and then and occasionally I went to church. My attendance at Christmas-tree parties on Christmas Eve, at ice-cream socials, at watermelon feeds, at church suppers, and at church picnics was practically 100 per cent.

The picnics were usually considered to be for the young people and they were well chaperoned. Sometimes we hiked across the new bridge that spanned the Salt River out into the rocky desert, in the area now called Papago Park. There we toasted wieners and marshmallows and sang songs. Some of the older and bolder boys sneaked off to smoke cigarettes and others tried to lure Samantha

Duncan out into the bushes. Now and then one of the farmer parishioners furnished a hay rack padded with hay and covered with a canvas tarp. The boys and girls, excited by thighs and shoulders pressing together, would be hauled out into the desert where they ate, played games, sang songs, made tentative passes at each other.

Ice-cream socials and watermelon feeds were, for the boys anyway, real orgies. I believe I have on many occasions downed at least a half gallon of ice cream and on other occasions I am convinced that I have got around two large watermelons.

I also loved the church suppers. These, I believe, were held to raise money. All the women baked their most exquisite dishes and they were laid out on a long table in the Odd Fellows' Hall above Birchett Brothers' Grocery. Mother always took Helen and me. I believe we were charged fifty cents for all we could eat. I still slaver as I think of the warm, nourishing smell of coffee and hot mashed potatoes, of roast beef and meat loaf, roast and fried chicken, roast turkey and duck and pork, of great luscious cakes, of myriad kinds of chow-chow and pickles, of great pots of red-brown frijoles, of apple, mince, lemon meringue, peach, apricot, raisin, and cream pies. And over all this magnificent provender fat, kindly, motherly women stood beaming and pressing larger and larger, more and more helpings on the customers. Sometimes I was barely able to waddle home. If anything was left over the matron who brought it was deeply hurt, and I, the kindest of boys, could not bear to see a look of disappointment on any of those plump, kindly faces. Some of the worst cooking in the United States is country cooking—but also some of the best!

JUST HOW MUCH difference there was between the various Protestant churches in Tempe in those days I do not know. I think the Presbyterians and the Congregationalists had more education on an average than did the Baptists, and were less inclined to shout when the Spirit was on them. The Baptists looked askance at the Methodists because they did not believe in dunking those who joined, but otherwise they were cut out of the same cloth. The

Christians struck me as being just as apt to belt out an amen or a hallelujah as the Baptists. The only "white" Catholic I can remember was Professor Fred Irish, who taught physics, chemistry, and military training at the normal. Everything the Pillsons did had to be high class. They were Episcopalians but there was no Episcopalian church in Tempe. They had to go to Phoenix to worship, as did the Levitskys, who were Jewish.

The Mormons had been among the first settlers in the Salt River valley. They had come into Arizona from Utah to the north, crossing unexplored deserts and undergoing incredible hardships. They settled along rivers, so that with their genius for communal activity they could dig ditches and divert water by building dams. The Mormon leaders preached industry, thrift, cooperation. A good Mormon was not supposed to smoke or drink tea, coffee, or alcoholic beverages. On the other hand, the church encouraged music and dancing. The Mormons I knew worked hard but they also had a good time.

Mormon missionaries had made many converts among the humble people of the Scandinavian countries and the British Isles. These they sent to the United States. Many of them had walked across the Great Plains to Utah. One old man I knew in my youth had been converted in England. He had pushed a handcart from the banks of the Mississippi to Salt Lake. On the way he had acquired three wives. He had just got well established in Utah when he and some others were ordered to go south to colonize Arizona. They did so by terrible toil. They let their wagons and their oxen down by long ropes into the canyon of the Colorado, upstream from what is thought of as the Grand Canyon, built rafts and ferried everything across, labored painfully over deserts, explored, built dams and houses.

Many of the Mormons still had more than one wife when I was growing up in Tempe. One very rich Mormon was reputed to have four, all living under one roof. If these women had been young, beautiful, and juicy little houris the menage would have been considered sinful, but the women were old and shriveled, with sagging jowls and drooping breasts. Because no one envied this rich old man his harem no one protested.

There was a certain amount of sub rosa polygamy among the Mormons of Arizona when I was a boy in Arizona, and the Mormons maintained colonies in the Sierra Madre Mountains of Mexico for polygamous families on whom Uncle Sam had put the heat in this country. George Romney, the present governor of Michigan, was born in one of those Mormon colonies in Chihuahua.

Mormon family arrangements used to puzzle non-Mormon schoolteachers. Two boys, both six years old, who said they were brothers but not twins and who listed the same man as their father, would show up for first grade, much to the bewilderment of the teacher. Once I had a date to take dancing a pretty Mormon girl who lived in Mesa. When I arrived at the appointed time the girl had been weeping and was plainly not ready to go anywhere. I was aware that not only the girl but the whole household was upset. I found out later that the girl's father had left hastily for Mexico just ahead of a warrant for his arrest. It seems he had two wives in Mesa and two more in Mexico.

Most of the Mormons I knew were admirable people and I had many friends among them. No matter what is said about the Book of Mormon and some of the early leaders, it is a good working religion that has done a great deal of good for a great number of people. The Mormons believe in education, just as they believe in abstinence, thrift, cooperation, and industry. Most of those I knew were not sophisticated people, even by Tempe standards of sophistication, but some of their children are very urbane indeed.

Even when I was growing up some of the younger Mormons did not adhere strictly to the Mormon law. They smoked, drank hard liquor, and gambled. These were known as Jack Mormons. Now, I am told, the flaunting of the Words of Wisdom is quite common among the more sophisticated Mormons in the larger cities. I have, alas, downed many a beaker of malt liquor and many a martini with Mormon friends in Mormon households.

The Mormons in the Salt River valley were almost entirely of British and Scandinavian descent. Most of them were blonds. The men were tall, strong, athletic, and the teams from Mesa High School were greatly feared in athletic competition. Many of the girls were very pretty.

Some of the pioneer Mormon patriarchs must have passed their genes around rather freely because many of the young Mormons I knew bore what might be called a family resemblance. Dozens of the young men were tall, strong, had light eyes, fair hair, and tended to become prematurely bald. The look is so characteristic that on several occasions I have identified people I have met hundreds of miles from Arizona as Salt River valley Mormons.

Back in the 1920's a national high-school basketball tournament was held annually at the University of Chicago, and the team that represented Arizona was usually composed of big, rugged Mormon boys from Mesa, Gilbert, or Chandler. One year the other contestants at the tournament filed an indignant protest against the Arizona team. They were all bona fide high-school students and not one of them was over nineteen, but the shortest one was six feet two and every one was bald. Not a one looked less than thirty-five. The high-school coaches there knew a bunch of ringers when they saw one!

# 18 · Grandfather Woolf's Last Days

My Grandfather Woolf was not a large man and as far as I know he came from small stock, as my great-uncles Frank and Bob Woolf, the only ones of my grandfather's brothers I ever saw, were probably smaller than my grandfather. He was only five feet eight, and would guess that he weighed around 145 or 150 pounds in his prime. My grandmother was likewise small, about five feet two, but one of her Confederate brothers who was shot by the Yankees during the Civil War was a six-footer as was her youngest brother, my Great-uncle Tom McConnell, who came out to Arizona on a visit about 1911. He was the president of a bank in Kentucky.

With the exception of my Uncle Jim Woolf, who was the family runt, all my Woolf uncles were taller than Grandfather. They must have got their height from the McConnells. My Uncle Charles was a six-footer, Uncle Arthur was five feet ten and a half or five feet eleven, John and Bill about five feet nine or ten. But Grandfather packed a lot of wiry strength and energy into a small frame. Some sort of physical activity was necessary to him. Even as an old man he walked with rapid steps. In his early sixties when he hunted quail he wore younger men down. Every time I saw him with his shirt off I was surprised at how large and muscular his biceps and forearms were.

I can never remember him when his hair was not white, but it was thick and wiry all his life. He wore his beard and mustache in the style that General U. S. Grant made famous. His beard was also white, but around his mouth it was always stained with tobacco juice. Like most members of his generation he was an inveterate tobacco chewer. His favorite was Horseshoe Cut Plug. When I was small I liked the little tin horseshoes that were imbedded in the plugs. Many tales are told about the spitting skill of the old tobacco chewers. They were supposed to be able to spit through a keyhole at twenty feet. Like the tales of Robin Hood's superhuman skill with the bow and the uncanny long-range shooting of the buffalo hunters, the epic performances of the tobacco spitters lost nothing in the telling. I never saw one that could be counted on to hit a spittoon every time at five feet. That is why spittoons always sat on rubber mats about two and a half feet in diameter. The spitters were in the four ring a lot more often than in the bull.

My grandfather's family owned a few slaves and were Democrats, but all were staunch Unionists, whereas my grandmother's people owned no slaves but were ardent Confederates and gladly shed their blood for the Confederate cause. Grandfather was only thirteen when the Civil War broke out, seventeen when it was over. In Crittenden County, Kentucky, where both Grandfather and Grandmother Woolf were born there were about as many Confederate sympathizers as Union sympathizers. Crittenden County men served on both sides, and two sons of the United States senator for whom the county was named, and who was the author of the Crittenden Compromise, were generals—one in the Confederate army and one in the Union army. Neither was a very good general.

My Great-grandfather Woolf sent my grandfather to Ohio to attend a college which must not have been much better than a high school. A few years before my grandmother's death I saw on her dresser a large, flat, diamond-shaped fraternity pin. Just to see what Grandmother would say, I asked her what it was. She told me it was the pin of Jeem's literary society. In the last year or so of the war my grandfather was either in the Union army or in some

Kentucky home-guard outfit. I suspect it was the latter, as he never joined the G.A.R. as far as I know.

But he was a lifelong Democrat. He was active in Democratic state politics almost from the time he moved to Arizona, and in the 1890's and early 1900's he served in the territorial legislature, a position that paid off largely in honor instead of money.

After my grandfather sold the ranch and retired he was bored and restless. Like many men who make money in one business he lost it in other businesses which seemed to him more romantic. I remember hearing my Uncle Charles Woolf say after Grandfather's death that he had lost fifty thousand dollars in the company he had formed to make puncture-proof, tubeless automobile tires. He invented a concrete headgate for irrigation ditches, but I doubt if either his gate or the cement company made any money. Other manufacturers quickly found ways to get around his patents on the gate, and the concrete blocks he manufactured had to compete with adobe bricks made from native soil and water by Mexicans who would work for a dollar a day. In the ten years between his retirement in 1905 until his death in 1915 my grandfather dropped a good deal of money.

When Woodrow Wilson was elected President in 1912, my grandfather decided he would like to be postmaster at Tempe. He had for many years been a heavy contributor to the Democratic Party, had been Democratic national committeeman for Arizona Territory, was a friend of all manner of bigwigs in the Democratic Party. Since in those days jobs as postmaster were up for grabs when a new party came into power, I don't suppose Grandfather had much difficulty in getting the appointment.

He approached the job with his characteristic energy and determination. He instituted the delivery of mail to homes. He had boxes put up to receive mail at various points in town so it was no longer necessary to go down to the post office to mail a letter. He worked hard himself, selling stamps, distributing mail. He seemed to think that I was a sort of an extension of his own personality and he quickly drafted me to help out at the post office. I too distributed mail, sold stamps, but I also helped the janitor. For this I was supposed to get a dollar a week, and I did on the weeks that my grandfather remembered to pay me.

Good, honest toil has always had a way of boring me, and I cannot say I worked at the post office with any great enthusiasm. Part of the job I found downright distasteful. I often had to sweep out the lobby. This was 1913, the year that I was eleven, and the year the beautiful Anna Levitsky, who was nineteen and with whom I was madly in love, ran away and got married. She used to come sailing into the post office every afternoon to get the Levitsky mail from a box. She always greeted me with a smile and a pleasant word, but it seared my soul to be caught by my love while I was performing such a menial and degrading task.

Another cross I had to bear was helping the janitor clean out the interior of the post office on Saturday mornings. All week, vast quantities of undeliverable newspapers, magazines, and advertising matter were thrown into big boxes. Then the three or four rural mail carriers, the city carriers, my grandfather, and the others who worked in the post office would squirt great gobs of tobacco juice over everything. The janitor and I would have to take this stinking, spittle-covered waste material out of the boxes and burn it. I cannot say I enjoyed working at the post office very much. Honest toil was not for me.

MY GRANDFATHER'S greatest joy and almost his only relaxation was hunting and fishing, and for years whenever it was feasible he took me with him, until the onset of his fatal illness. At first I only went along to pick up the birds he had knocked down. I learned to put my eye on the exact spot where the bird had fallen and then not take it off until I had found the bird. Mourning and whitewing doves used to lie where they fell, even if they were only wounded, but quail would run and hide as long as they could move. I learned to put a handkerchief, or something else that was easily seen, down at the spot I had marked and then search around it if the bird was not there. I became a very good retriever. Grandfather always told his friends that I was better than a bird dog.

Until Grandfather got the Overland touring car, our hunting expeditions always began by harnessing old Pet, his trotting mare, to the buggy. He buckled the harness on one side and I on the other. It has been over fifty years since I harnessed a horse to a buggy, but I believe if I had to do it I could manage it today.

Grandfather had a temper. He was also a good Christian man who did not believe in taking the Lord's name in vain or in cursing in general. Yet when he got his steam up he had to have some way of blowing it off. He compromised by adapting a private vocabulary of cuss words which were similar to the real ones but not identical. When Bossy the cow would try to kick the milk bucket over he would leap to his feet with his blue eyes blazing, kick the cow back, and shout: "Stop that, you goldurned old hut!" He used such words as durned, danged, son of a hitch, hut, dadblamed, goldurned. If anyone had told him that he was actually cursing and taking the name of the Lord in vain he would have been shocked.

About the time he sold his ranch Grandfather gave the Baptist church in Tempe ten thousand dollars toward building a new church, and I believe he donated the concrete blocks with which it was constructed. I think he was convinced that the gift had squared him with God from then on, as I can seldom remember him going to church. I think church services and the shouted sermons of the hillbilly preachers actually bored the hell out of him.

Nevertheless I am convinced that he died believing that he would go to heaven and that presently his wife Molly would show up to join him, not old and bitter, but young, pretty, curvaceous, and eager the way she must have been when they got married over a half century before. I am sure that he also believed his children and grandchildren would join him and that he would reign as a patriarch in grassy meadows filled with antelope and deer and that the heavenly guns he would use would never miss.

In his last years he still called me boy, but he talked to me more when we rode out to shoot doves or quail. He told me he had met Theodore Roosevelt but he didn't care for him. He liked many of Roosevelt's ideas, but said Roosevelt was basically a second-rate Kaiser Wilhelm. He didn't like Kaiser Wilhelm. He had met

William Howard Taft and had got along so famously with him that when Taft came through Arizona when he was campaigning in 1912 he remembered Grandfather and invited him to dinner on his private car, even though Grandfather was a dyed-in-the-wool Democrat.

We were driving out into the country to hunt doves one day in the summer of 1913 when he turned to me suddenly and said: "Boy, you go to Sunday school pretty regularly, don't you?" "Yes, sir," I said. "Do you believe everything you hear?" I paused for a moment in order to frame a tactful answer. "Well, not everything, I guess." We drove on for a mile or more. Then he said: "You've heard of evolution—about man not being created by the Lord and there not being a Garden of Eden and the world not being made in six days?" I said I had indeed heard of evolution. "Well," he demanded, "how does it sound to you?" "It sounds more logical than the Garden of Eden business," I said. We drove on for several minutes, then he said: "It does to me too, dad-rat it!"

I began to graduate from being a retriever only when I was nearing seven. Now and then my grandfather would hand me his 12-gauge double and say: "Boy, see that whitewing on the fence post? Well, here's the gun. Knock him off!" When the bird fell he would hold out his hand for the gun and say, "Good shot."

I was eight when he got me my 20-gauge single-shot Iver-Johnson. From then on he kept me in 20-gauge shells and coached me in wing shooting. By the summer of 1913 when I was eleven I was doing fairly well on both mourning doves and whitewings.

Much wheat was raised in the Salt River valley in those days. There were still thousands of acres of mesquite forests along the Salt and the Gila rivers and the birds flew in every spring from Mexico to nest and raise their squabs. In those lawless and short-sighted days shooting started as soon as the birds arrived and continued as long as they stayed, but before World War I the birds were in the valley by the hundred thousands, if not indeed by the millions. The whitewing hunt was famous among bird shots over the United States. Sports used to come in from California and even from the Eastern seaboard, establish luxurious tent camps with folding chairs, tables, and canvas bathtubs, iceboxes, imported cooks, quantities of wine, beer, and strong liquor.

Now and then Grandfather and I would pause at one of these camps and talk hunting and guns. He was always offered drinks but he always refused.

"Boy," he told me once as we rode off, "that's almost like offering a person poison. Don't ever drink. Rum is the curse of the world!"

I didn't tell Grandfather that I had drunk several small glasses of beer when I was with my Uncle Jim O'Connor and that Buddy Pillson and I had tasted the various kinds of wine and liqueurs at the Pillson house when his parents were out.

My grandfather was a firm prohibitionist. He believed that whiskey had its place as medicine, but as a beverage—*never!* Upon leaving Kentucky in 1875 he took with him a charred twenty-five gallon keg full of seven-year-old sour-mash bourbon. It traveled by train, wagon, and probably by packhorse from Kentucky to Colorado, from Colorado to New Mexico, from New Mexico to Arizona. As the years went by it was doled out when members of the family had bad colds, when Grandmother or one of the daughters had cramps, occasionally in the mountains of New Mexico when a neighbor arrived half frozen in the dead of winter. Not long before his last illness, he poured the last gallon of the whiskey into a jug. When he died Grandmother sold the big house and moved into a smaller house she had built beside my mother's place. The jug moved with her. In 1928 I was home for a visit with my young wife, Eleanor. My grandmother heard she had a bad case of cramps and came hobbling over with the very last of the whiskey in a pint bottle—two or three jiggers, enough for a stiff hot toddy for Eleanor and a taste for me. The moment the cork was out of the bottle the bouquet of that wonderful booze went all through the house.

Exactly when Tempe went dry I cannot remember, but it must have been about 1910 or 1912. My grandparents and my mother were against the wets, against the liquor traffic, against the saloon-keepers. They felt that when the saloon and the liquor traffic were abolished thriftless people would no longer waste their wages on booze. No drunks would start to stagger home to beat their wives and children and fall vomiting on the sidewalks before they got there. My Uncle Jim O'Connor laughed at the drys. "The only way they can make prohibition work," he said, "is to talk God into repealing fermentation. The damned fools will probably make the state dry and maybe the whole country, but it won't work!"

I DON'T REMEMBER when Grandfather decided to take the plunge and buy an automobile but it must have been about 1913. He loved horses and was fond of Pet, his trotting mare. But as the years went by more and more of his friends were buying automobiles and fewer and fewer horses were seen hitched in front of the stores on Mill Avenue. In Phoenix the wonderful horse-drawn fire engines were replaced by mechanical monsters with powerful, noisy motors that looked six feet long.

Grandfather went about the purchase of an automobile methodically. Many automobile salesmen from Phoenix called on him with shiny cars—Locomobiles, Simplexes, Mitchells, Pierce-Arrows, Packards, Wintons, Hupmobiles. At that time Central Avenue in Phoenix for several blocks north of Van Buren was automobile row. There must have been salesrooms of at least thirty makes of cars.

Grandfather finally decided on an Overland. It was a four-cylinder touring car. I believe it had a self-starter but I am not certain. Grandfather prepared for the coming of his automobile as carefully as a young woman prepares for the advent of her first-born. He had a garage built for it and in the middle of its concrete floor was a deep pit to make it easier for work on its mysterious underside.

At the time he bought the Overland Grandfather must have been about sixty-five, a bit old to change the habits of a lifetime and to start mastering a complicated mechanism like an automobile. The salesman spent an afternoon with him, teaching him what the various gadgets were for, how to shift gears, and whatnot. At the end of the afternoon Grandfather drove up to my mother's house and said: "Come on, Ida. Get the kids and I'll give you a ride. I can drive the dad-ratted thing!"

At that time and for a long time after that automobiles had a lever on the steering wheel regulating the spark and one regulating the flow of gas. When the car started the gas lever was supposed to be in a position where it would give the motor plenty of gasoline when it started to turn over. Grandfather could never remember that the gas lever on the steering wheel and the foot throttle on the floorboard had exactly the same function. He would get the Overland started, forget he had the gas lever down, and then discover to his horror that the damned thing wouldn't go less than twenty miles an hour—a speed he considered blinding and reckless.

That first ride was a bit hair-raising. Grandfather forgot to put the gas lever up. We started off with a fearful jerk as he took his foot off the clutch, and away we went with Grandfather hanging onto the steering wheel in the attitude of an ancient and dignified but apprehensive Roman competing in a chariot race. We skidded at the first turn and Grandfather, with a wild but determined look in his eyes, took a firm grip on the wheel. Old Grandpa Mullins, who had taken part in Pickett's charge, was slowly crossing the street, bent over by arthritis, cane in hand. It looked as if Grandpa Mullins and the Overland were on a collision course. The car was tearing along with Grandfather frozen to the wheel, apparently unable to remember what the various levers and pedals were for. Grandpa Mullins was somewhat deaf as well as crippled, but just in time he saw the Overland bearing down upon him and he sprang away. As we swept by he shook his fist at Grandfather.

"Dad-gummed old fool!" Grandfather said.

We kept sweeping down streets, skidding around corners. My sister Helen was crying and my mother's face wore a look of sheer terror. Grandfather apparently hoped to hang on and guide it after a fashion until it ran out of wind like a runaway horse.

My Uncle Jim O'Connor had given me lessons in handling an

automobile when I visited him in Florence. He had let me drive his big old lumbering 1908 Cadillac out in the country where I would not have to make any fast decisions. He had explained the various gadgets to me and I knew why the Overland would not slow down. I was in the front seat with Grandfather, and two or three times I had tried to tell him to push his gas lever back up. Each time he said: "Shut up, boy! Don't bother me! Can't you see this dad-blasted thing is acting up?" Finally I reached over and pushed the gas lever up. Instantly the car started to slow down. It almost stopped, and in a moment he had to step on the foot throttle to get it to proceed at a seemly ten miles an hour.

Grandfather never could remember about that gas lever. Once he had been to town, and because he had forgotten about the lever he headed wildly home at a breath-taking twenty-five miles an hour. He drove around the block several times trying to work up enough courage to take a shot at going into the garage at that speed. He couldn't stop fast enough, broke both headlights, crumpled the front fenders, bent the bumper. I think he was relieved that the Overland had to stay in the garage in Phoenix a couple of weeks for repairs.

But that first fall he had the car we could go farther afield for quail. Grandfather felt that twenty miles an hour was a decent cruising speed, but even at that it was a lot faster than a horse and buggy at three or four miles an hour. I have no doubt that there were seasons and bag limits in those days, but if there were I never heard of them. I am also quite certain that Grandfather never bought me a license. We considered fifty quail a fair bag for a day's hunt, seventy-five about right, and now and then we shot together more than a hundred. What Grandfather did with his share I have no idea, but my thrifty mother preserved many of ours in jars like fruit. They were delicious.

As long as I went hunting with him, my grandfather had to catheterize himself in order to urinate. He kept the catheter in a fruit jar filled with a carbolic-acid solution in the medicine cabinet in the downstairs bathroom, along with his spare set of false teeth, which were in another fruit jar. When we went hunting he took the catheter with him. In those days the operation for the removal of the prostate gland had not been perfected.

Eventually an infection set in, an infection that could easily have been cured with today's antibiotics or with sulfa. Grandfather went to bed in his study, grew thinner and thinner, weaker and weaker. Miss Williams, the trained nurse we always called in for serious illnesses, showed up in clean uniform and starched cap and stayed with him to the end.

I used to go over to see him almost every day. I would sit and read him hunting stories from *Outdoor Life* and *Field & Stream.* He would say: "Dad-rat it, boy. I want to get well. I want to take you up in British Columbia somewhere so we can shoot some of those northern sheep and maybe moose and caribou. You're old enough now!"

Once Miss Williams told me he had been asking for quail. I got on my bicycle and went out with my 20-gauge single barrel and shot a half dozen out of a covey. I also brought him doves and whitewings.

For some reason Miss Williams had a barber come in and shave off his beard and mustache. He didn't look like my grandfather any more. His eyes seemed bigger and deeper set and his cheeks were sunken. His skin was yellow wax.

One of the last times he talked to me he asked me to bring a chair and sit down beside his bed. Tears came into his eyes as he spoke.

"They haven't told me this, boy," he said, "but I know I am going to die. I get weaker all the time and I guess there is nothing the doctors can do. You are a good boy, Jack. I have always felt sorry that Ida and your father didn't make out. You've been sort of a son to me, maybe more of a son than any son I've had, because when I was young and my own boys were growing up I was too busy to pay very much attention to them. You are forgetful and dreamy but you're a good boy. You've got a good mother and you've got good blood on both sides. In some ways you're the smartest boy I've ever known . . . but just in some ways. Other ways you're not very smart but you're a good boy!" He closed his bright-blue eyes in those deep sockets for a moment. Then he took my hand. "I guess it is because you were my first grandson and always tagged around with me, but I have always loved you." He turned his head away and I could see that he was acutely embarrassed. I bent over and kissed him on his hot, dry forehead.

"I have always loved you, too, Grampa," I said. "I have always wanted to be like you!" As I tiptoed out of the room he had turned his head to the wall but I could tell he was weeping.

He was very sick the next day and Miss Williams wouldn't let anyone come in to see him. The day after that he rallied a little. He called me and my grandmother in and told Grandmother that he owed me at least fifty dollars for my work at the post office and that since I was the only one in the family who would appreciate it he wanted me to have his 12-gauge Purdey. Grandmother never paid me the fifty dollars, and as I have already recounted, she gave Uncle Charles, who never hunted, the Purdey. She never had much use for me because I had an Irish name.

The day after Grandfather talked to my grandmother and me he became delirious. It took him three days to die. Part of the time he lay quiet, unconscious, breathing heavily, but part of the time he talked and shouted in his delirium.

Along in midafternoon of that third terrible day Miss Williams came out of Grandfather's study into the living room and told us all that he had died. I went out into the orchard and bawled for a half hour or so. I didn't want anyone to see me. I didn't want to see the hearse come and take him away, so I cut across the pasture to Mother's house.

All the flags in Tempe were at half mast the day Grandfather was buried, and the normal and all the schools were dismissed. This was in 1915. I was thirteen then and my grandfather was sixty-eight when he died. He looked little and shrunken and waxen in his coffin. I was dry-eyed at the funeral, but when they took him out to the Double Buttes cemetery to bury him I refused to go. Instead I went home and lay on the bed and cried.

Grandmother sold the Overland. As soon as the estate was

settled she sold the big house and had a smaller house built next door to my mother's place on Forest Avenue. Grandfather's estate came to well over a hundred thousand dollars, enough to let Grandmother live comfortably the rest of her life and pass some money along to her eight living children.

She outlived Grandfather by nineteen years. In 1934 I went to the University of Arizona as its first professor of journalism. My wife went to St. Louis that Christmas to see her parents. I went into Sonora on a sheep and deer hunt. When I came back I drove to Tempe to spend New Year's with my mother. My grandmother was dying. She was fully conscious when I saw her in the afternoon. She met death calmly, coldly, without emotion, as she had met all the crises in her life.

When I went to see her she told me she was on her deathbed. She died during the night.

# 19 · Tempe Normal, 1915-17

IT really got under my mother's hide one time when she heard a professor from the University of Arizona refer to the Tempe Normal as an overgrown high school. She mentioned the slight several times and when she did so she always snorted: "The stuck-up snob!"

Actually the professor was right. The Tempe Normal in those days was not much better than a high school and neither was its sister institution, the Flagstaff Normal School in high, cool, and also thinly populated northern Arizona. If the truth were known, the University of Arizona wasn't a great deal better than a high school either. Because there were few high schools in Arizona all three institutions admitted high-school students in their preparatory or "academic" departments. Enrollments were small—probably not over two hundred at Flagstaff, perhaps three hundred or somewhat more at Tempe, and perhaps four hundred at the University of Arizona.

The Tempe Normal was established as a one-building institution in 1885, about the time my Grandfather Woolf moved to the Salt River valley. Because it was handy all the members of my mother's family attended the normal sooner or later. My mother and my two aunts all graduated with teachers' certificates. My Uncle

Charles Woolf went on to the University of Colorado, where he studied law, and my mother eventually got an A.B. and an M.A. at the University of Arizona.

The University of Arizona likewise began as a one-building institution in the same year as the Tempe Normal. It was located out on the caliche and greasewood desert a mile from the center of Tucson, and for a long time it was connected with Tucson only by a rickety streetcar line. The story is that, at the time the plums were passed out to the various Arizona towns by the territorial legislature, the representative from Tucson was on a seven-day drunk. When he sobered up he was horrified to discover that Yuma had got the state prison (it was later moved to Florence). Phoenix had come off with the lion's share—the state capitol and the insane asylum—and Tempe and Flagstaff had each got normal schools. As far as anyone knew there wasn't anything left to give the now desperate Tucson delegate. Then someone thought of a university. It was better than nothing. He went home with a small appropriation to start a building and to hire a principal. A public-spirited saloonkeeper threw in some worthless desert land east of town. It wasn't much but it was something, and it saved the legislator from being lynched.

During the many years I lived in Arizona professors and students at the university looked down their noses at the two normals, and consequently those who taught or studied at the normal school felt both resentful and inferior. The feeling probably still persists in spite of the fact that Tempe Normal is now Arizona State University and enrolls twenty thousand or more students and the Flagstaff Normal is now called Northern Arizona University and has seven thousand students.

Before World War I some of the departments at the University of Arizona were probably good. The college of engineering turned out competent civil and mining engineers. The college of agriculture no doubt had well-prepared and competent instructors in alfalfa raising and one-handed milking. However, by today's standards those who taught in the college of liberal arts were largely old-fashioned schoolmasters who were shy on both advanced degrees and scholarship.

At the Tempe Normal anyone with a bachelor's degree was considered very well prepared and anyone with a master's degree was looked upon as a scholar of breathtaking erudition. A. J. Matthews, the president of the normal, had acquired an honorary doctor's degree somewhere, but I doubt that he had never earned so much as an A.B. The only master's degree I can remember was attached to the teacher of geography. The head of the training school, the teachers of history and biology, and Fred Irish, who taught physics and chemistry, had bachelors' degrees. Most of the other teachers, including my mother, had gone to normal schools and had taken additional work mostly in education courses in summer schools.

If a student enrolled in the academic department right out of eighth grade he could go through the normal and graduate with a teaching certificate in five years. If, however, he entered after he finished high school he had to go two years. The first year's work for high-school graduates was largely a repetition of the senior year in high school, as many of the graduates of cow-town and mining-camp high schools were only marginally literate. In the "senior" year the students did their practice teaching and plowed through a jungle of education courses.

Most of the students at the normal were girls—perhaps three-fourths of them—as teaching was almost the only respectable work middle-class girls could do in the interval between school and marriage. Most of the students were from Arizona, but now and then a student who had asthma or a "weak chest" showed up from that fabulous land known as Back East. The Tempe winter climate was mild and sunny. Board and room cost only about twenty dollars a month. Nervous parents were assured that the virginity of the co-eds was carefully guarded. Unchaperoned evening dates were not allowed. Amorous lads could sit at night with co-eds in dormitory parlors or on well-lighted porches. Couples who wanted to see Friday- or Saturday-night movies at the Goodwin Opera House were convoyed from the dormitories to the show and back by the "preceptresses" from the girls' dormitories.

On Sunday afternoons it was the custom for both boys and girls to dress in their very finest clothes and parade up and down on the sidewalks on the campus, take pictures of each other with Brownie box cameras, or sit on the grass under the palm and olive trees. The girls wore taffeta dresses for these Sunday promenades, and the most fashionable shoe for females had a sharp toe and a high heel and was laced halfway up the calf. Glimpses of an inch or so of silk or lisle stocking above those shoe tops used to arouse the lustful fantasies of the young men. The males wore high shoes often with uppers of a different color, very tight trousers, tight jackets, shirts with high, detachable collars. Usually these were starched stiff and of the sort the handsome Arrow Collar Man wore in advertisements in the *Saturday Evening Post.* However, soft detachable collars were beginning to come in. Cravats were wide and it was fashionable to tie them with knots three or four inches long. The young men uniformly wore their hair unparted and long on top in a style called the pompadour. It was then considered very fashionable, at least in the circles in which I moved, to have the hair on the lower part of the head clipped very close so that the effect of the long hair was that of a toupee sitting on top of a bald head. Not many years before, peg-top pants had been the rage along with long suit coats with enormously padded shoulders that made weaklings look as if they could bend railroad rails with their bare hands. With this costume went high buttoned shoes with "bulldog" toes. This getup was looked upon with disfavor by the young sophisticates with whom I associated, but it was still worn in the less urbane areas in Arizona. Cheap magazines read by farm hands and cowboys carried advertisements by mail-order tailors that said: "Peg Top Pants a Specialty. No Extra Charge No Matter How Extreme You Order Them."

Since many of the students came from forlorn little mining camps and from remote cattle ranches where it was difficult to get through the grades and where they were many miles from high schools, some of them were far more advanced in years than they were in education. An occasional graduate of the academic department was twenty-one or twenty-two, and of the normal course twenty-five or twenty-six. There was always a sprinkling of students even older—sad young women whose husbands had died or who had been married and divorced. They generally had children to support and were looking for respectable and secure, if poorly paid, positions. Sometimes men in their thirties would enroll to take the two-year normal course and prepare themselves to teach. Occasionally they were arthritics who felt better in hot, dry Arizona. Sometimes they were recovered tuberculars who had been told that they should live out their lives in a mild climate. Often they were men who had been in business but who did not like male competition and preferred the largely female atmosphere of the schoolroom.

Tempe went dry by local option about 1912 and the whole state was dry before national prohibition came along in 1919. But Phoenix, a real Babylon, was wet until the whole state dried up. I listened with awe when older boys told me of drinking whiskey and gin in Phoenix, of seeing "leg shows" at the big city's three or four burlesque houses. If they were real hellers they sometimes wound up in one of the several parlor houses that existed to service the farm hands, cowboys, and miners. If one of the older boys got a "dose" it was a sign he was a real he-man. I remember one of the victims of *l'amour* at the normal, a lad about twenty whom I admired tremendously. He was an indifferent student but a good athlete and a famed rounder. He was alleged to have contracted a "bull-headed dose" from a girl named Billie at an establishment which I believe was called the Rex Arms. His affliction gave him a peculiar walk. I admired and envied this roistering fellow. I tried to dress like him, talk like him (his grammar was atrocious, and while I was in that stage of hero worship I almost drove my mother mad). I even envied him his famous bull-headed dose and tried to walk like him. My mother thought my underwear was too tight.

The pre-World War I normal did most of those who attended it a great deal of good. Even if it didn't teach them a great deal to teach, it taught them how to teach what little they did know. Mrs. Krause at the dining hall made it a point to correct their table manners. They were told not to eat with both elbows on the table, not to blow their noses on their napkins, not to shovel in food with their knives, not to dump hot coffee into the saucers, blow on it, and then drink it from the saucers, not to hold their forks like daggers or as if they were fingering the strings of a bull fiddle when they cut their meat, and not to pick their teeth in public. She also taught them that their hands had to be clean and they had to have neckties on when they were at the table.

The preceptresses who rode herd on the girls were mostly refined ladies in reduced circumstances. They taught the girls manners and deportment. The girls learned to curl their hair with curling irons which they heated by thrusting them into the chimneys of kerosene lamps. They experimented with a little lipstick and rouge cunningly applied. (If a preceptress was sure a girl was painting her face she sent her back upstairs to wash.) They traded information, gossip, and secrets with other girls, and in properly chaperoned groups they sometimes went to Phoenix to shop or even to see a matinee at the Elk's Theater, where a resident stock company put on three- and four-year-old Broadway hits. (A new show every week!)

In spite of their being so carefully chaperoned some of the girls managed to get themselves in trouble. Every year or so there was a scandal about a newborn infant wrapped in a dormitory towel being found dead in the bushes of the campus. Girls managed to slip away on Saturday afternoons and go with the boys into the concealing willows of the river bottom. Some of the more depraved girls spent weekends with nonexistent aunts in Phoenix and managed it with forged letters of permission from their parents and forged invitations from the "aunts."

MOST THIRTEEN-YEAR-OLD boys are pathetic creatures. Their faces are pimply, their voices are changing. They have become convinced that their parents are half-witted and that no one understands them. For a time they are suspended in a strange purgatory between boyhood and manhood. They have put aside childish games and gadgets but are not yet old enough for the pastimes of men. At thirteen I had discarded my bicycle as being too infantile for a person of my years to ride in public. I wouldn't have been caught dead playing marbles, spinning a top, or shooting an air rifle. My voice croaked and squeaked. The fuzz on my face started turning into hair. I first tried shaving with a piece of broken glass. When I told my mother I needed a razor she laughed at me and said it would be a year or two yet. My feelings were hurt. I was bitterly jealous when my pal Gordon Goodwin started shaving with his father's straight razor. I bought myself a Gillette, a brush, and a cake of shaving soap. I felt the purchase almost made a man of me.

I had entered the academic department of the Tempe Normal in 1915. I was then thirteen years old. I was tall for my age—probably about five feet seven inches. I wore knickerbockers and my long skinny legs were clad in black cotton stockings. Like the other members of my age group I wore my long blond hair in a pompadour, which I kept glossy-smooth by putting on a stocking cap when I slept and by judiciously applying olive oil.

I was keenly interested in girls but deathly afraid of them. Possibly because my first love had been the beautiful Anna Levitsky, who had run away with a rich gentile boy, I felt a little more at home with older girls than those of my own age. For some reason old maids of eighteen or nineteen paid a good deal of attention to me, but the girls nearer my own age looked upon me as a clumsy lout. I was growing so fast that I literally fell over my own feet, as today they weren't where they were yesterday.

As one who suffered through grammar school, high school, college, and graduate school and who has been a college and university teacher, I have long been struck by the very small percentage of really good teachers there are at any level. Many are stupid and poorly educated. Many are lazy. A high proportion of them are neurotic. But of all their shortcomings the most universal is that most of them are abysmally dull. In my four years as a college undergraduate and one as a graduate student, I had about a half dozen really good teachers. Two of the best were at the University of Missouri where I got a master's degree and a wife.

In my first year in the academic department I encountered three teachers who epitomize the pedagogical sins. Among them they influenced my life. In grade school I had been very good in arithmetic and in all my subjects. In those days a standardized series of examinations furnished by the state department of education was given to graduating eighth-graders. I got a grade of 100 on the arithmetic test, the only one in my class to do so, and, I believe, the only one in my state. A trick question which I happened to see through had confused everyone else.

Then I bumped into algebra. The teacher was a kindly old man, but he was not particularly interested in his students or his subject and the algebra class bored me stiff. How I did it I do not know, but I managed to get passing marks in the subject and later on in geometry, but being bored to desperation in those math classes served to close my mind against mathematics from that time on. Today I regret it.

I had looked forward to taking manual training and making all manner of useful things. The instructor was a lazy, unattractive, lethargic, dull little man with a fearful case of halitosis. He put me to squaring a board. I would plane on the damned thing, then check it with a square. When I thought I had it right I'd take it to him for approval. He would check it with his square and if he could find a microscopic error he'd send me back to work again. It took me months to get all four sides squared to his satisfaction and by that time what had started out as a large piece of wood had shrunk until the only possible use for it was a key rack.

The manual training teacher did nothing to make me see that squaring a board was important, nothing to stimulate his class. It would have been far better to let me make a footstool of a table with some slightly unsquare pieces of wood in it than to bore me to death by insisting that I plane day after day on that one miserable board. I never heard a cheerful word from the instructor, never saw him smile. He sat at his desk picking his teeth and belching. From that time on most things mechanical have given me chills and fever.

Another strange character, whom I have already mentioned, was Captain Fred Irish, the vice-president of the normal, the instructor in physics and chemistry, and the drill master of the cadet company. I had always loved guns and shooting. My Uncle Bill Woolf, of whom I was very fond, was a captain in the Arizona National Guard and a fine shot with shotgun or rifle. I thought that I would like military drill, which was held from eleven to twelve, three days a week.

I enjoyed target shooting with 1903 Springfield rifles in .30/06 caliber and did very well at it, but close-order drill bored me to death. It likewise bored my friend Gordon Goodwin. We cut it at every opportunity, and in all the time we suffered through it neither of us was ever anything but a buck private.

Fred Irish was a remarkable person, an intelligent, bitter, and very lonely man. As much as I loathed military training and abhorred the spit-and-polish tradition generally, I must admit that Irish was an excellent drill master. He had been told when he obtained his position at the normal that he had to organize and train a cadet company. He got all his information out of books. As I have said, I never saw him shoot a rifle and I doubt if he ever shot one, yet he did a good job of telling others how to shoot. Except for a few mavericks like Gordon and me, the cadets he trained learned a great deal. Many became officers in World War I.

Every year in the spring, the cadet company held an annual "encampment." They practiced tactical exercises, dug trenches, mounted guard, slept in pup tents, dug latrines, cooked their rations. Irish lived in his own tent, ate alone in it. No one ever saw Cap Irish with his hair mussed, sweating, or dirty. He was a tall man, something over six feet. He had thick, rather coarse gray hair—so thick that it looked like a toupee—brown eyes, a rather large nose, and very smooth shiny skin with something of the look of a wax apple used as a table decoration. He always stood straight, never unbent. The only time I ever saw him smile with his face and his eyes as well as his mouth was when he was inflicting pain.

For poor Cap Irish was impotent and a sadist. He had come to the normal as a young man just out of college. With him he brought a beautiful young woman, a bride of a few weeks. She and my mother became fast friends. I called her Aunt Kate. I loved her and she loved me. When I was about six years old I made sixty-seven valentines and gave every one of them to her. Years later my mother told me what had ailed Fred Irish. In his teens he had had the mumps. His sex glands became involved and he became completely impotent. After Kate had run off with another man and had filed suit for a divorce in Chicago, Irish's father testified on her behalf at the hearing that he had known his son was impotent but had hoped that somehow his marrying a beautiful young woman might help him.

Kate confided her troubles to my mother. In his rage and frustration Irish used to beat her. I remember her weeping and showing my mother some bruises once when I was quite small. The day Kate ran off with a friend of my grandfather's, the man she married as soon as she got a divorce, she told my mother what she planned to do, kissed Mother and me goodbye.

Irish continued to live in the same house where he had lived with the beautiful Kate. He rode a bicycle to the normal every morning, back every night. Often the lights burned late in his chemistry-physics laboratory, and it was thought that he was engaged in complicated and important experiments. He made his own breakfast, but during the school year he ate lunch and dinner at the dining hall. He drilled the cadet company three times a week, neat, military, correct in a perfectly tailored uniform with his captain's bars on his shoulders.

At exactly eleven fifty-five o'clock he manuevered the cadet company up to the Main Building, turned it over to the first sergeant, who dismissed it. Exactly at twelve ten he emerged from the door of his office completely changed into civilian clothes, neat, clean, composed, wearing a high stiff collar. As he walked out of his office the bell at the dining hall started to ring and exactly at twelve fifteen he entered the dining hall, found his table, and sat down. It was the custom for the faculty members who ate at the dining hall to sit with students. Irish did so. He was detached, cold, but perfunctorily pleasant.

Around 1915 Irish bought a Model T Ford. He drove it as carefully and as sedately as he had ridden his bicycle. His routine was the same throughout the school year. Even in the summer, he drove up to the science building on the normal campus, went into his laboratory, presumably still engaged in those important experiments. This strange man stayed at Tempe from the time he came there right after he got out of college until his death. He was there for the many years it was a normal school, when it became a teachers' college, when it became Arizona State College at Tempe. He had only a bachelor's degree, and when it became necessary that someone with a more advanced degree be head of his department, he asked if he could become registrar. As far as I know he was still registrar when his final illness began.

As a very young man he had found the warm little nest at the normal an environment in which he did not have to compete with the other males he feared and hated. He could always be a superior figure. Never again in his long life did he enter into an emotional relationship with a woman. Never did he compete with another male for the rights to one. When the United States got into World War I he could undoubtedly have secured a commission, as he was still less than fifty. He never applied for one.

He never returned to college for graduate work, as to do so would also require competition. When he no longer had the academic qualifications to be the head of the science department, he found his haven in the registrar's office where he could dominate his flock of fat and fluttering females.

When I was only thirteen I realized that he got joy in inflicting pain. I had been ill and had missed the final examination in chemistry. I was sitting in the lecture room writing the answers to a make-up examination and he was busying himself and keeping an eye on me so I would not cheat. A pretty girl who was entering the normal for the second semester came in and asked him where she could find Professor Beckwith so she could sign up for a biology course.

In her hand she had a printed slip. Irish took it away from her, told her to sit down.

"Your name is—?" he began.

"Iris Jones," she said.

"And you are from—?"

"Prescott," she said.

"You went to high school there?"

"Yes, sir."

"Reading is taught at Prescott High School, I presume?"

"Why, yes," the girl said, puzzled and a little frightened.

"And you, my dear young lady, in the course of your instruction learned to read?"

"Why, yes," she answered, her lips trembling.

"I presume you do not read very well?"

"I have always thought I read well enough." There were tears in her voice.

"Now, Miss Jones," Irish said. "Right here in my hand I have the slip which you were carrying when you interrupted me, distracted this rather dull young man who is attempting to concentrate on a make-up examination. The slip says that Mr. Beckwith is to be found in Room 202. My dear Miss Jones, if you had only bothered your pretty and empty little head to look and if, indeed, you are able to read at all, you would have seen on the door of this room in very large numerals the number 10. In case this problem ever arises again the figure "1" followed by a *zero* means ten."

The girl could no longer hold back the tears. She began to sob.

For the first time I saw Irish smile with his eyes and the rest of his face. As the girl walked out of the lecture room, tears streaming down her cheeks, he was beaming.

Later on that year I was hauled before what was called the

discipline committee for some peccadillo—possibly for playing some inane practical joke but more probably for cutting Cap Irish's military drill too often. The several faculty members on the committee in my presence discussed what they should do with me. "How is he doing in his classes otherwise?" A. J. Matthews, the president of the normal, asked. "Very well in my class," one of the committee members said.

"I have just read his mid-term examination in chemistry," Irish said. "It was a joke. He has learned nothing!"

I was shocked. Here was an adult whom I had respected and who had an honorable and responsible position and he was telling a lie. At various times I have not done very well in subjects that bored me but when I am interested in a subject I have usually done well in it. And I was interested in chemistry. The examination had seemed rather easy to me, and a few days later when Irish returned the papers my grade was 88. I was aware then that Irish was a very strange man indeed.

I often wondered why this unhappy man disliked me so. I had worshipped the beautiful woman who had been his wife with her pretty face and her shimmering cloud of fair hair, and she had liked me as a motherly woman would like a small admiring boy. Possibly one reason was that the man who had been his wife's lover and who was later her husband was a friend of my grandfather. Possibly Irish suspected that Kate had told my mother what the seat of his troubles was and that she had told me. In reality she did not tell me until many years later. There was no particular reason why he should like me, as I was an awkward, gawky, pimply-faced lout given to daydreaming and falling over my own feet. Nevertheless he disliked me above and beyond the call of duty.

I cannot remember when I saw Fred Irish last, but he must have been at least seventy. He had changed very little. His gray hair was still thick. He still wore rimless glasses. His face had few lines in it and still had the slick, waxy look of an artificial apple. He saw me through the window of the registrar's office and came out to greet me.

"I have been following your career," he said. "I must say that you have done surprisingly well!"

"I am sure you *were* surprised, Captain Irish," I said.

"Yes," he said, with his cold, withdrawn smile. "I must admit I was!"

I HAD ALWAYS LIKED to draw and I am told that I was making recognizable pictures of men and animals before I was three. I had at one time thought of being a cartoonist. I read all the comic strips and particularly liked the style of George McManus, who drew Jiggs in "Bringing Up Father." I could draw Jiggs and his wife Maggie and their pretty comic-strip daughter as well as McManus. I could also draw what I considered hilariously funny cartoons. Nevertheless by the time of which I write I was aware that my sister Helen, who was four years younger than I, was far more talented. My reaction was to say to hell with art—I have never wanted to be an artist anyway. Nevertheless the art teacher, a dark little Armenian woman, insisted that I make drawings for the normal annual, a fearfully dull book put out by students with no journalistic aptitude whatsoever. It contained individual pictures of the seniors and members of the faculty and group pictures of the other classes and of the athletic teams. Otherwise it was filled with dull jokes stolen from magazines and with windy, pointless, and insincere essays. One year I made all the drawings for the division pages. They must have been pretty terrible.

I had always thought it would be pleasant to make a living by writing, and the year I entered the normal I got my first pushes in that direction. I chose the mountain lion as the subject for my term paper in biology. I read everything I could find in the library about the big cats, dug through my grandfather's files of hunting and fishing magazines, put in incidents I had gleaned in conversations with my grandfather, my uncles, and various cowboys. The teacher gave me an A on the paper and had me read it to the class. Afterward in his office he told me that many of my words were misspelled and my punctuation was shaky but that I was a natural storyteller. My English teacher turned many of my themes over to *The Tempe Normal Student,* the school newspaper. Since the editors had four five-column pages to fill every two weeks and little to fill them with, they were desperate for copy. In the *Student* I got my first by-lines.

I remember how proud I was to be a published author and how quickly I was let down. When the *Student* with my first story in it was distributed in the Main Building one of the older boys saw that the whole back page was taken up by an opus of mine. " 'Rescue from the Indians' by Jack O'Connor," he read. "What the hell is this? Who in the hell is Jack O'Connor?" The second boy said: "He's that smart-aleck little bastard that runs around in short pants. You know who I mean. He's a town kid and his old lady teaches in the training school."

"Oh," said the first student. "That little prick!" He threw the paper on the floor.

I HAD A GREAT many crosses to bear that school year of 1915–16. I had jumped from the training school, where I was one of the big kids, to the normal, where I was at the very bottom of the pecking order—a freshman in the academic department. I was thirteen and many of the students at the normal were in their twenties. The First World War was on in Europe and prices were beginning to go up in the United States, whereas my mother's salary did not. The financial strain made her nervous and short-tempered. My beloved Grandfather Woolf became ill and died that spring.

All this was bad enough but in addition my mother kept me in short pants. She not only wouldn't buy me a suit with long pants but she wouldn't let me spend the money I had earned during the previous summer for long pants. She gave many good reasons. Suits with long pants cost half again as much as suits with short pants and, heaven knows, short pants suits were dear enough. Hadn't my last one, the handsome tweed I had worn to eighth-grade graduation, cost fifteen dollars? That was fantastic. For another thing, I was growing like a weed, and if I got a long-pants suit the bottoms of the pants would be halfway up to my knees in no time. They would look silly whereas a pair of knickerbockers such as I had been wearing had a great deal of leeway. And in addition, she told me, I must remember that I was only thirteen years old! She considered fifteen a good age for graduation to long pants —maybe even sixteen! I must not rush things, she said. Boyhood is short enough anyway!

Before the First World War the donning of long pants was an important milestone in a boy's life. When he put them on he took the first step toward manhood. The possession of that first pair of long pants then occupied the place that a boy's getting his first driver's license and being permitted to use the family car does today. It had the same significance of the puberty rites which young savages endure—rites which they begin as boys and from which they emerge as warriors and men. In all the Tempe Normal there were but two boys in short pants and I was one of the two. The other lad was about my age but much smaller. His name was Cecil Leeson and in later years he became a saxophonist of note. We used to commiserate with each other, but his parents were as adamant as my mother was.

Somewhere, unless they have been destroyed, is a series of pictures that were made of me when I was two and a half or three years old. I was wearing a sailor suit and I had ribbons in my long golden curls. Many times my mother used to take out those pictures, look at them, and tell me what a darling *little* boy I was. When, not long after the pictures were taken, my father took me to a barbershop and had my hair cut, she wept. I think she subconsciously wanted me to remain her little boy with golden curls and she spent a great deal of effort resisting some of my steps toward adulthood. I am certain the reason she let me stay out of school until I was eight was that she felt I remained her little boy a bit longer. She opposed my getting my first air rifle. My Grandfather Woolf heard the arguments and bought me one. The reasons she gave for keeping me in short pants were extremely logical, but I am certain that the real reason was that she didn't want me to grow up.

I was no great social success, but instead of shining in society I shot a great many ducks down on the river. I trapped skunks and coyotes, thought up involved practical jokes. I was anxious to learn to dance, to be a gay blade and grasp delectable young females around the waist. But I was frightfully shy. Finally I decided to take the plunge and learn to dance. Gordon Goodwin offered to teach me, said there wasn't much to it. When you waltzed, he said, you did like this: one-two-three, one-two-three. Simple! When you one-stepped you just walked around. When you turned a corner you just pointed the girl at a right angle, gave her a push and followed her. When you foxtrotted you just sort of walked and jiggled up and down. It didn't sound too tough. While Gordon watched and coached I went through the motions of waltzing, one-stepping, and foxtrotting. He pronounced me practically perfect. I joined the Wallflower Club (annual dues, one dollar) and the next time a dance was held I showed up. But there were unforeseen problems. In the first place, I could not tell a waltz from a one-step and I had to ask the girls. In the second place, I discovered that it was much more difficult to dance with girls than to dance alone. The trouble was that the only way to get the dumb girls to follow was to hold them close, and when I held them close and tried to dance my knee went between their legs. I had heard what girls had between their legs and was acutely embarrassed by the knowledge. This would never do! I tried holding them at arm's length but that didn't work very well. I compromised by trying to straddle the girl, with both her legs in the middle and mine on the outside.

I saw a very pretty but much older girl laughing as I shuffled awkwardly by. She was a senior, and she must have been all of twenty or twenty-one. Her name was Nora O'Neill and she was one of the few people who ever commented on my stories in the Tempe Normal *Student*. Because she paid some attention to me, treated me as if I were grown-up, besides was very pretty, I had a sort of a crush on her.

When that dance was over Nora walked up to me with her date. "This is the young man I was telling you about," she told him. "The boy who writes those nice stories in the *Student*." Then she turned to me. "I have told Joe he's going to have to sit out some dances, that I am going to dance with you!"

Joe did not seem to mind.

"I have been watching you," she said as we started off. "You're afraid to touch a girl. You're afraid to put your knee between a girl's legs. There's nothing down there that's going to bite you!" I wasn't so sure about that. I blushed. "Now look," she said, "a man has to hold a girl fairly close. If he doesn't she can't follow well. Like this!" She put my right arm around her waist, extended my left arm, put her right hand in my left. I became acutely conscious that Nora O'Neill had breasts—not little, not great big, not hard, not soft. Just right! Nora was a tall girl for those days, about five feet seven, just my height. Her breasts hit me smack in the chest. I danced three dances with Nora. She was right. Nothing bit me. When she turned me over to dance with girls my own age I did a lot better!

# 20 · L'Envoi

WHEN the war began in Europe in August 1914, it seemed about as remote from Tempe, Arizona, and the Salt River valley as anything one could imagine. Those of us who were twelve, thirteen, and fourteen years old at the time talked about it, read about it in the Phoenix *Gazette,* the *Arizona Republic,* the *Literary Digest,* and the *Saturday Evening Post.* We even took sides, as it is the nature of all children to take sides. Some of us were pro-German, some pro-Allies. Probably most of us were pro-German in that we were anti-English. We had read in all of our United States history books how the Americans had to fight the English in order to found this country. We had also read how the English picked on the young United States and how their high-handed methods had brought about the War of 1812.

In addition I had heard from the Irish branch of the family how the English had pushed the Irish around. None of the O'Connors was bitter but occasionally they talked about the long and often muddle-headed struggle of the Irish to free themselves from the English yoke. I heard about Robert Emmett, Patrick Sarsfield, Wolfe Tone, how under Cromwell the English butchered the Irish, and how under Victoria the English allowed the Irish to starve by the tens of thousands during the potato famine. When my Uncle

Jim O'Connor and I were sitting around in the back yard after dinner on hot summer nights and while he was working on his second brandy and had lit his second cigar, he sometimes spun for me tales of Irish history, told me something of the O'Connors, the Nevilles, the Heffernans, and the Fitzgeralds, and their past. He could reel off lists of distinguished Irishmen and Irish-Americans—from John L. Sullivan to the Duke of Wellington, and from the Confederate General Patrick Cleburne to Oliver Goldsmith.

Jim O'Connor was not a professional Irishman—professional Irishmen bored him—but he was not ashamed of his Irish blood and the fact that he was proud of his Irish lineage kept me from being ashamed of mine—no matter how hard my Grandmother Woolf worked on me. American history, the tales of how my English forebears had pushed my Irish forebears around, and the fact that I knew and liked some people who were German-born—all combined to make me mildly pro-German.

Then we all switched to the other side when we began to read how the Germans raped nuns and cut the hands off of Belgian children. We learned to call the Germans Huns. We heard of Americans who went to Canada to join the Princess Pats. Others joined the Royal Canadian Flying Corps. I must have read a book by an Englishman named Guy Empey called *Over the Top* sometime in 1915. Somehow I got the notion that fighting the Hun in the muddy trenches of Flanders would be rather romantic.

But what I really thought I'd like was to pilot a fighter plane in the Royal Flying Corps. Those R.F.C. uniforms were very attractive. The pilots wore cute caps on the sides of their heads, Sam Browne belts, pilot's wings turned upside down, goodlooking jackets. Some of them had snappy-looking mustaches. I tried to grow one but all I managed was some fuzz and three or four long hairs.

And what a life those young pilots led! They would put on their flying suits, jump into the Sopwith Camels, zip aloft to shoot down a Hun. Then they would return to the luxurious château where they were housed. Obsequious orderlies helped them off with their flying suits, drew their baths, laid out fresh clothes. Then the gay young pilots drank martinis and whiskey, ate delicious dinners. Then most of them went out to hop in the hay with gay French shopgirls or with lovely French countesses. The next day, after mowing down a couple of hundred Germans in a strafing run or perhaps shooting down another plane or two, the young R.F.C. pilots flew over the German airdromes and dropped flowers on the graves of the Germans they had shot down the day before. The German planes in the air waggled their wings at them. It was all very sporting and very touching. Oh for the life of the R.F.C.!

IN SPITE OF THE FACT that we read so much about the European War, as it was then called, and of the great seesaw battles on the western front, I believe most of us in Arizona were actually somewhat surprised when the United States finally got into it.

We had been expecting some sort of war with Mexico. The national guard regiments of many states, including the First Arizona Infantry, had been called into the federal service and stationed along the Mexican border after Pancho Villa's raid on Columbus, New Mexico, in 1916. One of the song hits of 1916 went about as follows:

I want to go-O-O
To Mexico-O-O
Beneath the Stars and Stripes
To fight the foe-O-O-O!

Many Arizonans were pretty badly shaken up by the trouble in Mexico and were afraid that the crazy Mexicans would raid one of the Arizona border cities—Douglas or Nogales. In 1915 or 1916 two Mexican factions battled near Nogales, Sonora. The commander of the faction that got the worst of it (Villistas, I believe) cleared out of Nogales with about half his men. The stragglers who remained behind looted the bars and cantinas, got drunk, started indiscriminate looting, shooting at passers-by, and setting fires. A regiment of American infantrymen of the regular army was stationed at Nogales and was strung along the "line" that separated the

United States and Mexico. When some of the Mexican stragglers started taking pot shots at Americans across the border in Arizona, the regulars shot back. The result was pretty one-sided. The American infantrymen were trained riflemen and they were sober. The Mexicans were untrained and were drunk.

Tempe and Phoenix were almost two hundred miles by road from Mexico and there were troops stationed at Nogales, Douglas, and Ajo, and the whole border was patrolled. Even if he had wanted to, any Mexican general who would have attempted a raid that far into American territory with hostile troops behind him would have been half-witted. Nevertheless, people in the valley were nervous. Householders kept their shotguns and their .30/30's handy and laid in a few extra boxes of ammunition.

In Tempe Captain Fred Irish sprang into the breach in the summer of 1916 and organized a home guard. Middle-aged men with potbellies, flat feet, and bunions turned out two or three times a week and learned to do close-order drill and the manual of arms on the athletic field at the normal. How Pancho Villa or any other raider would be intimidated by fat old men doing the manual of arms no one said.

If Woodrow Wilson had listened to the people of southern Arizona, the United States would have invaded Mexico instead of chasing over to Europe and getting mixed up with the Germans. American-owned mines in Mexico had been seized. American-owned cattle were stolen. Americans who had settled in Mexico in good faith had to get out and leave all they possessed behind them. I spent some time in the border city of Nogales in 1916. The town was full of well-to-do Mexicans who had fled from the chaos of the revolution, just as Florida today is full of Cubans who have run away from Castro. Many times I heard border Americans say that we were going to have to send an army down there and teach those damned crazy Mexicans how to run a country and that it would be a good idea if we took over the whole shebang.

The husband of one of my father's sisters was a victim of the Mexican revolution. He had made a good deal of money in California and owned extensive rice lands and walnut groves in the Sacramento valley. He got the idea that California property was overpriced and that the California boom was shortly to peter out. He sold all his California property, bought a silver mine in the Mexican state of Durango. One of the revolutionary regimes seized his mine. He still had some money left so he decided to recoup his fortunes by raising winter tomatoes for the American market in southern Sonora. Two Mexican armies fought a battle among his tomatoes, killed his foreman and most of his peasants, and filled his wells with dead Mexicans. He was an ardent believer in American intervention.

I BELIEVE IT WAS LENIN who said that war is the locomotive of history. It is certainly one of the principal bringers of change. World War I just barely clipped my home town and my Arizona on the jaw and made it a little groggy. World War II finished it.

Before the First World War broke out the Salt River valley was largely devoted to the raising of wheat and alfalfa and the feeding of cattle. But the war made the raising of long-staple cotton immensely profitable. Before the bottom dropped out of the cotton market in 1920 all the old wheat fields and many of the alfalfa fields had been plowed up and planted to cotton. Cotton was even raised on vacant lots in Tempe and Phoenix.

A few men became quickly rich on cotton. Others who could have been rich but held on too long because they were too greedy went bankrupt. Cattle raising was likewise wildly profitable. Men who had worked hard all their lives, whose standard costume had for many years been a battered old ten-gallon hat, a faded blue work shirt, a pair of levi pants and jacket, and worn high-heeled boots, men who wondered from year to year if they could sell their yearlings for enough to pay back the bank loan, men who rolled their own cigarettes from five-cent sacks of Bull Durham suddenly found themselves rich. Some quietly sold out their spreads and went to Long Beach, California, to take it easy. But most wanted to get richer. They went into debt at the banks to get control of more land, to buy more cattle. They smoked big expensive cigars, drove Cadillacs, Pierce-Arrows, Wintons, Packard Twin-Sixes. Arizona was dry then but they bought good bootleg Scotch and bourbon that had been run in from California. They gave high-class floosies fifty- and hundred-dollar bills instead of the fives and tens they had got before. The price of cattle went down after the war and a bad drought hit in 1921. Most of the high-flying cattlemen went broke and many who had thought they were millionaires in 1919 considered themselves lucky the banks didn't sell them out in 1921.

I am not certain when boyhood ends. Probably mine ended in 1917. I put on long pants then and joined the army. My Uncle Jim O'Connor bought me my first pair of long pants. He simply said: "For Christ's sake, Jack, has Ida still got you in short pants? That's a hell of a note for a kid as big as you are!" I joined the army in that first pair of long pants. I have forgotten how much I weighed but I was fifteen years old, had 20/20 vision, and was five feet nine and a half inches tall. I was at Camp Kearney near San Diego, California, trying to learn to be a machine-gunner a few months later when I received word that my beloved Uncle Jim O'Connor had died suddenly of a heart attack. Within two years I had lost both of the father figures in my life. I owe much to my Grandfather Woolf and my Uncle Jim O'Connor. If I have managed to stick with one wife for over forty years, to be reasonably responsible, industrious, and courageous I owe it at least partly to their example. May their souls rest in peace!

As I have said in a previous chapter, I lived at home and went to the Tempe Normal from the fall of 1921 until the spring of 1923. At that time Phoenix had grown a great deal but Tempe was still much as it was during my childhood. Old-timers died and were buried out in the Double Buttes cemetery. Many members of the younger generation moved to Phoenix or Los Angeles to get jobs. New people settled in Tempe to send their children to the normal, because someone in the family had arthritis or lung trouble, or simply because they wanted to get away from cold winters.

During the generation-long span of years between the end of

World War I and the beginning of World War II, Tempe changed very little. It was still the town where I grew up—quiet, sleepy, rather dowdy. The streets were paved, and the normal, which by then had become a four-year college, had added a few new buildings and its enrollment had probably doubled. The city had built a municipal swimming pool just off of Mill Avenue near the river, and boys no longer dived off the Point of Rocks into the river.

In the winter the town was fragrant with wood smoke and warm and bright with December and January sunshine even when the high mountains to the north were white with deep snow. In the summer it was always slow-paced, sleepy, filled with green trees and clamorous with the voices of nesting mourning and whitewing doves. The business section was not very different in 1940 from what it had been in 1917. The only time I lived in Tempe after I finished the two-year course at the normal was from September 1937 until early June 1938. I took a year's leave of absence from my job as a professor of journalism at the University of Arizona to finish a novel called *Boom Town* and to wind up another book called *Game in the Desert.* I lived with my family in the house my Grandmother Woolf had built next door to my mother's place. My mother inherited it when Grandmother died in late December 1934.

Tempe and the whole Salt River valley was still slow, sleepy, depression-ridden. In the fall I used to write every morning until about eleven thirty. Then my wife and I would take our shotguns and drive through the little village of Scottsdale and through the Fort McDowell Indian reservation to a favorite area along the lower Verde River, where we ate a picnic lunch and then hunted quail. We shot almost every day during the long season and all that time I don't suppose we saw five other hunters. During the depression not many felt that they could afford to buy shotgun shells to shoot at anything as small and as hard to hit as a quail.

TODAY I AM A STRANGER in my old home town. Phoenix has become a great city that has engulfed much of the pleasant

Salt River valley countryside. Tempe itself now has about fifty thousand people. There are luxurious winter homes on the sides of Camelback Mountain, where my Grandfather Woolf shot the big desert bighorn ram he was so proud of. The last drop of water has been squeezed out of the Salt River for irrigation, and instead of clear water, clean sand, and willows the river bed is dusty waste filled with rusty automobile bodies, worn-out tires, jerry-built warehouses, piles of junk and garbage. The country between the river and Scottsdale, where I used to shoot doves and quail, is now solid with houses, all with television antennas, and all exactly alike.

The Tempe Normal has become Arizona State University. Its enrollment is over twenty thousand and it fields powerful football teams. Its stadium, where its hired gladiators battle other hired gladiators for the glory of the alumni of old Arizona State, is by the Little Butte and hard by the slew I used to cross to hunt ducks and to trap coons. Actually the Little Butte has just about vanished, as it was used as a rock quarry and then as the site of the stadium. The big Tempe Butte itself is looking pretty seedy. At one time it wore a big "N" for normal. Later the "N" was demolished, and a big "T" for Tempe State Teachers College was put up. Now it wears an enormous white "A" for Arizona State University. Reminding anyone that the "university" was once a humble normal school is like bringing up the subject of someone's idiot uncle.

The explosive growth of the university has eaten the heart out of old Tempe. The humble adobe houses of Mexican Town have long since been torn down and the Mexican Town area is part of the campus. My mother died in 1962 when my wife and I were on safari in Mozambique. She was almost eighty-nine. Her house has now disappeared and so has the house my Grandmother Woolf built beside it. The ground has been made into a parking lot. The last time I was in Tempe my Grandfather Woolf's big concrete block house was still standing. It looked seedy and was, I believe, a roominghouse, but the university continues to grow and its days are numbered.

My old home town, the quiet frontier village of 1907–17 where

I grew up, has vanished, a casualty of war, of the westward shift of population, of technological change. But nevertheless, the beloved home town of my youth, the center of my world, still lives in memory—every house, every tree, every eccentric character—like an ancient insect preserved in Baltic amber!

## *A NOTE ABOUT THE AUTHOR*

JACK O'CONNOR was born and spent his boyhood in Tempe, Arizona. He was educated at the University of Arizona and the University of Arkansas, where he was graduated in 1925. He received his M.A. degree from the University of Missouri in 1927. Since then he has been a newspaperman, a director of public relations, a novelist, and a professor of journalism at the University of Arizona. He is the author of two novels, and as a free-lance writer he has contributed articles to all of the leading outdoor magazines and to general magazines as well. Since 1937 he has written only for *Outdoor Life* and has been its Arms and Ammunition Editor since 1941.

Other books by Mr. O'Connor are *The Art of Hunting Big Game in North America, The Big-Game Rifle, The Rifle Book, The Shotgun Book.*

Mr. O'Connor is married and lives in Lewiston, Idaho.

# *A NOTE ON THE TYPE*

THE TEXT of this book was set on the Linotype in Garamond (No. 3), a modern rendering of the type first cut in the sixteenth century by Claude Garamond (1510–61). He was a pupil of Geoffroy Troy and is believed to have based his letters on the Venetian models, although he introduced a number of important differences, and it is to him we owe the letter which we know as Old Style. He gave to his letters a certain elegance and a feeling of movement which won for their creator an immediate reputation and the patronage of the French King, Francis I.

*Composed, printed, and bound by*
*The Book Press, Brattleboro, Vermont*

*Typography by Kenneth Miyamoto*